Adolescent Relationships and Drug Use

LEA's SERIES ON PERSONAL RELATIONSHIPS
Steve Duck, Series Editor

Miller/Alberts/Hecht/Trost/Krizek • Adolescent Relationships and Drug Use

Adolescent Relationships and Drug Use

Michelle A. Miller
The Pennsylvania State University

Jess K. Alberts
Arizona State University

Michael L. Hecht
The Pennsylvania State University

Melanie R. Trost
Arizona State University

Robert L. Krizek
Saint Louis University

Ψ Psychology Press
Taylor & Francis Group

New York   London

First Published by
Lawrence Erlbaum Associates, Inc., Publishers
10 Industrial Avenue
Mahwah, NJ 07430

Transferred to Digital Printing 2009 by Psychology Press
270 Madison Ave, New York NY 10016
27 Church Road, Hove, East Sussex, BN3 2FA

Cover design by Kathryn Houghtaling Lacey

Library of Congress Cataloging-in-Publication Data

Adolescent relationships and drug use / Michelle Miller ...
[et al.].
         p.   cm. — (LEA's personal relationships series)
      Includes bibliographical references and index.
ISBN 0-8058-3435-4 (alk. paper). — ISBN 0-8058-3436-2
(pbk. : alk. paper)
1. Youth—Drug Use. 2. Drug use—Prevention. 3. Interpersonal relations. I. Miller, Michelle, 1960– . II. Series.
HV5824.Y68A315   1999
362.29'17'0835'0973—dc21
                                                    99-34292
                                                    CIP

Publisher's Note
The publisher has gone to great lengths to ensure the quality of this
reprint but points out that some imperfections in the original may
be apparent.

Contents

vi CONTENTS

6 Conclusions 107

Appendix A Methods 123

Appendix B Decision-Making Questionnaire 139

Appendix C Formula for Determining Risk Factors 144

Appendix D Development and Implementation 148
of a Peer-Based Prevention Program

Appendix E Killing Time 160

Appendix F Discussion Guide 189

Appendix G Perception of Performance Scale 191

References 193

Author Index 215

Subject Index 224

Series Editor's Foreword

Steve Duck
University of Iowa

This new series on personal relationships from Lawrence Erlbaum Associates is intended to review the progress in the academic work on relationships in respect to a broad array of issues, and to do so in an accessible manner that also illustrates its practical value. This series will also include books intended to pass on the accumulated scholarship to the next generation of students and to those who deal with relationship issues in the broader world beyond the academy. This series will thus comprise not only monographs and other academic resources exemplifying the multidisciplinary nature of this area, but also textbooks suitable for use in the growing numbers of courses on relationships.

Additionally, this series will provide a comprehensive and current survey of theory and research in personal relationships through the careful analysis of the problems encountered and solved in research, yet it will also consider the systematic application of that work in a practical context. These resources are intended to serve not only as comprehensive assessments of progress on particular topics, but also as significant influences on the future directions and development of the study of personal relationships.

Although each volume will be focused and centered, authors will attempt to place the respective topics in the broader context of other research on relationships and with a range of wider disciplinary traditions. Thus, the series will not only offer incisive and forward-looking reviews, but will also demonstrate the broader theoretical implications of relationships for the range of disciplines from which the research originates. Series volumes will include original studies, reviews of relevant theory and research, and new theories oriented toward the understanding of personal relationships both in themselves and within the context of broader theories of family process, social psychology, and communication.

Reflecting the diverse composition of personal relationship study, readers in numerous disciplines—social psychology, communication, sociology, family studies, developmental psychology, clinical psychology, personality, counseling, women's studies, gerontology, and others—will find valuable and insightful perspectives in the series. Apart from the academic scholars who research the dynamics and processes of relationships, there are many other people whose work takes them up against the operation of relationships in the real world. For such people as nurses, police officers, teachers, therapists, lawyers, drug and alcohol counselors, marital counselors, and caregivers for the elderly, a number of issues routinely arise concerning the ways in which relationships affect the people whom they serve. Examples include the role of loneliness in illness and the ways to circumvent it, the complex impact of family and peer relationships upon a drug-dependent's attempts to give up the drug, the role of playground unpopularity on a child's learning, the issues involved in dealing with the relational side of chronic illness, the management of conflict in marriage, the establishment of good rapport between physicians and seriously ill patients, the support of the bereaved, and the correction of violent styles of behavior in dating or marriage. Each of these is a problem that may confront some of the above professionals as part of their daily concerns, and each demonstrates the far-reaching influences of relationship processes on much else in life that is presently theorized independently of relationship considerations.

The present volume is an excellent case in point because it clearly shows that the use of drugs and the prevention of such use can each be more fully understood if professionals attend to the relational infrastructure within which decisions about drugs are made by individuals. Yet how do individuals "just say no" and stay friends with those to whom they are close, who may be the persons offering them drugs in the first place? How do an adolescent's concerns with fitting into the group play into the whole issue of drug usage and drug resistance? This book reviews many different strands of research to do with drugs, persuasion strategies, peer relationships, and the general contexts provided by culture, and then presents findings of research that manages to pull all these separate ideas together and place the whole in the context of peer relationships inside and outside of school. Not only do the authors show an impressive range of knowledge about a disparate set of research findings from a broad set of scholarly disciplines, but their own application of their scholarship to the practical problems of today's youth is equally convincing. The book offers a whole new set of insights into the problems of drugs in teenage culture and offers some well-grounded advice on the ways in which to present resistance strategies in light of the nature of relationships and relationship concerns amongst adolescents. There could be no better way to launch this series than with such a great combination of analysis, research, and practical implications for several different academic disciplines and practitioners.

Preface

This book describes the communicative and relational features of adolescent drug use. It is written for people who care about adolescents and are concerned about their drug use problems; people like researchers, practitioners, parents, teachers, and others. In writing this book we hope to provide information about drugs, adolescents, and their social world—a world filled with peer pressure, emerging and fragile self-identities, the need for approval, and acceptance, cliques, identification with peers and peer norms, and attempts to balance a relationship with parents. Although other scholars have focused on the properties of drugs, peer norms, risk and protective factors, and other aspects of adolescent drug use, the work represented here extends this focus to include how drugs are offered to adolescents. We are interested in learning who makes drugs available to adolescents and how they are resisted. In short, we want to know how alcohol and other drug offers are communicated in the context of adolescent social relationships.

This volume summarizes several studies funded by a series of grants from the National Institute on Drug Abuse. We include the work of others where relevant. Resisting drugs is treated as a relational and communicative competency as we explore how adolescents maintain and negotiate relationships while successfully refusing drug offers. Our attempt is to describe adolescent behaviors and thoughts in the United States, and in a world that includes drugs and drug offers from peers, family members, and others in a variety of social contexts. Our particular focus is on adolescent drug-related decisions and strategies to refuse offers of drugs while maintaining a self-identity and friendships.

A model of relational competence and narrative theory is used to guide this research. This volume describes adolescent stories of how, when offered drugs, they balance peer pressures, self-image, relational concerns, and the desire to say no in order to find successful refusal strategies. This volume also summarizes research findings and explains their implications for relational and communication theory, and for developing drug prevention interventions. The major contributions include the following:

1. Placement of the drug offer resistance episode in a living, relational context.
2. The first comprehensive communication and relational approach to drug resistance.
3. The first detailed analysis of drug resistance that considers the relationship between offerer and resister, different types of drugs, the language used by adolescents, family and peer group relationships, personality, and situations.
4. Arguments for a relational and communication competence model of drug resistance.
5. Recommendation of a unique relational and communication approach to drug prevention customizing video and live performance to present resistance models created from adolescents' own words.

WHY THIS BOOK IS IMPORTANT

This book is important because it applies the theories and principles of communication competence to a significant social concern, drug abuse. The application of such theories and principles emphasizes that theories operate in adolescents' daily relational worlds and are not mere research abstractions. Adolescents face relational dilemmas of acceptance by peers, and they need to be relationally and communicatively competent to manage peer relationships in the context of drug issues. While these relational concerns are not exclusive to adolescence, they typify this developmental period and are magnified during this developmental stage of life. By placing the management of drug issues in a relational and developmental framework, the book:

• informs relationship, communication, and psychology researchers by extending their theories.

- assists drug and health researchers by presenting them with a new way of looking at the topic.
- enlightens drug practitioners by demonstrating a new approach to prevention, and inform parents by helping them understand their teens.

Models of communication and relational competence have been developed on a limited range of relational and communication experiences. Rarely have relationship researchers studied the competencies necessary to deal with important life situations such as drug offers. Rejecting offers of drugs can brand one an outsider, particularly among adolescents for whom peer pressure is a very real concern. By applying a competence model to these situations, the book extends our understanding of communication and relational skills.

Research has recognized that drug use is tied to peer pressure and that teaching resistance skills is one of the keys to effective drug prevention. This book is the first to make the connection of peer pressure to the relationships between peers and hence to the large literature on relationships that can help illuminate the processes of peer pressure once that link is made.

This volume first describes the social and relational processes of drug resistance and then links intervention techniques to the adolescents' relational world. We advocate prevention and intervention from the adolescent perspective as expressed in their personal stories of drug resistance. Excerpts from these stories bring the drug resistance process to life and reveal the resistance strategies that teens say they use when refusing drugs while maintaining relationships.

CHAPTER OUTLINES

Chapter One: Drug Use in the United States: A Communication Perspective

The first chapter provides the relational context for drug offers by describing drug use in the United States. Patterns of use are presented as well as previous findings for attitudes, social norms, and family patterns. This chapter sets the scene for our discussion of adolescents' relationships and drug use by providing an overview of drug use patterns, some reasons for use, and key perspectives on adolescent drug use. The Spitzberg and Cupach relational competence model (knowledge, motivation, skills, outcomes) is explained and applied to drug use and resistance.

Chapter one also provides an introduction to certain factors that put teens at risk to abuse drugs. Finally, the chapter provides some direction for communication researchers regarding prevention and changing adolescent drug use through communication and relationship-based intervention.

Chapter Two: Adolescent Relationships and Drug Use: Family and Peer Influences

Central to the thesis of this book is the study of relationships. This chapter outlines family and peer influences on adolescent alcohol and other drug use choices. Family communication, peer pressure, norms, and communication competence as they relate to interpersonal skill in adolescent's handling drug offers are introduced to set the stage for how adolescent relationships facilitate or impede drug use.

Chapter Three: The Social Processes of Drug Resistance in a Relational Context

This chapter presents the findings of a series of studies that identify the social processes of alcohol and other drug offers and refusals. Based on data collected across middle school, high school, and college populations, we discuss the relational competencies necessary for teens to successfully resist offers of alcohol and other drugs while maintaining relationships.

Excerpts from adolescents' narrative accounts are used to illustrate how teens offer to other teens, how they accept or refuse offers, and how they resist offers in groups whose social norms support use. The REAL system (Refuse [simple no], Explain, Avoid, and Leave) is described for resisting drug offers without losing friends. This focus on sustaining relationships in the drug offer context is central to the relational competence model of adolescent drug use.

Chapter Four: Metaphor, Culture, and Action: The Symbolic Construction of Adolescent Drug Use

This chapter describes how metaphors operate in drug use and prevention, and presents our analysis of the language used when talking about drugs. For example, one of the controversial conclusions of this analysis is that the war metaphor does not appear in the language of teens and, therefore, has been unsuccessful in this arena. Instead, we present metaphors that are used by high- and low-risk adolescents and we consider their use in assessment, treatment, and prevention.

Chapter Five: A Narrative and Relational Approach to Drug Prevention in the Drug Resistance Strategies Project

Chapter five argues that media attempt to externally impose the truth about drugs on adolescents, rather than starting with the actual experiences of adolescents within their own social milieu. As a result, prevention campaigns may be perceived by students as lacking authenticity. This perception, in turn, may inhibit the overall impact of the programs. The authors argue that this kind of program content communicates disrespect by denying the adolescents' own experience. This disrespect is compounded by attempting to establish a nonexpert as the conveyor of knowledge. These programs fail to consider the relationship between the adolescents' experience and the message being conveyed by the program's structure and source.

These shortcomings are addressed in this chapter while arguing for a narrative, relational, and communication-based, peer modeling program that relies on the insider status of peer experience. Drawing from performance and narrative theory, this chapter describes the development, implementation, and evaluation of the Drug Resistance Strategies Project prevention program.

Chapter Six: Conclusions

In this final chapter, the findings from several studies in the Drug Resistance Strategies Project are situated in theories of relational communication competence. Conclusions are discussed regarding how teens engage in drug resistance while maintaining relationships and several directions for future research are presented.

This volume seeks to fill a gap in the scholarly literature. Relationship and communication texts are rarely problem-centered and have not focused on drug resistance. Books in the drug prevention area are derived from psychological, physical science, or health science perspectives. The focus on relationships and communication in drug resistance will provide an important application and extension for relational scholars and a new focus for drug researchers.

—*Michelle A. Miller*
—*Jess K. Alberts*
—*Michael L. Hecht*
—*Melanie R. Trost*
—*Robert L. Krizek*

The Drug Resistance Strategies Project maintains a web site with information about the program as well as video clips, sample curriculum, and other materials. It is located at www.la.psu.edu/speech/drsp/drsp.htm

Acknowledgments

We would like to thank the many people who contributed to this book. Steve Duck initially encouraged us to write about adolescent relationships and drug use and provided insightful editorial comments. William Bukoski and Raquel Crider of the National Institute of Drug Abuse have been helpful and encouraging from the beginning of our drug resistance research. The Shelby County Sheriff's Department has been instrumental in providing financial support. Janet Soper and the Publication Assistance Center at Arizona State University provided invaluable assistance preparing this book. Thanks, also, to Linda Bathgate for her patience and help, and to those who provided input and support including David MacKinnon, Karol Kumpfer, Judith Weiner, Carrie Barrett, Sandra Petronio, Steve Corman, Jim Stiff, Dean Scheibel, and Vicki Tarulis. We would be remiss if we did not acknowledge the staff and students of Southwind Middle School, the Memphis Boys and Girls Club, Red Mountain High School, the middle schools of Phoenix, and especially Barbara Lane and Chris Hberra Van Hilsen, without whom this project would not be possible.

~~~~~

I acknowledge and thank my sons, Jordan and Joshua, for their resiliency and adaptability. I have learned more about love and life from them than I ever imagined. As I wrote these chapters I kept my 13-year-old son in mind and his experiences resonate in these pages. I wish both of my boys a smooth path in an often rough journey through adolescence.

I also want to thank my husband and friend, L. Edward Day, my mother, and my deceased father for their never-ending love and commitment to family communication. Finally, I would be remiss if I did not thank Michael Hecht for believing in me when we first pursued this project. I do not believe he had the faintest idea of the depth and breadth that his involvement would reach. I thank him for taking the ball and running, and for being my colleague and friend.

—*Michelle A. Miller*

I am indebted to Meredith, Serena, Jilaine, and Aaron for keeping me informed about adolescent experiences. I have been privileged to watch Meredith and Serena grow up and to be a part of their lives; it has brought me nothing but joy. I cannot thank Aaron and Jilaine enough for so readily accepting me into their lives and for being such wonderful people. They all make adolescence look much easier than I remember it being. And, of course, I must thank Jim who brought Jilaine and Aaron into my life and who has patiently listened to me as I talked through various parts of this book; he has heard more about adolescent relationships and drug resistance than he ever cared to hear. Thank you all; I love you very much.

—*Jess K. Alberts*

I would like to thank my son Jim, who taught me more about adolescents than I ever wanted to know, and more about life than anyone else, and has been a constant source of inspiration and love. I also would like to thank Ann, companion, lover, and friend.

To Donnie and Lenore, thanks for all your support. Rebecca's striving and goal directness is exhilarating. Thanks, also, to Albie, Susan, and Bella for their thoughts, insight and love. And thanks to Melanie Trost and Margaret Kehoe for their work and to Flavio Marsiglia, without whose efforts this project would not be continuing and whose friendship has helped keep me sane through difficult times. Finally, my gratitude goes out to Michelle Miller, without whom this project would not have taken place and without whose friendship my own life would be diminished.

—*Michael L. Hecht*

Although we are moved and changed in some way by every face we meet, a handful of people have had a significant impact on my involvement in this project and in life, in general. Thank you, Michael, for asking me to join your research team and for providing the support and encouragement to take my own path in examining relationship issues in adolescent drug use; you have been a great mentor and will, I hope, remain a great friend. Thanks also to the multitude of colleagues, graduate, and undergraduate students who assisted in the data collection efforts for the studies described herein; we would have nothing to share without your dedication and effort. My parents, siblings, and extended family continue to provide the ties that strengthen. I am deeply grateful to have been born into a family that is such a dependable source of love, nurturance, and friendship. Finally, thank you to my collaborator and friend, Douglas Kenrick, without your support and guidance I might still be waitressing at The Bacchus Pub in Bozeman, no less happy, maybe, but certainly less fulfilled.

—*Melanie R. Trost*

My deepest appreciation goes out to Michelle, Jess, Michael, and Melanie. It was their hard work and perseverance that brought this project through to its completion. Thank you for including me. I would be remiss, however, if I did not also acknowledge all the adolescents who, sometimes to my surprise, rather openly and honestly shared their experiences with me in our interview "conversations." It was their willingness to discuss very private and personal matters that allowed us to capture and, hopefully, begin to understand a part of what it is like to be very young and facing the mounting pressures of the social environment of the late twentieth century. I am encouraged by what I heard. I also want to thank these young people for helping me become a better researcher/interviewer. Although I had read about the importance of certain "research skills" in various texts, these young people taught me the value of patience, the importance of trust, and the centrality of listening in the interview exchange. I thank you all.

—*Robert L. Krizek*

1

Drug Use in the United States: A Communication Perspective

Despite more than 30 years of research and effort, drug abuse continues to be a prevalent problem in the United States. Most national attention has focused on adolescent drug prevention and intervention, with the hope that preventing adolescent use will decrease the number of adult abusers and the severity of their abuse. This hope has seemed well placed. We know that early drug use puts individuals at greater risk for use later in life (Johnston, O'Malley, & Bachman, 1987, 1996; Newcomb, Maddahian, & Bentler, 1986) and that nearly all drug use begins in the preadolescent or adolescent years. It is rare for anyone to try a new drug after reaching the age of 21 (Kandel, 1983). An examination of drug initiation (age of first use) curves reveals that typically youths are introduced to illicit drugs in early adolescence, the rate of initiation peaks at around 16 years of age, then begins a negative acceleration and levels off soon after (Oetting & Beauvais, 1983). The age of first use is getting younger (Johnston et al., 1994), with initiation rates falling among the middle school grades. Thus, although serious drug problems may not emerge until later in life, those problems likely had origins in the adolescent years.

To examine the drug resistance process among adolescents, the word *adolescent* must be clarified. Many studies focus on older students (e.g., high school seniors) because there are generally higher proportions of older students using substances (National Institute on Drug Abuse, 1992). In this book, we refer to adolescents as those youth from 11 to 18 years of age, crossing the span from middle school and high school to early years in college. It is necessary to delineate when we are talking about younger middle school youth and when we are talking about young college-age youth to understand the complexity of the drug resistance process as youth move through the adolescent cycle of their lives.

This book is about these youthful users; it is about the social processes of drug offers to adolescents and the relationships within which these offers occur. In addition, it examines the relationships that inhibit and promote drug use and the social and relational processes involved in preventing such use. Drug use does not occur in isolation. Except for those rare instances in which the substance is harvested or synthesized by the user, drug use is a social process that is part of the ongoing relational life of the adolescent. Because peer interaction relationships are vital to adolescents, we focus on these relationships as well as on the influence of family interaction on adolescent drug choices.

We acknowledge that psychosocial issues affect adolescent drug behavior, and these issues are not ignored. Yet we believe communication within the context of social relationships plays such a central role in adolescent drug choices that it justifies the primary focus of this book.

In this chapter, we present the background for an understanding of the social and particularly the relational processes of drug use and drug prevention. We discuss general demographic, individual, and social factors in drug use, and we argue for a communicative approach to the study of use and prevention. This approach is important because it allows us to explore the social and relational processes of drug offers.

ADOLESCENT DRUG USE PATTERNS

Many images in U.S. culture encourage alcohol and other drug use among adolescents. Specifically, media messages strongly influence attitudes, expectancies, intentions, and behaviors that then affect individual decisions about drug use. These media messages both reflect and shape the image of drug use among our youth. For example, the *story* of drug use that emerges when talking with adolescents contains images of the user as mature and unconventional and the act of engaging in drug use as a way of "killing time" (Alberts, Miller-Rassulo, & Hecht, 1991; Jessor, Chase, & Donovan, 1980; Jessor & Jessor, 1978).

In an attempt to counteract media influences, various campaigns to persuade teens to avoid drug use have been developed; these have given rise to media products such as "Reefer Madness" and "Just Say No." Unfortunately, few of these efforts have met with uniform and sustained success. Numerous and diverse studies suggest that the scare tactics of the 1950s and

1960s and the information campaigns of the 1970s and 1980s have had little effect on drug consumption by teenagers (Hanson, 1980; Johnston, O'Malley, & Bachman, 1987). There was a slight decline in illegal drug use among adolescents in the early 1980s, then a significant increase in use between 1992 and 1996, leading to a leveling off for most drugs by 1998. Although this plateau in the prevalence data is encouraging, overall use of alcohol and controlled substances among adolescents is still a problem. Tracking the prevalence of substance use among adolescents over the past seven years, the Monitoring the Future Study, which began in 1975 at the University of Michigan's Survey Research Center, provides a picture of adolescent drug use in the U.S. during the past few decades. Beginning in 1975 the study first focused on high school seniors and then in 1991 the annual survey was expanded to also include 8th- and 10th-graders. At each grade level the students are drawn to be representative of all students in public and private secondary schools nationwide (Johnston, O'Malley, & Bachman, 1998). The 1998 sample consisted of nearly 50,000 students in 422 public and private secondary schools and a sampling of the results indicate the following prevalence statistics for 1998.

- Among the class of 12th-graders, 54.1% of students had used an illicit drug by the time they reached their senior year. Of those students, 41.4% had used an illicit drug in the past 12 months.
- Forty-five per cent of 10th-graders report using illicit drugs in their lifetime compared to 29% of 9th graders.
- Among the class of 12th-graders, within the past year 37.5% had used marijuana/hashish, 74.3% had used alcohol, 52% report being drunk, and around 10% of these seniors had used hallucinogens or stimulants.
- During the 1990s, smoking rates among American teens rose to the highest levels in nearly 20 years.
- In 1998 the proportion of students reporting smoking any cigarettes in the prior 30 days was 19.1% of the 8th-graders, 27.6% of the 10th-graders, and 35.1% of the 12th-graders.
- In 1998 the proportion of students reporting smoking cigarettes daily was 8.8% of the 8th-graders, 15.8% of the 10th-graders, and 22.4% of the 12th-graders. Additionally, the 1998 proportion of students that smoked more than half a pack of cigarettes per day was 3.6% of the 8th-graders, 7.9% of the 10th-graders, and 12.6% of the 12th-graders.

- Among students in 8th, 10th, and 12th grades who are current smokers, Marlboro is by far the most common brand that they usually smoke. By Grade 12 nearly two-thirds (65%) of youngsters who are current smokers (i.e., have smoked any cigarettes in the prior 30 days), smoke Marlboro. (Among White 12th-graders, this proportion reaches 70%.)

- As early as eighth grade, the majority of youngsters who smoke—some 90%—can name a usual brand. And among those who have already established a half-pack-a-day-habit in eighth grade, 98% name a usual brand.

- The proportion of students who reported drinking five or more alcoholic drinks in the last two weeks was 13.7% of the 8th-graders, 24.3% of the 10th-graders, and 31.5% of the 12th-graders.

- The proportion of students who believe that drinking one to two alcoholic drinks per day is harmful was 30.3% of the 8th-graders, 31.9% of the 10th-graders, and only 24.3% of the 12th-graders believed frequent drinking is harmful.

- The proportion of students who believe that alcohol is fairly easy or very easy to get was 73.1% of the 8th-graders and 88% of the 10th-graders.

- The proportion of students who believe that marijuana is fairly easy or very easy to get was 50.6% of the 8th-graders, 77.9% of the 10th-graders, and 90.4% of the 12th-graders. This reflects the increased availability of drugs to adolescents that has steadily increased over the past decade.

The effects of drug and alcohol use on students can be both immediate and long term. A study of 813 students in Grades 5 to 12 revealed that only 25% of students receiving primarily As and Bs used drugs as compared with 100% of students receiving Ds and Fs (Coventry Drug and Alcohol Council, 1987). It is sobering to note that approximately 3.5 million adolescents have problems with alcohol, ranging from poor school performance to severe family conflicts (Forney, Forney, & Ripley, 1989) to truancy (Arizona Criminal Justice Commission, 1994) and delinquent and criminal behavior (Watts & Wright, 1990).

The risk of adolescent use is particularly acute for alcohol. Part of the problem with adolescent drinking behavior involves positive societal attitudes toward drinking. The trend in the United States for drinking to be symbolically associated with adult status encourages adolescent consumption. Youths believe they appear more adult when they drink and often use initiation into drinking as a rite of passage. Perhaps as a result, young people display more positive attitudes toward alcohol than other drugs. In particular, alcohol differs from tobacco and marijuana in its widespread acceptability; college students classify alcohol with prescription medicine as socially acceptable (Ellickson, 1984).

Perception of risk may also be a salient attitudinal factor in alcohol use. Research indicates that significant health and behavioral risks are associated with adolescent consumption (Hansen, Graham, Wolkenstein, Lundy, Pearson, Flay, & Johnson, 1988), yet teenagers perceive alcohol to be less risky than other drugs. Between 1975 and 1988, the difference in perceptions of risk between alcohol and other drugs increased. Although the perceptions of risk of using marijuana and cocaine on a regular basis have increased (from 43% to 77% and 73% to 89%, respectively), the perception of risk for regular use of alcohol remained almost static over the 13-year period.

We cannot ignore that there are perceived benefits of alcohol and other drug use.[1] Longitudinal studies indicate that alcohol consumption consistently precedes the use of illicit drugs (Andrews, Hops, Ary, Lichtenstein, & Tildesley, 1991). Adolescents often move from alcohol consumption into experimentation with marijuana with no expectations of negative consequences. Baumrind (1991b) suggested that experimental use of marijuana in nondelinquent populations is associated with positive characteristics such as friendliness, intelligence, and self-confidence. In fact, " ... drug use appears to be more a function of social and peer factors, whereas *abuse* appears to be more of a function of biological and psychological processes" (Glantz & Pickens, 1991, p. 9).

More important, teens also perceive positive consequences from the use of both alcohol and other drugs, although they cite different benefits for each. College-age women drink as an organized activity to relax, celebrate, and enhance enjoyment of eating (Hunter, 1990); college students also report that they drink for the taste (Barber & Gritching, 1987). Younger teens say they drink to get away from problems and "deal with" frustration and anger (National Institute on Alcohol Abuse and Alcoholism, 1986; Newcomb, 1995a). Reasons given for marijuana use include relaxation, pleasure, and because one's friends do (Toohey, Dezelsky, & Baffi, 1982).

---

[1]From this point on, except when stipulated, the term *drug* is an inclusive term referring to alcohol and other illicit drugs such as marijuana, cocaine, inhalants, and prescription medication.

Teens also say they drink to experience pleasure, create favorable peer impressions, and display a positive portrayal of self (Braucht, 1978). Some adolescents try drugs because they are curious (Bailey, Flewelling, & Rachal, 1992) or expect heightened sexual functioning by becoming drunk (Brown, Goldman, Inn, & Anderson, 1980). Several studies suggest that the consequences young people expect from drinking are associated with their drinking behavior (Jessor & Jessor, 1977). Thus, these positive attitudes and expectations likely encourage adolescent drug use.

There are three distinctive transitions in drug use among adolescents (Duncan & Petosa, 1995). The first transition is from nonuse to use, the second from use to abuse, and the third transition may be from abuse back to use or nonuse. The initiation of drug use does not necessarily lead to abuse; in fact, "the transition from nonuse to use of some drugs is a normative part of adolescent development in American culture" (Duncan & Petosa, 1995, p. 57). They suggest, however, that the transition from use to abuse is maladaptive and may carry social and health consequences.

Adolescents generally have difficulty assessing drug use risk or ascertaining the potential negative outcomes of use. Thus, adolescents continue to use drugs at alarming levels and with severe social, psychological, and physical implications. Associated with this use and abuse are positive attitudes about drugs and their consequences that support use. This can lead to destructive behavior and possible abuse. The next section reviews some of the central perspectives concerning adolescent drug use.

AN OVERVIEW OF PERSPECTIVES
ON ADOLESCENT DRUG USE

In an attempt to address adolescent drug use more effectively, a wide range of research has examined influences on adolescent substance use. Social explanations argue that drug use is a symptom of underlying social problems, whereas psychological explanations suggest drug use meets personal needs or compensates for personal problems. Psychosocial explanations are those that include characteristics of both the social environment and characteristics of the person (Oetting & Beauvais, 1983). Many adolescents experiment with drugs, but not all misuse or transition into abusing drugs. The remainder of this chapter and chapter 2 discuss certain factors that have been found to be related to substance use and misuse. This chapter looks specifically at demographic and individual factors. Chapter 2 addresses family and peer factors in detail.

Factors Associated With Drug Use

Drug Use and Demographic Factors. Research on the effects of demographics on drug use are mixed. For example, studies indicate that drug use among teenagers is higher when the family is not intact, when the adolescent does not live with his or her parents, and when there is little or no religious identification (Needle, McCuggin, Wilson, Reineck, Lazar, & Mederer, 1986). However, general population studies do not find an overt link between socioeconomic status (SES) and drug use. Although higher rates of drug use are found and can be attributed to the effects of extremely low SES (Padilla, Morales, & Olmedo, 1979), SES above this level appears to have little influence on drug use. However, SES can influence where a family lives, and environment can affect adolescents in several ways: by providing deviant role models, providing easier access to drugs, and encouraging youths to join gangs who often use drugs (Oetting & Beavais, 1987).

Relatedly, research consistently suggests that ethnicity plays a role in the use of alcohol and drugs. Earlier research indicated that members of certain ethnic groups are more at risk for use and the negative consequences of use than others (Bachman, Wallace, & O'Malley, 1991; Dryfoos, 1987; Kumpfer, 1989; Kumpfer & Turner, 1990; Newcomb, Maddahian, & Bentler, 1986; Pentz, Cormack, Flay, Hansen, & Johnson, 1986), and that members of various ethnic groups hold different attitudes toward drugs (Korzenny, McClure, & Rzyttki, 1990).

Ethnicity has been framed as a sociocultural factor in substance use. Although the use and abuse of licit and illicit drugs have been implicated as a primary cause for the disproportionate share of African-Americans and Latinos/as in drug and alcohol treatment (Secretary's Task Force on Black and Minority Health, 1986), surveys on drug use in adolescent populations indicate drug use between African-American and Latino/a youth is comparable to, if not lower than, that reported by White youth (Johnston et al., 1998; Wallace, Bachman, O'Malley, & Johnston, 1995). In addition, data from high school seniors do not indicate higher usage of licit or illicit drugs among minority ethnic groups. Trimble and Fleming (1989) also found no association between ethnic identity and drug/alcohol use for these groups. However, Wallace et al. (1995) posited that African-American and Latino/a youths are more suspicious of self-reports and confidentiality than Anglo populations, which may lead to an underestimation of actual alcohol and drug use for those groups. It is also possible that more minorities drop out of high school. Therefore, the sampling of high school seniors in these studies includes only those minority students who stayed in school. This excludes a large set of high-risk youth.

Hecht, Trost, Bator, and MacKinnon (1997) reported that Latino/as received drug offers at a significantly higher rate than either Whites or African Americans. Latinas, in particular, were at more risk than other females of receiving a drug offer. Other differences involve the location of drug offers and the adolescent's relationship to the offerer. More studies are needed on the etiological factors that influence drug use among youth from all racial/ethnic groups (Botvin, Schinke, & Orlandi, 1995; Collins, 1995; Escobedo, Remington, & Anda, 1989; Felix-Ortiz & Newcomb, 1995).

We are only just beginning to learn about the intersection among socioeconomic, environmental factors, and ethnicity. We do not fully understand the resiliency or protective factors that allow many members of such groups to avoid drug problems. Furthermore, by treating ethnic cultures as demographic groupings, we lose the diversity within collectivities and treat ancestry rather than culture as the relevant factor. Thus, we need to complement our group-based understanding with a focus on individual factors that influence adolescent drug use to more fully describe all of the multiple influences on adolescent drug use.

Drug Use and Individual Differences. Individual differences are believed to influence adolescents' risk for developing drug abuse, although the correlations between personality traits and drug use tend to be small (Wingard, Huba, & Bentler, 1979). Simons, Whitbeck, & Conger (1991) argued that psychological distress is only likely to increase the frequency of drug use if such behavior is approved by one's peer. However, youths who experience low self-esteem and/or depression do appear to be slightly more likely to use drugs, and there is a moderate correlation (.25) between drug use and chronic anger (Oetting & Beauvais, 1987). Whatever the psychological problems of adolescents, when they lead to feelings of social rejection and/or chronic anger, they increase the likelihood that the teenager will deviate and associate with deviant peers who use drugs.

Other personality factors associated with drug use are conformity, lack of future-oriented goals, and risk taking. Males who report that they often go along with the crowd, who feel a strong need to be liked, and who are followers rather than leaders drink more frequently than other males (McBride, Joe, & Simpson, 1991). As well, youth who lack future goals are more likely to be attracted to the excitement and danger associated with deviant groups (Simons, Conger, & Whitbeck, 1988). A study of adolescent reference groups found that higher sensation-seeking youth were more likely to report various sensations reminiscent of being high and were more likely to engage in drug use. Related tolerance for deviance has been found to be associated with adolescent drug use. Jessor and Jessor (1977) found that adolescent problem drinkers had greater tolerance for deviance, although this association was not found for college-age students. This led the authors to propose that tolerance for deviance is important when drinking is not socially or legally sanctioned.

Poor impulse control, difficult childhood temperament, lack of commitment to school, and low religiosity are all individual factors associated with greater risk for drug use (Brooke, Brooke, Gordon, Whiteman, & Cohen, 1990; Norman, 1995). Norman (1995) provided a nice overview of the personal attributes related to risk and resiliency.

Another important individual difference that is thought to impact students' drug habits is social skills. Youths with poor social skills (e.g., coercive personality styles) more often experience academic failure, are disruptive, and engage in troublesome behavior (Patterson, 1986). Such difficulties in school are likely to lead to negative labeling and rejection by conventional peers. Once rejected by their peers, these youths tend to drift into association with one another and form deviant peer groups. In addition, associative pairing occurs when youths who are more concerned with independence and excitement than with prosocial values are attracted to and form friendships with one another.

In addition, studies indicate a relationship between adolescents' social behavior (skills) and peer acceptance and rejection; most unaccepted children report social skills problems. Peer dislike has been found to be associated with specific negative responses and not simply with the absence of positive behavior (Coie, Dodge, & Coppotelli, 1982). Poor social skills are thought to be a determinant of poor coping patterns. Individuals who have difficulty forming close friendships, who are uncomfortable expressing their feelings, or who tend to be either under or overly assertive often are unable to use certain coping strategies. For example, they find it difficult to appropriately confront people who are sources of social stress or to mobilize social support (i.e., advice, assistance, reassurance) in response to a stressor. They also have difficulty responding appropriately to persuasive interactions (Simons et al., 1988).

All of the factors discussed in this chapter function together to predict and explain an individual's choice to use drugs. This choice is enacted in interaction, typically with peers. It is on this context of peer interaction that this book focuses to paint a clearer picture of adolescent drug use and relationships. Family and peer relationships are discussed in greater detail in chapter 2.

CHANGING ADOLESCENT DRUG USE

Although adolescent drug use likely has multiple causes, not all of the causes are equally easy to influence to prevent drug use. Individual skills have been the most accessible and direct avenue for effecting change. Early drug prevention approaches emphasize drug information and self-esteem. However, a variety of studies indicate that social skills training is the most effective means for altering adolescents' drug use patterns. Such training programs are grounded in the belief that peer pressure impacts attitudes, perceived norms, and behavior, and that specific refusal skills are necessary for adolescents to handle peer pressures (Bukoski, 1985; McCurdy, 1986). Tobler (1986, 1989) reported that social skills or peer programs are superior to other programs for the magnitude of effect size obtained; they produced the only results that show change toward the ultimate goal of reducing drug-abusing behaviors. However, it is also clear from more recent research that normative changes must accompany skill development.

Social Skills

The aim of social skills programs is to inoculate students against the pressure to use drugs by teaching them refusal skills. This approach involves: (a) making students aware of potential social influences, (b) teaching specific skills such as how to say no, and (c) correcting misperceptions of social norms (Botvin, 1986). This approach assumes that students' resistance to social pressure is improved by making them aware of the influences on them and by providing them with the opportunity to develop skills for resisting those influences.

The ability to say no competently is an important part of most prevention programs. However, effective refusal skills involve more than simply being able to say no. For a speaker to refuse competently, he or she must be able to say no in such a way that the relationship between the offerer and refuser is maintained. This is especially important to adolescents, for whom peer relationships are perceived to be both important and fragile. However, for the adolescent to be a competent communicator, he or she must take into account variations in the other's psychological characteristics or subjective perspective. The ability to make attributions concerning others' intentions, emotions, psychological characteristics, and subjective perspectives is necessarily intertwined with the development of communication effectiveness (Ritter, 1979).

Unfortunately, although adolescents possess the cognitive ability to take another's perspective, they often do not do so. Due to the particular egocentricism of adolescence, teenagers frequently have difficulty exercising their social perspective-taking skills to provide listener-adapted communication. This egocentricism emerges because adolescents are exceedingly self-aware and self-centered. Their self-awareness is such that they construct an imaginary audience who constantly and closely observe their actions. At the same time, their self-centeredness encourages them to develop personal narratives that highlight their uniqueness (Rawlins, 1992). Therefore, they believe others are as preoccupied with them as they are, yet they come to regard their own feelings as unique. Thus, although the adolescent tends to think of him or herself as having feelings no one else does, he or she simultaneously believes everyone sees the world as he or she does (Ritter, 1979).

This failure to take the other's perspective is particularly strong during early adolescence. Consequently, younger adolescents, who are subject to the most peer pressure, are the least competent to take others' perspectives and develop appropriate responses to drug and alcohol offers.

Despite their general failure to take others' perspectives, adolescents have the cognitive ability to do so. Although there is a relationship between age and perspective taking, there is none between age and cognitive complexity (Ritter, 1979). This suggests that training and experience can provide adolescents with the ability to take others' perspectives and can improve their ability to fashion appropriate refusal responses.

Many of the social skills training programs that have been developed thus far are based on Bandura's (1976) social learning work. Bandura's work suggests that adolescents may be taught to resist drugs and alcohol through modeling resistance skills for situations in which they are likely to find themselves. The theory explains how communication competence is developed and how new competencies may be taught via peer modeling. In addition, the theory posits that behavior is a function of social learning and that behavior change occurs when the target (adolescent) is provided with reasons to alter his or her behavior as well as the means and resources to do so (Bandura, 1990). Through modeling effective resistance skills, youth are provided with information, skills, and self-efficacy to master these skills (Bandura, 1990; Decker & Nathan, 1985).

Self-Efficacy and Competence in Resisting Drug Offers

Bandura (1990) defined *self-efficacy* as a positive perception of one's competence to perform certain tasks. The perception that the world is manageable and hopeful, and that one has control over one's fate, instills confidence. Self-efficacy is closely aligned with the concept of locus of control. If an adolescent feels that he or she has some influence over environmental circumstances and one's future destiny (Kumpfer, 1993), this provides a sense of mastery over one's life and choices. In the drug use context, this self-efficacy and perception of competence is particularly important. Ellickson, Hays, and Bell (1992) discovered that adolescents who *believed* that they had the competence to resist offers of drugs were more likely to actually do so.

Adolescents rarely begin drug use on their own, and most are initiated into drug use by their friends rather than strangers (Finnegan, 1979; Miller, 1998). For females, the friend most likely to offer a drug is a male partner (Hser, Anglin, & McGlothlin, 1987). Having a relationship with an offerer may make it difficult to resist offers while maintaining the integrity of the relationship.

One of the most common routes to adolescent drug use is through peer influence (Alberts, Hecht, Miller-Rassulo, & Krizek, 1992; Dielman, Butchart, & Shope, 1993). Oetting and Beauvais (1987) found that the influence of peers accounted for 95% of the variance in adolescents' drug use. Coombs, Paulson, and Richardson (1991) also found that those who used drugs were more susceptible when their peers used drugs. Peer influence is often conceptualized as occurring when strangers or acquaintances make drug offers; much less often is it cast as a relational event that occurs among friends.

During adolescence, friendship begins to play a more significant role in an individual's life. Consequently, adolescents may want to refuse drugs but are highly invested in preserving their relationship with the offerer and other friends in the vicinity. Social exchange theorists argue that individuals will not stay in a friendship if the costs outweigh the rewards, but other research suggests that children and adolescents will display loyalty toward their friends regardless of the costs involved (LaGapia & Wood, 1981). Perceptions of use by peers and family members may influence the acceptability and tolerance of drug use behavior and allow adolescents to integrate drug use into their friendships.

Norms are viewed as an adolescent's perception about the prevalence of drug use between peers and friends (Hansen, 1991). These peer norms are influential in early experimentation, whereas parental norms are influential in decisions to try other and more dangerous drugs (Hansen, 1991).

Norms

Norms can be seen as the motivational component of drug resistance competence. Cialdini, Reno, and Kallgren (1990) norm focus theory distinguishes among three types of norms: injunctive, descriptive, and personal. *Injunctive norms* describe what people should do; they are approval-oriented and externally imposed by others (e.g., the society at large, parents, peers, etc.). Injunctive norms motivate behavior by promising either rewards or punishments (sanctions). An example would be the typical edict from parents and authorities that "drugs are bad, don't do them." *Descriptive norms* describe what most people do. They provide frequency information about the behavior of important reference figures or groups and motivate behavior by providing information about what is most effective and adaptive in the situation. For instance, college students who perceive drinking to be excessive and widespread on their campus are more likely to be problem drinkers than those students who hold a more realistic, moderate perception of community norms regarding drinking (Berkowitz & Perkins, 1988). As is seen, simply changing these descriptive norms can have a powerful effect on subsequent drug use. *Personal norms* (Schwartz, 1977) are internalized values and expectations for one's own behavior irrespective of external reward or evidence. Moral obligations typically flow from personal norms. Students are expressing personal norms when they declare that "I'm not the type of person who does drugs."

The Cialdini et al. (1990) norm focus theory suggests that one's behavior is driven by the norm that is made most salient in the situation under consideration. They found that they could instantiate a descriptive norm about littering simply by placing a single piece of trash in an otherwise clean environment. One piece of trash is very salient in a clean environment, triggering the "people don't litter here" norm and decreasing littering behavior. Conversely, a littered environment can trigger the "everyone's doing it" norm, thereby inviting more littering behavior. They were also able to trigger an injunctive norm and reduce littering by sweeping a large pile of litter to the side of the lot ("littering is bad and must be cleaned up"). As noted earlier, two or more conflicting norms may be operating in any given situation, blurring what is appropriate behavior.

Norm focus theory also suggests that the most prominent norm in one's mind guides behavior. For instance, offers of beer in a dating context could trigger a "please your partner and go along" norm, an "I don't do drugs" norm, or an "all of my friends drink with their partners" norm. The norm that is primed may help determine drug use in that situation. Cialdini et al. (1990) found that injunctive norms—those that sanction undesirable behaviors—are more effective than the other two types across a wider variety of situations. They also found that two types of norms working toward the same behavioral goal are more effective than one. This finding has important implications for drug resistance training, which has recently emphasized modifying descriptive norms more than instilling relevant injunctive norms. Combined with descriptive norms, injunctive norms offer an equally important strategy that can use the sanctions of the peer group to regulate and reduce undesirable behaviors. Also, distinguishing among injunctive, descriptive, and personal norms acknowledges the complexity of normative processes. It is easy to commingle the separate effects of descriptive and injunctive norms, which is usually done, and it is usually approved of by others. However, distinguishing among them emphasizes their unique contribution to motivating behavior and the potential for enhancing the power of norms when two different types are activated with the same goal in mind (i.e., helping adolescents establish connections between appropriate norms may enhance their power by priming related and reinforcing behavioral rules). These reinforced norms may then become more easily accessed norms and followed when situations present conflicting goals between two partners.

In addition to the problem of priming multiple norms, Guerra, Huesmann, and Hanish (1995) argued that normative beliefs may influence behavior at several different points in a decision-making cycle. According to their model, norms can affect what we attend to in the environment, trigger automatic responses, and filter out behaviors that are inconsistent with scripted behaviors. First, normative beliefs affect the salience of various cues in the situation and how those cues are evaluated. For instance, a student who has lost a friend to a drunk driver is particularly aware of a person who shows up drunk to a school event and more likely to view the drunk as a potential threat. Second, norms can act as retrieval cues causing people to respond automatically in situations based on their normative beliefs. Students who believe that it is okay to use drugs may automatically try a new substance without knowing or considering the potentially negative consequences of using it. This automatic responding is enhanced by the tendency of normative beliefs to filter out any behaviors that might violate those beliefs, such as questioning the potential side effects of an unknown substance. This model complicates our understanding of the potential impact of norms on behavior—the norm that is primed matters, as does the point in the behavioral sequence at which the norm is primed. Those norms that enter into behavior sequences early are those that are most ingrained, connected to the self-identity, and most influential in peer relationships.

COMMUNICATIVE NATURE OF DRUG RESISTANCE

Previous social skills programs have attempted to teach resistance methods. More recently, they have focused on perceptions of norms, yet these programs do not pay sufficient attention to the communicative nature of drug resistance. If one wishes to teach resistance and life skills, one must first understand how adolescents effectively say "no" by analyzing the communicative and social processes of resistance. Resistance is predicated on both the motivation to resist and the specific offer. Different response strategies are required for different influence attempts by different offerers in different settings. The type of message used to offer a substance—be it peer pressure based or otherwise—is likely to figure prominently in determining the appropriate response for intervention.

Narrative Theory

Because resistance is a communicative phenomenon, we cannot ignore the perspective of the actor—the adolescent—in the resistance process. However, the majority of existing programs advocate resistance skills, which were developed by adults with the belief that they are appropriate to adolescents' experiences. Because the measurement of the efficacy of these programs has involved imagined encounters or appraisal of knowledge, there is inadequate proof that these skills are applicable to the real-life experiences that adolescents must confront. Bandura (1976) and Miller-Rassulo and Hecht (1988) argued that the success of role modeling is dependent on both realism and involvement. Bandura's work suggests that peer modeling of situations from the adolescent's own experience facilitates transference of identification and learning into behavior change. In addition, social influence research reports differences between imposing lists of strategies on respondents and allowing respondents to generate their own strategies (Burleson, Wilson, Waltman, Goering, Ely, & Whaley, 1988).

Narrative theory suggests that adolescents organize and make sense of their world through the development of their own personal narratives. Narratives are the talk organized around consequential events (Neimeyer, 1995), with a protagonist "inspirited with intentionality, undertaking some action, within the story itself" (Russell & Lucariello, 1992, p. 671), and with implicit or explicit end points (Gergen & Gergen, 1986). Narratives are also strongly tied into one's speech community, such as youth culture, and serve as an organizing principle for behavior (Botvin et al., 1995).

Narratives contextualize historical acts and provide structures of meaning that allow the person to understand their social roles, relationships, and wider social plot of which they are a part (Neimeyer & Stewart, 1996). The stories that adolescents tell themselves and others reflect personal attitudes, beliefs, and understandings of group norms. These narratives consist of language that structures experience and provides a framework for reality (Riessman, 1993). It is also through the reception of narratives in one's own social group (e.g., family, peer, ethnic) that adolescents learn of the experiences of others, learn group expectations and norms, and, through identification with group narratives, learn new behaviors.

The role modeling inherent in social learning theory is dependent on both the realism and involvement of culturally specific narratives. Narrative accounts of substance use experiences in the youth culture, from the adolescent's own perspective, provides narrative knowledge of adolescent drug use and misuse. This narrative knowledge informs our understanding of the drug resistance process and allows us to develop prevention efforts that model a conservative image of drug use.

Relational Communication Competence

All communication occurs within the context of some form of relationship. However, past resistance programs have developed their methods without a clear picture of how drugs are offered, who offers them, the strategies teens use to resist, and the circumstances under which they are resisted. Communication research suggests that, to be maximally effective, messages must be adapted to the audience and situation. Therefore, to be effective, resistance strategies must be developed and taught that are specific to the types of situations, relationships, and offers adolescents experience.

If resistance is an adolescent's goal, communication competence in the context of relational considerations is central to that process. Dillard (1990) and Clark and Delia (1979) provided a framework for a communication perspective of drug use. Their model addresses relational and identity goals in interaction. Dillard suggested that adolescents may have primary goals (e.g., offer a drug, accept or reject the drug) as well as secondary goals of identity and interpersonal relationship management. In this goal-focused model, communication is seen as strategic and directed toward goal attainment. Within this framework, an effective resistance strategy is one that satisfies the primary goal (refusal) and both parties' relational and identity goals (Harrington, 1995). However, recent research indicates that junior high students may not have a large or sophisticated repertoire of drug resistance strategies (Hecht, Trost, Bator, & MacKinnon, 1997; Miller, 1998). In fact, most of these students typically use a simple "no" to reject both initial and repeated offers of drugs. Unfortunately, this response is the one most likely to be followed up with additional pressure to take drugs (Alberts et al., 1991, 1992).

Successful drug resistance requires communication competencies in which messages are constructed to resist social influence while maintaining the relationship. A theoretical model of communication competence (Spitzberg & Cupach, 1984; Spitzberg & Hecht, 1984) argues that competence is a relational phenomenon that requires four components: knowledge, motivation, skills, and outcomes. Relational competence stresses the outcomes for both parties; it suggests that communication that optimizes mutual outcomes is maximally effective. When cast into a drug resistance framework (e.g., if Chris offers marijuana to Jordan and Jordan's reply both resists the offer and does not offend Chris), continued pressure is less likely, resistance is successful, and the relationship is maintained. These components of relational communicative competence mirror elements of successful drug prevention:

- *Knowledge* typically includes understanding the effects of drugs, the context, and the topic.
- *Motivation* entails perceptions of peer norms, attitudes, and consequences, and a desire to engage in resistance.
- *Skills* are life skills and the messages used to refuse drugs.
- *Outcomes* are the consequences for self, other, and the relationship.

Thus, to competently resist offers of drugs, adolescents need adequate knowledge, appropriate motivation, and skills to produce desirable outcomes.

This emphasis on the relational aspects of the situation follows from an interactionist perspective on drug use—the notion that drug use occurs in an interdependent episode to which both partners bring needs and goals. The relational competence model emphasizes that successful communication is: (a) effective in achieving personal objectives, and (b) appropriate to the relationship and the social context (Spitzberg & Cupach, 1984; Spitzberg & Hecht, 1984). Communication is effective when a message is sent and received as intended; it is appropriate when it does not violate valued rules, norms, or expectations. A unique aspect of this model extends the current prevention approaches by evaluating communication competence at the dyadic level (i.e., by considering whether the goals of effectiveness and appropriateness are met for both participants in the interaction.). For instance, being assailed with insults for politely refusing a joint is an instance in which communication is unsuccessful and unsatisfactory for both partners. Hence, even a typically competent communicator can have an incompetent episode with a hostile or noncommunicative partner. The positivity of interactions with a partner is one determinant of whether a relationship continues to become more intimate. If one partner is encouraging drug use when the other partner wants to avoid drug use, dyadic effectiveness is difficult to achieve unless the person who is offered can refuse in a manner that is also satisfying to the person who offered.

This book uses the framework of relational communication competence, along with narrative theory, to examine adolescents' own successful and unsuccessful drug communication strategies, situate those strategies in interaction, and use those strategies to develop an effective communication competency, skills training prevention program.

After discussing adolescent family and peer relationships in general, the remainder of this book describes the research findings of a series of studies we conducted and of other researchers pursuing similar goals. Through these studies, we extend narrative theory into the substance use arena and describe the communicative competence associated with drug resistance—the knowledge, motivation, and skills that adolescents need to refrain from drugs and maintain relationships.

SUGGESTED READINGS ON FACTORS INFLUENCING ADOLESCENT DRUG USE

Demographics

Bachman et al., 1991, 1997; Beauvais et al., 1996; Behnke et al., 1997; Downs & Robertson, 1987/1988; Flannery et al., 1994; Hawkins et al., 1991, 1992, 1994; Johnston et al., 1989; Jones & Battjes, 1985; Kallan, 1998; Marston et al., 1988;

NIDA, 1992, 1996; Oetting & Beauvais, 1987; Padilla et al., 1979; Warheit et al., 1996

Ethnicity

Amey et al., 1998; Bachman et al., 1991; Bass, 1993; Botvin et al., 1995; Botvin & Schinke, 1997; Dryfoos, 1987; Felix-Ortiz & Newcomb, 1995; Gil, Vega, & Biafora, 1998; Hecht et al., 1997; Johnston et al., 1993, 1996, 1998; Korzenny et al., 1990; Kumpfer, 1989; Kumpfer & Turner, 1990, 1991; Longshore et al., 1997; Newcomb, 1995a,; Parker, 1995a, 1995b; Pentz et al., 1990; Trimble, 1995; Vega et al., 1993; Vega & Gil, 1998; Wallace, 1994; Watts & Wright, 1990; Yates, 1987

Individual Differences

Coie et al., 1982; Dryfoos, 1990; Forney et al.,1989; Gullota et al., 1995; Hansen & Ponton, 1996; Hawkins et al., 1992; Hecht & Driscoll, 1994; Jessor & Jessor, 1978; Kumpfer & Turner, 1990; McBride et al., 1991; Felix-Ortiz & Newcomb, 1995; Novaceck, Raskin, & Hogan,1991; Oetting & Beauvais, 1987; Osgood et al., 1996; Patterson, 1986; Schinka et al., 1999; Simons et al., 1991

2

Adolescent Relationships and Drug Use: Family and Peer Influences

A primary goal of this book is to examine how an adolescent's relationships can either facilitate or impede drug use. By nature, humans are social animals; we live and thrive in groups that provide us with a sense of affiliation and identification. The primary group with which we identify tends to change over the course of our lives, moving from an exclusive identification with our family members to an identity that is not only expressed through our family connection, but also through our choice of friends, romantic partners, and work environments. These influences are not always complementary, and adolescents must manage shifting loyalties and overlapping identities. Mismanagement can have serious consequences; choosing to belong to a clique of drug users facilitates subsequent drug use. In an effort to better understand the impact of various relationships on adolescent behavior, this chapter provides an overview of how adolescents' families, peers, and romantic partners affect drug use and resistance.

FAMILY INFLUENCES

Because the family is the social unit primarily responsible for modeling communication behavior and teaching social skills, family interactions should also provide models for competencies related to drug resistance and use. In fact, research consistently points out that, although peers play a crucial role in levels of current adolescent drug use, it is the attitudes and behaviors of parents, the quality of family life, and the relationship between the parent and child that play the most crucial role in initiation and experimentation with alcohol, tobacco, and other drugs (Baumrind, 1983; Kumpfer & Alvarado, 1995).

Before children engage in relationships with peers, they have relationships with family members. Family members' behaviors, in particular, have lasting effects on children, especially in shaping their drug attitudes and values (Newcomb, 1995b). According to Kandel (1996), scholars who view family influences as less important than peer influences are ignorant of the central role of family relationships in influencing adolescents' values, norms, and peer group selection.

Family relationships may influence adolescents in a myriad of ways. With regard to drug use, parental and sibling drug use behavior, the quality of parenting skills, and the quality of the parent–adolescent relationship are of particular concern.

Family Member Drug Use

Parental use is one of the four factors that increases the probability that adolescent experimentation will escalate into drug abuse (Willis & Vaughn, 1989). Perceptions of fathers and mothers drinking, and the fathers actual drinking, are the strongest influences on adolescent males' alcohol use. A father's drinking also influences females' drinking practices, whereas a mother's does not (Wilks, Callan, & Austin, 1989). Clearly, drugs and alcohol are much more likely to be available in the home when parents indulge.

Both parental history of drug use and the current status of parental drug use are positively correlated with an increased risk factor for children (Baumrind, 1990; Cutter & Fisher, 1980). In fact, McLaughlin, Bauer, Burnside, & Pokorny (1985) found that parental alcohol use was the best predictor of adolescent alcohol use. Kafka and London (1991) and Query (1985) suggested that family members may be a primary source of socialization into drug abuse.

Older siblings may be even more important than parents as role models for younger adolescents ages 11 to 13. Adolescents with older, drug-using siblings start using drugs at an earlier age than do other similarly aged adolescents who do not have older siblings or whose older siblings do not use drugs. Although parental use does predict adolescent use of cigarettes and beer, older sibling use predicts adolescent use for all substances (Needle et al., 1986).

Family use may provide availability and modeling opportunities for use and misuse, and the interpersonal relationships of parents to each other and with their children are strongly related to adolescent substance use and abuse. Over and over again, the quality of family life emerges as a salient influence on adolescent substance use behavior (Gullotta, Adams, & Montemayor, 1995; Hawkins et al., 1992).

Family Relationships

Family correlates of drug use beyond parental and sibling drug use include: poor socialization practices, poor supervision, poor discipline skills, poor parent–child relationships, excessive marital discord, family chaos and stress, poor parental mental health, family isolation, poor family acculturation, family stability, safety of the neighborhood in which a family resides, favorable family norms toward drug use, and family communication (Catalano, Haggerty, Gainey, & Hoppe, 1997; Coombs, Paulson, & Richardson, 1991; Kumpfer, Molgaard, & Spoth, 1996; Newcomb, 1992; Turner, 1995). Werner and Smith (1992) discovered that the death of a significant adult in a child's life before he or she reaches the age of 11 also increases the risk of adolescent substance use and misuse.

Not all parental variables, however, demonstrate a linear relationship with adolescent drug use. Parental socioeconomics appear to have a curvilinear effect on drug participation among youths. A number of unique findings contribute to that conclusion. First, adolescents in the lower socioeconomic strata or the offspring of unemployed parents are at greater risk of drug use (National Institute on Drug Abuse, 1989a). Second, although the frequency of adolescent drinking has been found to be positively related to social class (Gossett, Lewis, & Austin-Phillips 1980), Kaplan (1979) concluded that the adolescent members of upper income families were more likely to become alcohol abusers. McLaughlin et al. (1985) and Turner (1995) suggested that in both socioeconomic extremes, there is a greater likelihood for both parents to work or otherwise be occupied outside the home, thereby providing less supervision of adolescent behavior.

The more risk factors to which a child is exposed (e.g., demographic, individual, family), the more protective factors that child needs to offset these stressors (Catalano, Haggerty, Gainey, & Hoppe, 1997; Durlack, 1995; Hawkins et al., 1992; Kumpfer, 1989; Newcomb, 1992; Turner, 1995). Risk factors can be considered predictors of substance abuse. Much research has focused on eliminating, reducing, or mitigating those factors that are linked with substance use (Hawkins, Catalano, & Miller, 1992).

An alternative area of productive research effort, however, has been in the area of protective and resiliency factors. A focus on resiliency seeks to enhance factors that protect against vulnerability in the face of life's stressors (Masten, Best, & Garmezy, 1990). Norman (1995) suggested that an emphasis on coping rather than risk shifts our perspective from fatalism to opportunity. With this opportunity comes the necessity to distinguish resiliency factors and protective factors.

Kumpfer (1993) provided a working model that characterizes resiliency factors as an individual characteristic. Some of these resiliency factors have been identified as self-esteem, easy temperament, academic achievement, humor, empathy, age, self-efficacy, and communication skills (Norman, 1995). Conversely, this same model presents protective factors as characteristics of the environment (Kumpfer, 1993). Some protective factors that have been identified include:

- parent education
- availability of school, family, and community resources
- positive, warm, and caring parenting
- clear parental expectations
- given family responsibilities
- good parenting skills and supervision
- family traditions and rituals
- extended family support networks (Turner, 1995, pp. 43–51).

Many treatment evaluations suggest that when families are included in prevention programs, risk factors can be reduced and family skills improved. In this way, the chance of onset of use is diminished (Bry, 1983; Bry, Catalano, Kumpfer, Lochman, & Szapocznik, 1999; Glynn & Haenlein, 1988). These treatment programs often utilize family systems approaches, where family processes such as adaptability, cohesion, and closeness are central to prevention and intervention (Palmer & Liddle, 1994). We know that secure, nurturing attachments with caregivers and a structured, consistent environment are strong protective factors for children (Werner, 1990). Similarly, Dodge (1991) found that nurturing and consistent parenting leads to more accurate encoding and interpretation of social cues by children. In the frame of social influence, this may affect the communicative competence of an adolescent to interpret offers and encode refusals.

In family therapy, the structural and strategic therapeutic family approaches are systematically evaluated to assess efficacy. The Oregon Social Learning Center (OSLC) targets parent management practices as part of

their therapeutic approach (Dishion & Kavenaugh, 1999). The parent training interventions emerge from the social learning principals of social learning theory (Bandura, 1986), where it is suggested that behavior is learned
through the process of modeling and reinforcement. Therefore, targeting
the parental unit may result in changes in adolescent behavior. Robins,
Helzer, Croughan, and Ratcliff (1981) situated problem-solving training in
the family-based environment and found that it reduced drug use and
school problems. Joanning, Quinn, Thomas, and Mullen (1992) compared
family-based interventions against nonfamily-based interventions and
found that the family-based were most effective. Liddle (1996) found similar results.

Family relationships affect an adolescent's attitudes, skills, choices, and
behaviors concerning alcohol and other drug use. A social development
model suggests that parents who are unskilled or feel helpless in controlling
their child's behavior will possibly stop monitoring what that child does.
This lack of monitoring may establish fertile ground for problem behavior
(Patterson, Reid, & Dishion, 1992). Family conflict is strongly associated
with higher levels of drug use risk, whereas family cohesion may function
as a protective factor (Duncan, Duncan, & Hops, 1994).

Research suggests that the impact that family members' unhealthy habits
have on their children may be minimized if family members engage in communication about use and abuse. Communication is inherent in family systems, family therapy, social learning, and social development approaches.
In most family intervention programs, problem-solving skills and communication skills are promoted. Yet communication is often conceptualized
and operationalized in terms of style rather than substance.

Family Communication and Drugs

A National Center on Addictions and Substance Abuse study finds that over
half of the parents surveyed expect their children to try illegal drugs, but
only 14% hold themselves accountable (Califano, 1997). Although the
family is the social unit primarily responsible for childrearing functions
(Bruner, 1990; Dishion, 1997; Fitzpatrick & Badzinski, 1994) and family
interaction is clearly influential on a child's behavior (Baumrind, 1966,
1978, 1983, 1989, 1990; Noller, 1994; Patterson, 1982; Patterson &
Yoerger, 1997; Socha & Stamp, 1995), actual communicative interaction
between parents and adolescents about risky behavior such as drug use may
be quite low. A Children's Defense Fund (1994) study suggested that one in
five teens have not spoken to either parent for more than 10 minutes during

the last month. This is a cause for concern when we consider that parental influence has been reported as more important than peer influence regarding youths' reasons for nonuse (Coombs, Paulson, & Richardson, 1991).

ABC News and the *Washington Post* surveyed a random sample of 1,145 parents and children and found that 85% of parents report talking with their children about illegal drugs, but only 45% of their children can recall such a conversation. Although some parents believe that discussing drugs will condone their use, other parents leave drug education up to the schools because they do not feel they have the expert advice needed.

Beyond this media research, certain intervention research has focused on parental communication strategies to influence drug attitudes (Beck & Lockhart, 1992; Klingle & Miller, 1998). Throughout adolescence, parents continue to impact their sons and daughters. Although peers play a crucial role in levels of current adolescent drug use, it is the attitudes and behaviors of parents, the quality of family life, and the relationship between the parent and child that play a critical role (Kumpfer & Alvarado, 1995).

Bry et al. (1999), Catalano et al. (1997), Conger and Elder (1994), Dishion (1997), and Kumpfer (1998) are a few of the many scholars in the drug abuse prevention area that support family-based prevention strategies and interventions as the most effective approach for reducing adolescent substance abuse and associated problem behaviors. Improving parenting practices and understanding family dynamics is central to effective family interventions. In fact, according to the Center for Substance Abuse Prevention (CSAP; 1998), only three family approaches appear to meet the National Institute on Medicine's criteria for effectiveness. Those three approaches are: behavioral parent training, family therapy, and family skills training approaches to prevention. Exemplary programs in these areas are Strengthening Families (Kumpfer, 1998), Focus on Families (Catalano et al., 1997), and Family Effectiveness Training (Szapocznik & Kurtines, 1989). These family programs encourage family members to increase family communication and reduce family conflict (Kumpfer, 1998).

Klingle and Miller (1998) found that family members' communication of antidrug messages significantly affected drug use. These scholars suggested that family communication of information, clear norms, and values serve as a protective factor against youth drug use and misuse. This finding was particularly important for younger children. However, for the older adolescents in their study (e.g., 12th grade), family communication aimed at deterrence did not appear to be an effective protective factor (Klingle & Miller, 1998).

Miller (1998) examined African-American and European-American adolescents' perceptions of their parent–child communication about alcohol, tobacco, and other drug use. The results indicate that parent–child drug conversations may not actually occur for many adolescents. Out of the 67 adolescent respondents 43.3% indicated they had communicated about alcohol, tobacco, and other drug use with their parent(s). Hence, 56.7% have *not* communicated about alcohol, tobacco, and other drug use with their parent(s). Forty-five percent of African-American youth report talking with their parents compared with 39.1% of European-American youth.

Regardless of ethnicity, the adolescents in Miller's (1998) study felt more comfortable talking with mothers than any other family member about important topics such as alcohol, tobacco, and other drug use. Almost 70% of all respondents reported that they felt closest with their mothers, even when controlling for the presence of fathers in their lives. The following illustrates the importance of mothers in these adolescents' lives (Miller, 1998, p. 10).

Charles: I can talk with my mom the best. She can understand me a lot better. She is my best friend ... my mom.

Kevin: My mom is the only one. She says that African-Americans use more [drugs] because the White people try to make us look bad. They got us to do it.

Pick and Palos (1995) reported that the mothers in their study showed higher overall levels of communication with children than did fathers. In addition, fathers consistently overestimated their level of communication with their children (Apter, 1993; Pick & Palos, 1995). Although children may be more likely to engage in conversation with mothers about risky topics, other research indicates that children are more likely to obey their fathers (Grusec & Goodnow, 1994). Moon, Jackson, and Hecht (in press) discovered that resiliency plays a large role in the age of first use and overall drug use. Resiliency factors such as satisfying family relations, low parental permissiveness, and perceived neighborhood safety had significant direct effects on drug use. This seemed, however, to be more important for males than females.

In studies that have linked parental norms—typically maternal and child alcohol use norms—parental norms have been assessed by the children's perceptions of their parents norms rather than the parents' reports of their own norms (Jessor, Donovan, & Costa, 1991). Brody and colleagues (1998) addressed this gap with a study of parents' self-reported alcohol use norms and their child's alcohol use norms. The authors found that as children got older they were more likely to develop more liberal norms of the larger society, but youth who developed norms that defined alcohol use during adolescence as unacceptable experienced the onset of drinking at older ages. This study found that frequent parent–child discussions in which both parents' and children's perspectives were aired would orient children to more conservative norms for alcohol use (Brody, Flor, Hollett-Wright, & McCoy, 1998). They discovered that frequent and bidirectional parent–child discussions were linked with abstinence-based alcohol use norms.

Scholars have been calling for more family-focused prevention efforts since the 1980s (Kaufmann & Borders, 1988; Kumpfer & Alvarado, 1995; Rose, Battjes, & Leukefeld, 1984). Yet few studies focus on prevention tactics that take into consideration the bidirectional, transactional nature of communication in the family. Communication is a symbolic transactional process in which both participants affect and are affected by the interaction. The transactional approach emphasizes the interdependence of relationships in understanding parent–child communication. Lollis and Kuczynski (1997), Petit and Lollis (1997), and O'Connor, Hetherington, and Clingempeel (1997) suggested that the bidirectional, transactional dynamic in the parent–child interaction has been neglected in empirical research.

Although much more needs to be systematically examined, there are several organizations that offer tips for parents on how to talk with youth about alcohol and other drug issues. Two of the top organizations that focus on drug education that have excellent web sites are the National Institute on Drug Abuse (NIDA; *www.nida.nih.gov/BacktoSchool*) and the Partnership for a Drug Free America (*www.drugfreeamerica.org/tips.html*).

The NIDA site offers a "Mind over Matter" curriculum that guide adolescents into making their own decisions, slide teaching packets, information documents in both spanish and english (National Institutes on Health, 1997). The Partnership site offers tips for parents, education on a variety of drugs, physical and emotional signs of drug abuse, and links to organizations involving parents. Some key advice from this site encourages parents to teach values to their children, set and enforce rules, teach children how to follow rules, listen carefully, let kids know that it is okay to act independently, role play how to say "no," encourage choice, provide age-appropriate information, establish a clear family position on drugs, and set a good example for their children.

Future research efforts still need to examine family discussions about norms, values, boundaries, and sanctions regarding adolescent drug use. We need to understand who participates in these family discussions, who initiates them and how, where they occur, and the motivations or catalysts for these discussions. Regarding content, additional research should focus on the content and relational messages that are included in these discussions, the specific content of the discussions, whether personal and family norms are complementary or contradictory, the communication strategies employed during these discussions, and comparisons of drug talks among different dyadic pairs (i.e., parent–child, sibling–sibling, peer–peer). Before we can look at these questions, however, a more general discussion of parent–child communication is warranted.

General Parent–Child Communication

Parental Communication Styles.   Diane Baumrind (1966, 1978, 1983, 1989, 1990) has pioneered the study of parenting styles. Baumrind (1990) extended her examination of parenting styles to include the relationship between style and adolescent drug use. She found that nonauthoritarian but directive styles of parenting demonstrated the lowest occurrence of adolescent drug use. Nonauthoritarian refers to a style that is less intrusive on children than authoritarian families; Although there is parental control, it is not without explanation. These families tend to be directive as well, indicating a parental style that is disciplined, orderly, and where the children are monitored. Interestingly enough, relatively high adolescent drug use was found in democratic style families whose parenting is supportive, caring, and responsive, but has less conventional control and indirect demands. Democratic parents tend to use more alcohol, tobacco, and other drugs than do other parents and were rather permissive and tolerant in their attitudes toward drug use. The homes with the most adolescent drug use were the unengaged. These families were neither demanding, structured, nor responsive. The families were disorganized and had a high divorce rate.

There is mounting evidence that coercive strategies are counterproductive for encouraging long-term features of social competence in children (Hoffman, 1980; Peterson & Zill, 1986). Coercive strategies tend to minimize and discourage internalization or commitment to parents' perspectives and the tendency to become self-efficacious—self-responsible for their own actions. Conversely, parenting that is warm, open, sensitive, and responsive and provides general support, physical affection, acceptance, and companionship is associated with competence. Communication competence is linked to social perspective taking and having an internal locus of control. Yet this research is typically not culturally sensitive.

Parenting Strategies and Orientation.   When discussing parental communication, induction as a parental strategy is worth noting. Induction is used by parents to explain how a child's actions have either positive or negative consequences for both themselves and others (Hoffman, 1980). Power may be examined bidirectionally as a child effect as well as a parent effect within the parent–child relationship (Peterson & Rollins, 1987). This strategy uses minimal imposition of authority; it gives children an opportunity to engage in two-way communication and express viewpoints that differ from parents' perspective. Induction is an attempt by parents to seek compliance from their children by appealing to the children's innate rationality, empathy, and pride.

Current research suggests that parental induction may foster higher self-esteem in children—an important cognitive resource for social competence (Openshaw, Thomas, & Rollins, 1983). The use of induction as a childrearing behavior often communicates to children their ability to (a) engage in dialogue with parents, (b) be treated with respect, (c) evaluate the consequences of their own behavior, and (d) to make decisions based on these judgments (Peterson & Rollins, 1987).

In addition to induction, two parent–child communication orientations have been identified in the family literature: conformity orientation and conversation orientation (Ritchie & Fitzpatrick, 1990). A family whose communication emphasizes cooperation and family harmony are said to have a *conformity orientation,* whereas a *conversation orientation* emphasizes conversation and open exchange of ideas. Ritchie and Fitzpatrick (1990) found that children in families who have a strong conformity orientation are more susceptible to outside influence than children in families with a conversational orientation. A strong conversational orientation may open the window for new ideas and encourage an adjustment of old ideas.

Miller (1998) reported that mothers are most likely to talk with their children about alcohol and other drug use. Mothers are also most likely to emphasize the conversation orientation over conformity (Wood, 1996). Conversation orientation may teach a way of communicating and thinking that encourages consideration of new ideas, questioning others opinions, and actively pursuing information. Dixson (1995) actually found conversational orientation to be the best single predictor of family satisfaction.

Research on parent–child communication about drug use raises a number of questions: Do parents and children avoid or ignore this type of communication interaction, or are parents proactive with their messages to engender interpersonal competence and self-agency in their children? Conversely, are parents proactive with their messages, but nonetheless motivated by the need to ensure compliance? Baumrind (1983) pointed out that this approach by parents emphasizes external compliance and internal conformity to parental expectation. Then again, are parents or children reactive to these topics to protect and retain the balance in the family (i.e., safety, comfort, power) or reactive to punish and regain power in the family? What are the motivations behind parent–child communicative interaction about drug use?

Another way in which parents may affect adolescents drug use patterns is through their influence on teenagers' peer relationships. Parents can play a large role in their children's success or lack of success with their peers. Peer rejection is associated with certain family backgrounds, such as family instability (e.g., divorce), low socioeconomic status (SES; Patterson, Vaden, & Kuperschmidt, 1991), poor maternal attachment, and parental warmth and conflict style, among others (Cohn, Patterson, & Christopoulos, 1991).

Parental influences on children's peer relations are important because of the strong influence peers have on adolescent drug habits. An examination of the influence of various risk factors on adolescent drug use indicates that poor relationships with parents accounted for 16% of the variance, whereas peer use accounted for 41% (Newcomb, et al., 1986). Indeed, parents can impact their children's drug use in several ways, including indirectly by influencing their adolescent's social skills, which then influence peer relations and subsequent substance use. A variety of research indicates that youth who are heavy substance users are those who engage in deviant behavior, associate with deviant peers, and have experienced social failure or rejections (Kandel, 1983; Patterson & Yoeger, 1997). Peer relationships are discussed next. These relationships hold particular power over the beliefs and behaviors of most individuals, particularly adolescents.

Drug Use and Peer Relationships

Among the most important tasks associated with adolescence is the development of identity, intimacy, and appropriate public behavior (Rawlins, 1992). For adolescents to accomplish these tasks, they need relationships with peers who act as models, mirrors, helpers, testers, and foils (Douvan & Adelson, 1966). Healthy development in adolescence requires teens to become independent of their parents and become socially integrated with their peers (Christopher, 1994). Affiliation with a peer group provides a context wherein adolescents can increasingly develop their self-images. Through relations with peers, they create an understanding of their world by debating, discussing, compromising and negotiating. Thus, learning friendship becomes one of the primary challenges and rewards of the teen years.

PEER INFLUENCES

The peer group is a strong reference group for most adolescents. They discover that friends can provide significant emotional, moral, and communicative grounding and skills (Douvan & Adelson, 1966). However, when researchers write about adolescent peer groups, they are not always writing about the same set or subset of individuals. There may be as many as four different groups referenced by the term *peer group*. These groups, in turn, may be labeled with a variety of terms. At the broadest level is the peer cohort—that is, other individuals who are roughly in the adolescent's age range. This group may affect individual's behaviors by influencing their perceptions about the degree of drug use among other individuals their age; this may, in turn, influence their beliefs about what is acceptable or appropriate. Within this broad cohort exists a smaller, more specific peer group that Mosback and Leventhal (1988) labeled the *reference group* and that Brown, Lohr, and McClenahan (1986) called a *crowd*. These peers are a reputation-based group of similarly stereotyped individuals (such as *jocks* or *dirts*). Within the reference group exists *peer clusters* (Oetting & Beauvais, 1987), which are small, cohesive groups of individuals who share attitudes, beliefs, and sometimes drug use. Finally, these clusters tend to break down into *dyads* or best friend pairs.

Each of these peer groups may influence an individual's drug use habits. Although research on peer influences consistently reveals it to be a strong influence, inconsistencies among some of the findings are likely attributable to the different groups being referenced by the term *peers*.

The peer cohort is strongly influential in establishing adolescent group norms of drug use. Adolescents develop beliefs and norms about drug use partially as a result of their perceptions of what adolescents their age believe and which behaviors they engage in. Adolescents' perceptions of their cohorts' attitudes toward substance use are more strongly correlated with actual use than are their perceptions of their parents' and siblings' attitudes (Needle et al., 1986). Unfortunately, adolescents' perceptions of their cohorts' attitudes are often inaccurate. A variety of research indicates that adolescents consistently overestimate the degree of drug use and acceptance by their cohorts (MacKinnon, Johnson, Pentz, Dwyer, Hansen, Flay, & Wang, 1991).

A more direct influence on adolescents' drug use is their reference group. These groups may be particularly influential because efforts to achieve group identity make teens especially sensitive to peer pressure and expectations; such expectations transmit and enforce group norms. A variety of studies have identified different types of reference groups in school settings: social, academic, and delinquent (Downs & Rose, 1991). Other studies have included groups called *regulars* or *jocks* (Mosback & Leventhal, 1988). The salience and recognizability of these groups have been demonstrated in several studies. Downs and Rose (1991) derived their categories from students' reports of group labels in their high schools, whereas Mosback and Leventhals' (1988) respondents recognized the various groups as present in their schools and were able to identify the group with whom they were most likely to socialize.

These groups may be an important contributing factor to adolescents' psychosocial problems. For example, students who belong to or identify with delinquent groups tend to show higher levels of alcohol and drug use. The type of peer group with whom an adolescent associates is a strong predictor both of drug use and deviant behavior; the group variously labeled as *druggies/losers/rejects* engages in more alcohol use, is more likely to use a variety of drugs, and has significantly higher levels of delinquent behavior (Downs & Rose, 1991).

Even stronger associations have been found between adolescents drug use and peer clusters or cliques. A *peer cluster* (clique) is the primary base of group interaction; it is composed of a small number of similar individuals, often from 5 to 10. Members of these groups tend to be of the same age and socioeconomic class. They generally exert strong influence over the attitudes and behavior of members. Within these clusters, drug use can play an important role in group membership and identification.

When drugs are used, it is almost always within a peer context. Most frequently, peers initiate one another into drug use, provide drugs, talk with each other, model drug use, and help shape attitudes. Generally, the peer cluster develops a consensus about where, when, the types of drugs to be used, and so on. Peer clusters or clique members tend to be similar in their drug use. Cohesiveness within the group is built on maintaining norms that the members have constructed. Members of the clique exert pressure to conform to group norms by offering desirable rewards, such as status within the group hierarchy, and undesirable sanctions, such as exclusion (Youniss & Haynie, 1992).

Much of the research that examines peer influences on drug use has focused on the clique or cluster. Many of the studies ask respondents to report on their friends' substance use or have compared the patterns of use of self-selected good friends. The relationship between reported drug usage by friends (both good and best) and self-reported drug use is much stronger than that between perceived use by other same-age peers (the cohort) and self-reported usage. As well, close or good friends (the clique) are particularly influential (by means of example and approval) in the initiation of drug use (Morgan & Grube, 1991).

Finally, best friends (both opposite and same sex) provide a uniquely strong influence on adolescents' patterns of drug use. Best friend's drinking is the strongest predictor of both male and female adolescents' drinking habits (Wilks et al., 1989). Best friend's use of other drugs is more strongly related to adolescent use than other good friends. In fact, best friend's use is a strong and significant predictor after controlling for other friend's and peer use. This is especially true in the case of maintenance of drug use. Although good friends are important to the introduction of drug use, the habits of the best friend are the strongest predictors of continued use of a substance; this is true for smoking, drinking, and illicit drug use (Morgan & Grube, 1991). Additional research indicates that females are more often introduced to and provided with drugs by their boyfriends than their same-sex friends. In contrast, males' same-sex friends are more likely to influence their initiation and maintenance of drug use (Kumpfer & Turner, 1993).

Researchers often argue that friendships with peers, especially deviant ones, lead to or cause drug use. However, the relationship between friendship and drug use is complicated, and causes are not easy to tease out. Adolescents engage in a process of interpersonal selection called *associative pairing,* in which youth with similar values seek each other out as friends. In turn, these groups of friends co-create values and norms that influence drug use. Findings from longitudinal studies suggest that two processes operate: Deviant youth tend to select deviant friends, and involvement with deviant friends serves to escalate participation in deviant behavior. Therefore, although many adolescents experiment with substance use in the process of growing up, the motivations and techniques associated with frequent drug use are often learned in a deviant peer group (Simons et al., 1988).

This discussion of peer influence naturally leads to a discussion of peer pressure. In both popular and scholarly literature, the prevailing opinion about peer pressure is entirely negative and suggests that peers exert strong influence over one another (Berndt, 1994). Peer pressure is generally thought of as some external power that operates directly on the will/behavior of others, especially adolescents. However, it is more useful to think of peer pressure as operating at two levels: directly and indirectly. Most research has focused on explicit peer pressure. Explicit peer pressure consists of overt attempts by one individual to persuade another to engage in an activity—in this case, substance use. However, it is likely that a more potent, frequent, and difficult manifestation of peer pressure exists implicitly.

Implicit peer pressure operates in two ways. First, groups develop norms; group cohesiveness and group identity are achieved through the maintenance of these norms. The pressure to conform and follow norms is particularly strong for adolescents; it is a period in their lives when they are moving toward and struggling with independence. During this stage, as the family decreases in strength as a source of support, values, and role norming, the peer group is substituted to meet these needs.

Second, once these norms have been internalized, they exert pressure on adolescents to conform regardless of whether someone has provided external pressure. In addition, adolescents typically gauge their actions in terms of their appeal to peers (Rawlins, 1992). Thus, adolescents may accept a drink or smoke a joint because they believe they are expected to and that others will disregard them if they do not. Therefore, it is likely that peer groups encourage group members to drink by instilling the expectation that they will be more liked and their peers will be more friendly to them if they drink. Males have been found to be particularly susceptible to this internal pressure. Young males report they drink because of social expectations (norms), whereas young women are more likely to report they use alcohol because of personal choice (preference); (Wilks et al., 1989). This finding is supported by a host of literature showing that males begin to drink earlier and drink more than do females throughout adolescence (Forney et al., 1989; Kumpfer & Turner, 1993).

The Development of Peer Influence in Adolescents' Lives

Adolescence is a time of rapid change and adaptation. It begins with the biological upheaval presented by puberty and ends, typically, with an adult child leaving the family home to establish an independent existence. Adolescents must deal with a variety of confusing issues: The changes in their physical appearance changes the way others interact with them, they have adult sexual urges but it is not socially acceptable to act on them, they are physically mature but still live under the control of their parents and other agents of society (e.g., teachers), their same-sex playmates are being supplanted by mixed-sex crowds and opposite-sex romantic partners, and they are expected to act like an adult without the cognitive, social, or emotional maturity that characterizes adulthood. In fact, Erickson (1968) described adolescence as a period of identity crisis, during which children must develop an identity that integrates their various selves or remain confused as to their role in life. To create a sense of identity, adolescents typically experiment with a variety of possibilities (Markus & Nurius, 1986). Thus, we have the serious student, wild partier, loyal friend, and good kid sometimes all in the same individual. As identity stabilizes, adolescents enter young adulthood with an integrated sense of self. During this time of exploration and flux, however, relationships with peers are of paramount importance.

Throughout childhood, the focal relationships are with parents and siblings; relationships with peers tend to be more activity focused. As children enter adolescence, however, the quality of their relationships with peers improves as they begin to experience trust, intimacy, and closeness with friends as well as family members (Collins & Repinski, 1994). This shift has been interpreted in various ways by developmental theorists. In general, the psychoanalytic perspective views the years of adolescence as a time of necessary conflict with parents that leads to separation from them and allows for the assumption of adult roles. Therefore, adolescence is viewed as a time during which children struggle to establish themselves as autonomous, independent individuals from their parents. More contemporary perspectives on development conceptualize adolescence as a time of transition—when children integrate the overlapping systems of social influence presented by their parents and peers (Hartup & van Lieshout, 1995). The ability to consolidate parental and peer influences can be particularly problematic when they clash with each other, however. When disagreements do occur, parents often find, much to their chagrin, that the opinions of their teenagers' friends are more influential than their own.

Pressure to conform to peer group standards increases steadily through childhood and preadolescence, peaking at about age 14 or 15. The effects of peer pressure then gradually decline, as adolescents become less dependent on an exclusive peer group (Berndt & Zinn, 1988) and are more likely to become attached to a romantic partner (Dunphy, 1963). These developmental trends are reflected in the effects of peers on drug use. One of the most common routes to adolescent drug use is through peer influence. Adolescents rarely begin drug use on their own, and most are initiated into drug use by their friends (Finnegan, 1979; Freeland & Campbell, 1973). Peer pressure is especially important for the initiation of drug use, as perceived disapproval by friends has a greater impact on starting to use drugs than perceived disapproval by parents (Bailey et al., 1992). Moreover, when parents' attitudes toward drug use conflict with peers' attitudes, peers are more influential (Kandel, 1990).

Adolescents whose friends use drugs are more likely to use drugs themselves (Flannery, Vazsonyi, Torquati, & Fridrich, 1994; Johnston et al., 1994; Kaplan, Martin, & Robbins, 1982). Among 10 risk factors that assessed a variety of personal and social characteristics, peer drug use was the single best predictor of drug use by high school respondents (Newcomb et al., 1986). Therefore, using drugs and drinking alcohol is typically a social activity that occurs in interaction with others. In fact, one of the two most frequently provided explanations for using drugs is social cohesion (Newcomb, Chou, Bentler, & Huba, 1988) or belonging, particularly among middle school students (e.g., to make me more popular with my friends; Novaceck, Raskin, & Hogan, 1991).

Adolescent Dating

The progression from childhood friendships to love relationships begins in pre- and early adolescence when children form groups of primarily same-sex friends (Dunphy, 1963). Although girls typically start to like boys before boys start to like girls, by the end of eighth grade both sexes are beginning to make contact with members of the opposite sex (Petersen, 1988). At about this time, their groups open to include members of the opposite sex (Dunphy, 1963). This mingling may be motivated by the emergence of the sexual desire that accompanies the hormonal changes occurring in their bodies. It allows children to learn to interact with members of the opposite sex in a comfortable environment while primary friendships remain same sex. By late adolescence, many children have coupled off with members of the opposite sex, beginning with casual relationships and moving to more stable relationships in which the partner becomes the primary friend and attachment figure (Dunphy, 1963). This progression from attachment to parents to attachment to same-sex friends to attachment to opposite-sex partners (in heterosexual relationships) differs by individual and can be influenced by a variety of factors, including one's culture, parental guidance, biological maturity, and relational experience (Furman & Wehner, 1994). Furman and Wehner (1994) found that adolescents' perceptions of friendships and romantic relationships were significantly correlated, indicating that how children experience friendships affects how they relate to romantic partners.

Learning to form healthy romantic relationships is an important step in developing into a well-adjusted adult. People who form loving relationships are happier and healthier than those who do not (Traupmann & Hatfield, 1981). These positive benefits are apparent even in high school, as adolescents in steady relationships have higher self-esteem and stronger sex role identity than those who are unattached (Samet & Kelly, 1987). There are other reasons for seeking out romantic relationships as well. Selecting the right partner can serve as a means of achieving status or provide information regarding status (Skipper & Nass, 1966). Some seek solace outside the home when divorce or separation disrupts family support systems (Newcomer & Udry, 1987). Although adults frequently discount the importance of relationships in high school, breaking up can be a traumatic experience. It may not only result in social withdrawal and poor academic performance, but can lead to feelings of personal failure and inadequacy, helplessness, loss of personal identity, depression, and suicide. It may also lead to self-medication with alcohol and/or drugs (Kaczmarek & Backlund, 1991). Therefore, intimacy with a romantic partner can play an important role in adolescents' lives.

According to Camarena, Sarigiani, and Petersen (1990), adolescent intimacy may differ from adult intimacy, which is typically demonstrated by increasing levels of self-disclosure to one's partner. The authors argued that emotional intimacy is characterized by feelings of connection or joint belonging. It is emotional closeness, which can be expressed in a variety of ways that go beyond self-disclosure. For instance, they found that both boys and girls self-disclose more as a relationship progresses, but boys are more likely than girls to take another path to emotional intimacy with their friends—through shared experiences such as sports and activities. Frydenberg and Lewis (1993) corroborated this observation; they found that boys' coping strategies were more likely to involve physical recreation and girls were more likely to seek social support and engage in wishful thinking. This gender difference could also lead to heightened drug use among males, who may view drug use as a shared experience with their friends. The development of intimate relationships during adolescence is critical to successful relationships as an adult. However, little is currently known about how drug use may affect the development of emotional intimacy because most research has focused on a more problematic issue—the effects of drug use on physical intimacy.

Drug Use With Romantic Partners

As noted earlier, the majority of males and females are introduced to drugs by a male (Freeland & Campbell, 1973). Circumstantial evidence indicates that these males are frequently romantic partners because females who date report higher marijuana use (Freeland & Campbell, 1973). Among female addicts, male partners play an important role in initiating and maintaining drug habits (Anglin, Hser, & McGlothlin, 1987; Eldred & Washington, 1976; Hser, Anglin, & McGlothlin, 1987; O'Donnell, Besteman, & Jones, 1967; Sutker, 1985).

As noted, most research on the relational consequences of drug use has neglected to examine the implications of use for relationship formation or the development of intimacy. Rather, research has jumped to drugs' effects on the most intimate of couple behaviors—sexuality. The general assumption has been that drug use has a disinhibiting effect and leads to more promiscuous sexual behavior, which is a common expectation among teenagers (Brown, Goldman, Inn, & Anderson, 1980). Certainly the correlation between drug use and sexual involvement during late adolescence is high (McGee & Newcomb, 1992). Rosenbaum and Kandel (1990) found that a more advanced stage of drug involvement and early onset of drug use predicted early sexual activity for both White and Hispanic adolescents. Elliott and Morse (1989) also found a progression of deviant behavior from delinquency to drug use to sexual intercourse in adolescents.

However, the causal nature of the relationship between drug use and sexual activity is in dispute. Using causal modeling techniques, Newcomb and Bentler (1988) found that, for both women and men, there were virtually no direct effects of teenage drug use on sexual behavior in young adulthood—except to increase the number of intimate relationships. Teenage drug use was significantly related to early sexual involvement as a teenager and to a high rate of intercourse, contracting a venereal disease, having an abortion (for women), and ineffective birth control (for men) by young adulthood. However, the effect of drug use was mediated by both teenage sexual behavior and social conformity, supporting Donovan and Jessor's

(1985) argument that a general underlying construct of nonconformity motivates deviant behaviors (see also McGee & Newcomb, 1992).

Although sexual involvement is an important component of romantic relationships, the desire to please one's partner should produce its own propensity toward using drugs when offered by a partner, especially among females who tend to be more nurturing (Eagly, 1987) and defined by their relationships with others (Wood, 1996). These types of relational consequences deserve more investigation. For example, among adult drug addicts, evidence indicates that women are frequently initiated into drug use by men with whom they are living or romantically involved (Hser, Anglin, & McGlothlin, 1987; O'Donnell et al., 1967). In addition, females who date engage in higher levels of marijuana use (Freeland & Campbell, 1973). Newcomb and Bentler (1988) found that young adults' sexual precocity did not predict their satisfaction with intimacy, providing some evidence that developing active sexual relationships and healthy intimate relationships are independent processes.

However, it is the evidence that links drug use to relational violence, that provides a compelling reason for better understanding how to resist offers of drugs in dating relationships. Males who use drugs are generally more aggressive than those who do not (Flannery et al., 1994), and drinking alcohol also temporarily facilitates male aggression against females (Richardson, 1981). The relational consequences of this heightened aggressiveness can be dangerous and even deadly. Drug abuse can inflame or prolong jealousy episodes, which are one of the most common precursors to domestic violence and homicide (White & Mullen, 1989). In addition, drug use—and particularly alcohol—enables date rape and sexual violence. Both men and women cite intoxication as one of the precursors to unwanted sexual activity (Craig, Kalichman, & Follingstad, 1989; Muehlenhard & Cook, 1988; Muehlenhard & Linton, 1987), and a survey of teenagers indicated that sexual assault is justified if a girl is stoned or drunk (Goodchilds & Zellman, 1984). In general, the relationship between drugs and dating can be debilitating not only from an emotional development perspective, but from a physical safety perspective as well.

MODELS OF DRUG USE

Two of the clearest directional models of drug use were developed by Oetting and Beauvais (1987) and Kumpfer and Turner (1990). Oetting and Beauvais model suggests that family strength shapes both adolescent school adjustment and religious ties, which in turn affect peer choices (and peer-related drug use), which then impact the individual's drug use. Kumpfer and Turner's model posits that family and school climate mutually influence one another and together influence the adolescents' self-efficacy, school bonding, peer choices/effects, and finally drug use. Both of these models reflect the current view that adolescent drug use is affected by a variety of variables that influence one another and ultimately affect the adolescent's drug habits.

Kumpfer and Turner (1993) further suggested that, despite the influence of demographic variables on substance use, those adolescents who possess effective resistance skills are less vulnerable to drug use. These resistance skills appear to be a resiliency factor that ameliorates or even blocks the effects of risk factors.

Overall then, two primary influencing factors on substance use and misuse are family and peer relationships. Families serve as a foundation and source of early attitudes and values that peer relations further shape. These external influences interact with the specific adolescent's skills and personality to create specific instances of beliefs and behaviors.

There is a need for normative education and resistance skills training in communities and families (Botvin et al., 1995; Bukoski, 1985). This chapter suggests that scholars and professionals extend previous research by including communication competence (Spitzberg & Cupach, 1984; Spitzberg & Hecht, 1984) in the framework for examining family and peer interaction.

This book extends the Oetting and Beauvais (1987) and Kumpfer and Turner (1990) models by focusing on a series of studies that explore relational communication competence, describing the communicative and relational features of drug resistance. Resisting drugs or saying no is treated as a communication and relational competency, exploring how teens maintain and negotiate relationships in the context of drug offers and refusals. The competence model may also extend our knowledge of risk and resiliency by focusing on the process of communication in establishing family and personal norms (motivation to resist) and the knowledge of how to do so (resistance skills). It is in the context of interaction that this book attempts to paint a clearer picture of adolescent drug use and relationships.

SUGGESTED READINGS

Family Relationships

Aktan et al., 1996; Amey et al., 1998; Andrews et al., 1991, 1993; Ashery et al, 1999; Bachman et al, 1997; Baumrind, 1989, 1991; Brody et al., 1998; Brook et al., 1990; Bry et al., 1999; Catalano et al., 1992, 1997, 1999; Coombs et al., 1991; Dielman et al., 1993; Dishion et al., 1995; Foxcroft & Lowe, 1995; Gil, Vega, & Biafora, 1998; Graber et al., 1996; Gullota et al., 1995; Haggerty et al., 1991; Hawkins et al., 1992, 1994; Kameoka & Lecar, 1996; Kandel, 1990; Kumpfer et al., 1989–1999; Lamb, 1996; Miller, 1998; Newcomb, 1992; Peterson & Leigh, 1990; Pick & Palos, 1995; Spoth et al., 1995; Steinberg, 1990; Szapocznik & Kurtines, 1989; Turner, 1995; Werner, 1990; William & Smith, 1993; Zelvin, 1999.

3

The Social Processes of Drug Resistance in a Relational Context

"Eh, want some beer?"

"No, I don't."

"Hey, ya gonna be at my party—if you're gonna stay here, you gotta drink something."

"I don't know man. I don't want it. I didn't drive here. I don't have any way home."

(Pushing drink into my hand) "Here, it's yours."

" I don't want it … let me just sit here by myself. Go to your guests and enjoy your party. You won't even know that I'm here."

He grabs a hold of my shoulder and starts pulling on me. He pulls me out the door, shuts it, and says, "If you're not going to drink, you're getting out of here."

Great, it's winter time and I don't have my jacket. I'm gonna freeze.

The ability to say "no" both gracefully and convincingly has been shown to be a vital aspect of drug abuse and smoking prevention programs (Biglan, McConnell, Severson, Barry, &Ary, 1984; Gilchrist, Snow, Lodish, & Schinke, 1985). However, as the prior interview excerpt illustrates, effective refusal strategies entail more than simply saying "no." Numerous studies show that assertive refusers are perceived as offensive and unlikable (Kern, 1982; Wildman, 1986).

Most studies indicate that peers are an important part of the drug experience for adolescents and young adults (e.g., Hunter, 1990; Kandel, 1985). Peer influences are often stronger than religion, individual factors, and other predictors of drug use. However, beyond the claim that peers affect one another, the literature provides little insight into how peer effects take place and, consequently, what strategies can be used to change this behavior. Although we know the patterning of drug use, we know very little about how young adult peers offer drugs to one another; further, we know little about how this population succeeds or fails in resisting such offers (Perkins & Berkowitz, 1984).

Competently maintaining relationships with one's peers and sustaining a nonuse identity, while meeting one's own instrumental goals of refusal, is a difficult task to assume. Yet it is accomplished every day by a myriad of adolescents and young adults. Thus, for an individual to be effective in resisting drug offers, a specialized set of communication skills is needed—a set of skills that considers the relational context of the offer.

The previous chapters suggest that refusal skills are a type of communicative competence in which messages are constructed to resist social influence. It is certainly difficult to invoke a norm of resistance if teens lack the requisite skills to manifest normative behavior. Thus, a theoretical model of relational communication competence (Spitzberg & Cupach, 1984) is recommended, which argues that competence is a relational phenomenon. The model identifies four necessary components: knowledge, motivation, skills, and outcomes. This model is explained in chapter 1; however, a brief overview of the model is presented for the reader's convenience.

The concept of relational competence stresses that any conversation has outcomes for both parties and that communication that optimizes these mutual outcomes is maximally effective. When cast into a drug resistance framework, this means that if Chris offers cocaine to Jordan and Jordan's reply both resists the offer and does not offend Chris, continued pressure is less likely, resistance is successful, and the relationship is maintained. Knowledge includes understanding the effects of drugs, the context, the other, and the topic. Motivation entails understanding peer norms and attitudes, perceptions of consequences, and desire to engage in resistance. Skills are the messages used in refusal and outcomes are the consequences of these messages—including consequences for the self, other, and relationship. Thus, to competently resist offers of drugs, teens need adequate knowledge, appropriate motivation, and skills necessary to produce desirable outcomes.

Research on social influence communication (McLaughlin, Cody, & Robey, 1980) provides a framework for understanding competent resistance skills along a social acceptability dimension (Boster, 1988). However, most of this research focused on how compliance is obtained; much less is known about resistance. The little resistance research that exists primarily examines general social situations (e.g., buying a new suit, cutting down a tree) and public policy issues (e.g., legalization of heroin) rather than more significant personal issues such as drug and alcohol use. This leaves individuals more vulnerable to social influence over personal issues (McGuire, 1964). However, studies of smoking have addressed social influence processes and provided some initial understanding of effective resistance strategies (Reardon, Sussman, & Flay, 1989).

Given the degree of peer pressure commonly associated with drug offers, refusing such offers may require complex and sophisticated refusal skills. The refuser must balance the desire to resist the influence attempt with protecting his or her relationship with the offerer (Hecht, Alberts, & Miller-Rassulo, 1992; Kline & Floyd, 1990). Thus, resistance involves communication skills as well as sensitivity to the social network.

Successful resistance has been linked to planning and decision making as well as to the ability to assess prior success or failure in similar situations. Consequently, perspective taking may affect skills that influence individuals' ability to successfully say "no." Perspective taking refers to a person's ability to understand how others perceive a situation. It is a developmental process associated with social influence abilities in people of varying ages (Delia, Kline, & Burleson, 1979), and these abilities have been linked to general compliance resistance (McQuillen, 1986). Understanding the perspective of the person making a drug offer should facilitate the choice of an effective resistance strategy. Knowing why someone is making an offer, what the offer means to that person, and how he or she is likely to respond to refusals allows the recipient to form a refusal response that will minimize the continuing pressure that characterizes drug offers while maintaining the relationship. It is this ability to be effective in saying no while maintaining friendly relations with the offerer that leads to relational competence (Spitzberg & Cupach, 1984).

A second characteristic of refusal effectiveness may be resistance complexity. A complex communicator employs a variety of dimensions when perceiving an event and has a larger repertoire of strategies to choose from in the persuasion process (Daly, Bell, Glenn, & Lawrence, 1985; Hale, 1982; O'Keefe & Sypher, 1981). Resistance complexity concerns the size of the repertoire of refusal strategies for responding to drug offers. As children mature, more persuasive strategies typically become available to them (Clark, O'Dell, & Willinganz, 1986). In general, more complex people are more likely to resist unreasonable demands and do so with more sensitivity and success. Kline and Floyd (1990) demonstrated that complexity is related to sensitivity to the situation and the number of refusals enacted. Thus, greater refusal complexity should be associated with a better understanding of the situation and greater success in resistance.

Assertiveness has been linked to refusal skills as well (Kline & Floyd, 1990). Because implicit and explicit peer pressure play an important role in drug offers, particularly among this age group, assertiveness is likely to be a key skill in the refusal process. Teens lacking assertiveness may not have the strength to resist pressure from their peers.

Social, situational, and individual factors provide the framework within which drugs are offered and refused. Friendship and other relationships are at the heart of use and misuse, thus examining social factors is important to understanding resistance (Kandel, 1985). Further, both the importance of the situation and specific characteristics of the individual should also influence the unfolding of the interaction.

As an outgrowth of this burgeoning area of inquiry—relational communication competence—in the area of prevention, we conducted a series of studies that sought to describe the actual situations in which drugs were offered: (a) who, where, and how offers are made; (b) how adolescents responded to these offers; and (c) which responses worked and which did not.

The next few chapters present the findings of a series of studies conducted by our team of researchers from 1991 to 1998 as well as the research of others who examined the social processes of drug offers, refusals, and use in the context of relational interaction. These studies were conducted in several geographic regions of the United States and focused on different ethnic and socioeconomic populations. The perspective taken in our research is one that traditionally has been overlooked—that of the adolescent drug user in the context of his or her adolescent relationships. "After all," say the adolescents in our lives, "It's just a social thing."

> "I don't know what the big deal is (about binge drinking), it's just something that we all do, so we all have something to do together. It's fun."

> "Yeah, some people try it for the thrill of it, just to see what it feels like. But, after that, most people do it to fit in, to be nicer and more acceptable. You know, it's easier to approach people if you're buzzed."

> "I think I was afraid of how he would react to me (if I refused) because I had just met him in class, and I don't want people to not like me and stuff."

THE DRUG RESISTANCE STRATEGIES PROJECT

The studies in this project emerged out of a need to develop a more realistic and appropriate picture of relational communication competence in the process of drug offers and resistance. Derived from the adolescent perspective, we hoped to provide substantive information that could lead to the creation of a drug intervention program that would reflect and inform actual adolescent drug offer interactions in relational contexts. In the end, we hoped to contribute to the understanding of social influence in adolescence, particularly regarding drugs, and to identify a broader and more realistic range of resistance strategies that could be used in prevention programs.

In addition, we wanted to understand resistance strategies in a variety of drug domains (e.g., from alcohol resistance to controlled substance resistance). Social influence research shows that message strategies differ with the desired effect (Hecht, 1984) and situation (McLaughlin et al., 1980). The situational efficacy of message strategies suggests that researchers should explore similarities and differences between influence attempts and refusal strategies associated with alcohol and controlled substance offers. This assumption is supported by research showing that people use different drugs for different reasons (Jessor et al., 1980). Therefore, one can expect that the messages used to resist alcohol may differ in some fundamental aspects from those that successfully resist offers of cocaine. It is possible that the entire process—from motivation to offer to resistance—may differ across these domains.

Thus, in the Drug Resistance Strategies Project (DRSP), we sought to determine, from adolescents' own experiences, what drugs have been offered, which strategies have been successful, and which have failed in situ before we developed a program to teach drug resistance strategies. Toward that end, we conducted studies to help us to understand the social processes of substance resistance.

The remainder of the chapters focus on the findings of several studies in the DRSP as well as the work of other scholars who pursue similar goals in understanding the social processes of substance resistance. Table 3.1 outlines the DRSP studies, their number of participants, their methods, and the age groups targeted.

METHODS OVERVIEW

Two widespread, colloquial beliefs about drug offers and adolescents exist: Strangers approach teenagers on the street and try to persuade them to take

TABLE 3.1
Drug Resistance Strategies Project

Study	N	Methods	Age Group
Alberts, Miller-Rassulo, & Hecht (1991)	33	I	H
Alberts, Hecht, Miller-Rassulo, & Krizek (1992)	69	I	H
Hecht, Alberts, & Miller-Rassulo (1992)	452	S	Y
Hecht, Trost, Bator, & MacKinnon (1997)	158	I	M
Miller (1998)	83	I	M
Moon, Jackson, & Hecht (in press)	995	S	M
Moon, Hecht, Jackson, & Spellers (1998)	2622	S	M
Trost, Kellar-Guenther, & Bator (1997)	512	S	M
Trost, Langan, & Kellar-Guenther (1999)	2166	S	M

Methods: I = interview, S = survey, E = experiment. *Age Group*: M = middle school, H = high school, Y = young college age.

drugs and adolescents' friends provide them with drugs typically during school hours. In the initial studies of the DRSP, we asked students to tell us which, if either, of these scenarios was typical for drug offers because the situation and relationship between the offerer and recipient are likely to influence the unfolding of the interaction. Of course, we also wanted to hear which types of verbal strategies were successful and which failed during adolescents' attempts to refuse drugs.

In our later studies, we expanded our respondent pool to include two urban geographic locations and extended our focus on high school and young college-age students to include the experiences of middle school students. The rationale for moving into the middle schools was provided by the older respondents: They told us that first offers and initial experimentation happened during the younger years. Therefore, we needed to determine whether the younger adolescents' experiences differed from those of our young adults' and teenagers' experiences. Although the early and middle adolescent years are a more vulnerable time for most people, the young adult years continue to be a time when experimentation takes place and alcohol use as well as controlled substance use is illegal for most students.

Across all of the DRSP studies, the goal was to elicit specific information concerning who, what, where, how, age, gender, dialogue, and behavior of the offerer and refuser. Face-to-face interviews were conducted to
generate narrative accounts of previous offers and refusal interactions, and
surveys were ultimately constructed to measure offer strategies, refusal
strategies, relationships of interactants, amount of drug and alcohol use,
frequency of offers, change in consumption during the past 30 days, gender,
ethnicity, family income of respondent, and perceptions of norms.

Interviews

Interviews were conducted with adolescents from middle school, high
school, and college. The purpose of these interviews was to allow us to develop a typology of drug resistance strategies and create a more complete
understanding of drug offer interactions. That is, we wished to know who
was most likely to offer drugs to adolescents, in what situations, and to what
effects. Thus, we wished to know what was said as well as by whom and
where.

To elicit this information, all participants were asked a series of questions ranging (in earlier studies) from two general open-ended questions
combining alcohol with other drug offers (i.e., Would you tell me about a
time when you were offered drugs or alcohol and you turned down that offer? Would you tell me about a time when you were offered drugs or alcohol
and you wanted to say no but didn't?) to a complex interview schedule that
distinguishes offers of alcohol from offers of other drugs (see Appendix A).

Open-ended questions were used to elicit stories from the respondents.
We wanted to examine adolescents' subjective experience as portrayed in
their own experience-near concepts (Geertz, 1976; Hecht, Ribeau, &
Alberts, 1989). Such narrative discourse is an important resource that
young people use both to reflect and constitute their social world (Rawlins
& Holl, 1987). The value of this approach is that it allows an account to be
developed that captures more of the adolescent's view than that of the adult
culture.

The use of personal narratives contributed significantly to the value of
this study. As discussed in chapter 1, narrative is a meaning structure that
organizes events and human actions into a whole, thereby attributing significance to individual actions and events according to their effect on the
whole (Polkinghorne, 1988). The narrator configures the events in his or
her story so that parts in the whole become clear. The resulting narrative,

then, reflects the role of definitions and situational variables that guide behavior in social settings (Fisher, 1978).

In general, each narrative was read by multiple investigators, the location of the specific resistance story determined, and the essential narrative features identified. That is, a fully developed narrative includes an abstract (a summary telling what the story is all about), an orientation (who, what, when, where), a complicating action (then what happened), and the results (what finally occurred and the evaluation; Polkinghorne, 1988). Reflective of these elements, the following types of information were identified and a category or coding system developed for each:

1. Who made the drug/alcohol offer
2. What was offered (alcohol or controlled substance)
3. Where the offer was made
4. How the offer was made
5. How the narrator responded to the offer
6. Why the narrator made the choice (acceptance/refusal)

Surveys

After completing interviews with adolescent participants, an initial set of questionnaires was distributed to the young adult students. Half of the students described a situation in which they had turned down alcohol, and the other half described a situation in which they turned down other drugs (see Appendix B for a copy of the alcohol questionnaire). The requests were followed by 13 questions designed to elicit more specific information about the experience.

Because of the importance of risk factors to adolescent drug use and the likelihood that at-risk students may lack or possess different resistance skills from low-risk students, risk was incorporated into later studies. As a measure of risk state, scales were developed to assess the amount of drug and alcohol use, frequency of offers, and change in consumption during the past 30 days.

The results of these initial surveys led to more refined surveys that extended the earlier work by examining a younger population, describing ethnic and sex similarities and differences, norms, family communication, and risk and resiliency. A detailed account of the methodologies used in the various DRSP studies are included in Appendix A.

RESEARCH FINDINGS

Offers

Who Made the Offer.   Given the importance of interpersonal relationships to successful resistance, we were concerned with understanding the relationship between persons who make drug offers and the recipients of those offers. Four categories were derived from the data: friend, relative, acquaintance, and stranger. Friend included anyone who the recipient considered to be so, although it did not include friends of friends nor those identified only as classmates. Relative included people such as parents, siblings, aunts and uncles, and cousins. Acquaintance included classmates, neighbors, and people met through friends. Strangers were those with whom the recipient had no prior experience.

In general, our studies have consistently found that fears regarding stranger danger are unwarranted, but concerns about a teenager who is running with a wild crowd may be well placed. Friends exert more influence over drug use than any other category of relationship. Across all age groups, adolescents are offered drugs by their friends more than any other relational partner (Alberts et al., 1991; Hecht et al., 1997). In particular, same-sex friends were the most frequent offerers for both boys and girls, although girls were also frequently targeted by male friends (Trost et al., 1999). Moreover, offers are likely to involve some peer pressure—in one study, only 28% of the offers described did not involve any persuasive pressure from the offerer (Alberts et al., 1992). In the college sample, 48% of the offers or responses to refusals were accompanied by some pressure. Peer pressure also tends to be exerted more in social settings (parties or other gatherings with large numbers of people) than at home or school (where the number of people in the setting is typically smaller; Alberts et al., 1992). Middle school students described scenarios that typically involved the presence of at least one other friend or acquaintance besides the offerer (Hecht et al., 1997), and they were more likely to take the drug when with a small group of four to six people or a larger crowd of people (Kellar-Guenther, Moon, & Trost, 1998), indicating that social pressure does affect acquiescence.

It is primarily friends who offer friends alcohol and drugs, regardless of age. For middle school students in our interview studies, these friends were most likely to be males, although female friends were the next highest category (Alberts et al., 1991; Hecht et al., 1997; Miller, 1998). Although family members were not as prevalent in the older samples, in middle school, family members also offered drugs, including siblings, parents, cousins, or extended family elders (aunt, uncles, and grandparents). This is particularly evident in Latino/a and African-American populations (Miller, 1998; Moon, Hecht, Jackson, & Spellers, 1998). These offers, however, were almost always refused. As one teen suggests:

> *It is so funny that when I was exposed to it by my friends it was so much easier for me to say yes. I could just say okay, yet when I was offered it by somebody I loved, trusted, and was comfortable with (my mother and stepfather), I couldn't say okay.*

The large survey of junior high students also reported that offers from close family members (especially brothers and male cousins) were less frequent than those from friends. However, in this case, they reported that offers from family members were more potent and less likely to be resisted than those from friends (Trost et al., 1999). Boys, in particular, had difficulty resisting offers from their extended family elders and brothers or male cousins.

What Was Offered.   Beer represents the most frequently offered alcoholic beverage, and marijuana is the controlled substance that was most often accepted or refused. Of the controlled substance offers, few were of substances other than marijuana (predominantly cocaine, but also amphetamines and quaaludes). On average, however, 50% to 70% of adolescents in our middle school samples had been offered alcohol or another drug. The largest number of acceptances are for alcohol. Two thirds of the time, an offer of alcohol is accepted, but when the offer is of another drug, it is accepted less frequently.

Ethnicity seemed a salient variable when looking at what substance was offered. Across these studies, it seems that White adolescents are more likely to be offered cigarettes, followed by Latino/as and African-American adolescents. Latino/as were most likely to report an offer of beer, wine, or hard liquor, followed by Whites, and then African-Americans. Latino/a and African-American adolescents are more likely to be offered marijuana than White adolescents. Hard drugs are more likely to be offered to Latino/as than to Whites or African-Americans. Finally, Latino/a and White adolescents are more likely to be offered inhalants than African-American adolescents. These studies suggest that Latino/as are most likely to be offered drugs, with the exception of cigarettes, which were most likely to be offered to White adolescents.

Location of Offers. We were interested in where such offers were likely to be made. The prevalent notion is that drug offers are quite common at school and parties. We wished to discover if that were true. We derived three categories for setting: school, home, and social situation. School, of course, referred to any offer that occurred on school property. Home referred not just to the recipients' home but anyone's home. Social situation covered situations where the offer was made at a party, in a restaurant or bar, while cruising, or in any other social environment. Parties that occurred in a home were coded as a *social situation; home* was used to describe when the recipient was visiting others or was offered substances in his or her own home.

According to our data, offers of controlled substances occur less frequently at school than many adults would suspect. For adolescents, in order of frequency, most drug offers occurred in public places, on the street, or at a park; at school; at their own or a friend's home; or at a social setting such as a party. These offers were typically in the presence of known others. On average, 65% of the time at least one friend was present and 25% of the time there was at least one acquaintance in the setting (Miller, 1998; Hecht et al., 1997). Family members and strangers were also present at several of the offers.

Adolescents tend to be offered drugs in public at informal gatherings, whereas college students are more likely to receive offers at home. This may reflect the increased control young adults have over their personal space (i.e., college students have their own apartments). Nevertheless, the context of offers tends to change as children develop into young adults. The data also indicate that most middle school students were approached to use drugs in public places, high school students received most of their offers in social situations, and college students were more likely to receive offers at home or at a party.

> *I don't go to these parties to drink. I just go there to see my friends and people just drink at these parties.*
>
> *If you use it just to party with friends, socially, you're not abusing it and making it a main focus of your life. I do it mostly as a social thing to do.*
>
> *Well, ya know. I had nothing else to do. It's like, do your homework, go party with friends, smoke pot here, smoke pot there, go out to clubs, get stoned. That's it.*

Interestingly, none of the recipients admitted accepting offers at school. This could be reflective of an unwillingness to admit to such behavior or it could be a result of the fact that most acceptances were of alcohol. It could be that the larger number of offers that were declined at school is indicative that controlled substances are offered at school, whereas alcohol is offered more rarely. These findings also suggest that youth are twice as likely to accept as refuse an offer made in someone's home.

Types of Offers. In general, our research indicates that most drug offers are simple requests, such as, "Would you like a beer?" or "Do you want to smoke a joint?" This finding held for 97% of the middle school students who reported drug offers (Hecht et al., 1997), as well as the majority of high school students in both studies (Alberts et al., 1991, 1992) and 68% of the college students (Hecht, Alberts, & Miller-Rassulo, 1992). Interestingly, Alberts et al. (1991) found that 77% of the refused drug narratives involved a simple offer, whereas only 37% of the accepted drug narratives described simple offers. In other words, those who accepted the drug offer typically received a more complex appeal. In fact, those who accepted the drug were more likely to have received a stronger persuasive appeal (37%) than those who refused (only 16% described some persuasive attempt by the offerer; Trost et al., 1999). Other types of appeals include availability (the drug is available in the situation without any offer being made), minimization of the harmful effects, appeal to group norms ("everybody is doing it"), and statement of benefits of doing the drug ("It'll make you feel good"; Alberts et al., 1991).

Harrington (1995, 1996) built on the findings of the DRSP with her focus group and experimental research. Her focus group research sought to generate the competent communication strategies used to resist offers of alcohol among young college-age students. Her experimental manipulations placed college-age students and trained confederates in one-on-one interactions in the context of a simulated small party. The students' job in these experiments was to persuade the confederate to have an alcoholic beverage and the subjects were not aware that they were offering to a confederate. The confederates were trained to never accept the offer and were also trained in the use of four primary resistance strategies (i.e., direct refusal, suggestion of alternative, excuse, and explanation). These strategies were then coupled with the presence or absence of face support (polite refusal by rejecting the offer rather than the person; Harrington, 1996). The issue of face support is of particular interest to the relational focus of communication competence.

Harrington (1995) discovered that, in addition to the strategies of simple offers, availability, minimization, appeals to group norms, and statements of benefits, offerers used facilitation as a means to insinuate the substance on another through assistance ("Let me pour you one," "I'll drive you home").

Regarding the offers themselves, high school and college students described fairly diverse types of drug offers, whereas the middle school students' offers were very uniform. Although high school and college students most often heard a simple "Do you want some?", they also reported a variety of other offers, including drugs being merely available in the situation (but no overt pressure), offers that minimize the effects of drug use ("Just a drag won't hurt you"), appeals to group norms ("Everyone's doing it"), and statements that describe the benefits of use ("It makes you feel real good"). In comparison to this wide range of offers, 97% of the middle school students who were offered drugs experienced a straightforward offer (Hecht et al., 1997; Miller, 1998). In the middle school survey, 56.6% of the students reported a simple offer, but the next most frequent type of offer was a nonverbal pass (32.2% of the students)—that is, the student was just handed the drug (Trost et al., 1999).

Although these two types of offers may seem simple and even harmless, the nonverbal pass was effective 54.7% of the time, and the simple offer was effective 40.6% of the time (Trost et al., 1999). Refusing a nonverbal pass requires that one disrupt the flow of interaction and possibly even deflect an intrusion into one's personal space—both uncomfortable behaviors from an interpersonal perspective especially if the offerer is a close relational partner. As noted by McLaughlin et al. (1980), many of those who wish to resist compliance-gaining attempts have relational maintenance as their primary interpersonal goal especially when the appeal comes from an intimate. Therefore, a direct request challenges the target to construct a message that not only effectively resists the influence attempt, but pacifies the interaction partner as well. At this age, adolescents are not as adept as older students at constructing elaborate compliance-gaining or resistance messages (Delia et al., 1979; McQuillen, Higginbotham, & Cummings, 1984).

Other research (Alberts et al., 1992) indicated that the real pressure to take a drug did not occur on the initial offer; rather, it came as a response to the initial refusal. Alberts et al. (1992) asked the high school students to describe the offerer's response to their refusal. The pattern of results indicate that, as before, most offers were simple, and most refusals were either a simple no or a statement of no desire to do the drug. However, in most of the narratives, the offerer responded to those refusals with some sort of persuasive pressure especially if the initial offer involved any pressure. Thus, a simple "no" typically leads to additional pressure. For the middle school students in Hecht et al. (1997), 26% of the interviewed group reported follow-up pressure; only 2 of 23 students caved in on the second request, most simply said "no" and/or walked away, and 3 students threatened to report the offerer to an authority figure. From the middle school survey (Trost et al., 1999), we found that, on average, 2.48 different types of offers were used in the average narrative description, and the responses were significantly less complex (average of 1.59 resistance strategies reported). Moreover, those who received more complex offers were more likely to take the drug, and those who responded with more complex resistance scripts were more successful in refusing the drug offer. An analysis of college students' narratives (Hecht et al., 1992) showed that refusals of simple offers were not followed by any pressure, whereas persuasive offers were somewhat more likely to be followed by persuasive counteroffers. This indicates that older adolescents may exert less persuasive pressure to use drugs or alcohol than younger adolescents.

The role of pressure may be perceived more indirectly by adolescents, as when one respondent said she accepted a drug offer because she was "ashamed to say no. I wanted to be, you know, like my friends." Furthermore, as one teen experienced:

> I was caught off-guard, because I wasn't used to people just coming up and offering me stuff. I thought that if I wanted going to drink anything, I would have initiated it and asked someone for something. So, when I was offered it right away, I took it, but I really wasn't sure about whether I really wanted it. He never really pressured me, but, I said, "okay, thanks."

Response to Offers

Accepted Offer. For the situations in which respondents accepted an offer that they actually wanted to decline, we developed three categories of responses. These included: yes, just tried it, and hesitated then tried it. The *yes* category described those times that recipients simply said "yes" or "okay" and took the proffered drug or drink. *Just tried it* described occasions when the recipient simply accepted the offer without making a verbal statement. *Hesitated then tried it* referred to the times that the recipients decided to or said "no" but then went ahead and accepted the offer. For example, one respondent said "No...oh. all right," while another claimed, "I said no then I just started drinking."

In the majority of cases where respondents did accept an offer, little verbal discussion or explanation occurred. They simply said "yes" or took the offered drug or drink. However, in a sizable number of cases, the recipient hesitated and said "no" either to him or herself or to the offerer before giving in to the offer. It may be that adolescents either engage in relatively little reflection or have little ability to resist the pressure to indulge. As one teen suggests, "It's a harder situation (to say "no") when it's a friend who offers it to you." Alternatively, students may initially say "no" so they can feel as if they gave the appropriate response to a socially inappropriate behavior although they really want to take the drug (Trost et al., 1999). Examining the motives that underlie acceptance of drug offers may shed more light on this particular refusal-then-accept sequence.

Reasons for Accepting. Five categories of reasons for why the recipients accepted were found: peer pressure/acceptance, curiosity, rationalization, was upset, and role model behavior. *Peer pressure/acceptance* included those explanations that attributed the decision to accept to the persuasive efforts of others or to a fear of rejection by one's peers if one did not. This included explanations such as, "I wanted to be with the older guys," "everybody was doing it," and (I did it) "just to please them." It also included explanations referring to direct pressure such as (they said), "Oh come on, don't be out of the crowd." *Curiosity* described occasions when the respondents accepted to find out what the experience was like. *Rationalization* described those times when the recipient talked him or herself into trying the offered substance. This included statements such as, "I thought I'll do it a little bit; hey sure, what the hell," "one cup or drink won't really do anything … ," and "I kind of forgot about the reasons why I wasn't going to, thinking that it wouldn't hurt." The fourth category included occasions when respondents said they accepted drugs because they were *upset* or *feeling bad*. *Role model* described subjects' explanations that he or she accepted the substance because his or her parents or some other role model engages in such behavior and therefore it must be all right. For example, one respondent justified her decision by saying, "Well, my parents always drink."

The most frequent reason given for accepting concerned peer pressure with a large number of respondents also acknowledged that they talked themselves into it. Further, these explanations indicate that many of the respondents entered the situation without having their minds made up with reference to the decision, and therefore they were vulnerable to others or their own persuasive messages.

As one teen recommends:

You really just have to associate with the type of crowd that will accept a "no."
That's really it. Just avoid it unless , you know, you have a really good ability to
say no and you don't care about the others' attitudes or opinions.

Rejected Offer.   Relational communication competence suggests
that an optimally effective resistance strategy is one that accomplishes
the goal of resisting the offer of alcohol or other drug while satisfying
both parties' relational and identity goals (Harrington, 1995). In an offer
situation, individuals often want to maintain their image as a "nice" person and do not want to offend or hurt their relationship (or chance of a relationship) with the offerer. This concept seems central to the resistance
strategies that adolescents use when offered alcohol or other drugs.

Types of Refusals.   Given that most offers are simple requests, it
may not be surprising to know that most refusals are simply "no" (ranging from 56% in Alberts et al., 1991, to 81% in Hecht et al., 1997) or "no,
I have no desire" (Alberts et al., 1992). We developed a typology of resistance strategies out of our original study with high school students
(Alberts et al., 1991) that included the students' own descriptions of how
they refused offers of drugs. The strategies in the *REAL* system were refined and developed over the years and included:

- *Refuse:* A simple "no."
- *Explain:* "No" with an explanation. The two explanations of nonuse
  identity ("I'm not that kind of person") and fear of consequences were
  most common among White students, whereas nonuse identity and
  antidrug attitudes were the most common among the African-American students. The African-American adolescents in our
  samples did not mention fear of consequences. Rather, their explanations were much more along the lines of personal pride in their
  antidrug, nonuse stance.
- *Avoid:* Avoiding the situation by not exposing oneself to situations in
  which drugs are present or deception (holding a glass filled with beer,
  but not drinking it).
- *Leave:* Leaving the situation.

In the same way that middle school students experienced a narrow range
of drug offers, they also responded to drug offers with fewer resistance

strategies, with most of them voicing a simple "no." The few middle school students in the interview studies who did not use a simple "no" described leaving the scene, making a statement about their nonuse identity, or expressing fear of consequences. In the middle school survey, most students gave a simple "no," followed by leaving, avoiding the situation, and explaining their refusal. Fewer of the older students relied on a simple "no" strategy (40%–56% of high school students and 40% of college students, compared with 81% of junior high students). The older students reported using a wider variety of explanations, including fear of consequences, suggesting an alternate activity, claiming a dislike for the product, as well the immorality of drug use.

On the one hand, it is not surprising that junior high students did not engage more sophisticated or elaborate explanations given the overwhelming use of the simple request strategy. Others have also found that a simple request is most likely to be resisted by a simple "no" (Alberts et al., 1992; McQuillan et al., 1984). On the other hand, overreliance on this simple strategy will not serve the children well as they develop and enter high school. Alberts et al. (1992) found that, among high school students, a simple "no" response was likely to be followed by more concerted pressure to use drugs, and the younger adolescents are already facing a proportion of repeat offers similar to that reported by the older students. Moreover, as children age, those persuasive communications become more cognitively complex (Delia et al., 1979) and therefore more difficult to refuse. Interestingly, the older students did not respond to repeat offers with threats as did the junior high students. The older students appear able to deflect the second request with a more socially acceptable refusal. Consequently, the younger sample not only relies on a resistance strategy that will soon fade in effectiveness, but has fewer resistance techniques to draw on to decline either an initial or repeat drug offer.

The most common reasons that adolescents provide for resisting is the negative effect it could have on their body or mind and it does not fit into their personal identity as a nonuser. Other common reasons include personal preference (e.g., I just don't want to do that stuff), fear of the high, observation of negative effects of drugs on others, fear that drugs would adversely affect their own future, and fear that drugs would have a negative effect on their family relationships.

Among college students who reported refusal scenarios, a simple offer was most typically followed by a simple "no," whereas persuasive offers elicited more explanation such as dislike of the product or no desire (Hecht et al., 1992). Unfortunately, using these explanations typically led to more pressure in the offerer's response. Statements of dislike may invite defensive reactions because they place an evaluative judgment on the person who is partaking of the drug; stating a lack of desire may simply be seen as a weak response and an invitation for some encouragement. Suggesting an alternative activity such as dancing may be a more successful response, but it also requires more skill to enact. In general, the research indicates that just saying "no" is not particularly effective—for those who end up accepting a drug offer, many first say "no" (either in their minds or aloud to the offerer) and then take the drug anyway (Alberts et al., 1991).

One reliable finding was that nonusers were more likely to rely on a simple "no" strategy than users, indicating that nonusers in particular may benefit by learning a wider repertoire of refusal strategies (Alberts et al., 1992; Hecht et al., 1992). Consistent with the relational competence model, Alberts et al. (1992) found that having the motivation to resist offers of drugs that results in planning resistance before it is needed actually increases the efficiency of resistance.

For young adult students, simple offers were most typically followed by a simple "no," whereas persuasive offers were resisted through explanations such as dislike of product and no desire. It is important to note that resistance through statements of dislike for the product and no desire are more likely to lead to additional pressure. This interpersonal transaction of offer and refusal clearly has relational implications. In the interpersonal arena of drug offers and refusals, adolescents and young adults must negotiate their relationship. As one student states:

> My friends didn't know how to react to me (when I did drugs). I would get them to get high with me or just ignore them. Pretty soon I felt lost with them, people I had clung to and held on to, I felt they didn't want to be around me any more.

Saying that you dislike the substance or have no desire may be respected by the offerer, "My friends are my friends. Them doin' drugs doesn't really bother me. They're still my friends." However, these data indicate that additional pressure may follow these strategies irrespective of the interactants' relationship.

Harrington (1996) discovered that when young college-age students made repeated offers, the offerers drew on increasingly more sophisticated strategies to achieve their goal. Follow-up attempts to offer a substance tended to be more complex than initial attempts, but only on the third attempt. She found that, although the typical persuader is not very persistent, "a resister should be prepared to hold his or her ground" (Harrington, 1995, p. 238). She also found that offerers were more attracted to their partner and more satisfied with the relationship if they received resistance strategies containing messages of face support.

    Reasons for Rejecting Offer.   In the refusal condition, five categories or reasons were derived: fear, negative role model, don't need/want/like, it's bad, and morality. *Fear* was used as a reason by those who were concerned that they might become addicted or were afraid of being hurt by the experience. Many students reported fear that drugs would affect their future and have a negative effect on their family relationships. *Negative role model* was similar to the prior role model, except here subjects said they did not take controlled substances or drink alcohol because they knew people who had and they were negatively affected by the experience. For example, one recipient said, "Just because I see my dad and he used to drink a lot. He still does and I don't like how he gets, acts, when he gets to the house." Experiences such as the following understandably make a lasting impression:

> This guy sat next to a toilet, his girlfriend loved him and sat next to a toilet for three days and had a bag. He would shoot up, throw up, and then sit there and pass out. And every time he woke up I watched him do this again, and again.

Don't need/want/like were also reasons offered for not using such substances; the subjects simply did not want to partake of the offered substances. *It's bad* was used when respondents said they did not accept the offer because it is bad for one's body, for one's system, and because of the negative perceptions of users. *Morality* described reasons provided by those who said they refused controlled substances and alcohol for religious reasons or because it was wrong to do such things. One respondent said, "I was reborn a Christian so I can stay away from it...it's the right thing." Morality did not surface as a reason for Dutch adolescents. Dutch adolescents did not perceive drug use as a moral decision. Rather, they perceived it as a health issue or lifestyle choice. This finding persisted even for youth who did not use drugs, did not associate with drug users, and were strongly opposed to use.

    Interestingly, in none of the narratives did the participant state that he or she declined the offer because it was illegal or because his or her peers or parents would disapprove. However, one's *identity as a nonuser* played a large part in refusals particularly for African-American adolescents. The picture presented by these findings is a scenario wherein the adolescent had some sort of prior negative attitude and identity that may have influenced him or her to enter the social situation with a commitment to refusing these illicit substances or refuse once he or she encountered them, irrespective of his or her relationship to the offerer.

Reardon et al.'s (1989) ACE Model of Compliance Resistance talks about a similar system, where resistance strategies appeal to: (a) Appropriateness—what is right or expected (similar to our immoral category), (b) Consistency—what I typically do (similar to no desire and nonidentity), and (c) Effectiveness—outcomes (similar to our fear of consequences). The DRSP findings extend this model to include a greater array of responses across varying age groups.

ETHNIC SIMILARITIES AND DIFFERENCES

Overall, there were more similarities than differences among the three ethnic groups in our research. Latino/as, African-Americans, and Whites were most likely to receive offers from acquaintances or friends at a friend's home (Alberts et al., 1992; Hecht et al., 1992; Miller, 1998). All were most likely to use a simple no to resist offers, with relatively small repertoires of resistance strategies.

Some important ethnic difference did emerge, however. Latino/as reported more drug use and were significantly more likely to be offered drugs (49% of those offered). Whites (27%) were more likely to be offered drugs than African Americans (14%). Latino/as were more likely to be offered alcohol, marijuana, hard drugs, and inhalants at a party when other people are around. This group was more likely to be offered substances by peer family members (brother, sister, cousin) and least likely to be offered by their parents. Whites were more likely to be offered cigarettes by a male or female acquaintance through simple offers at a friend's home or on the street. African-Americans received about as many offers of marijuana as Latino/as. Otherwise, they received less offers of each type of drugs than the other groups. Offers to African-Americans were more likely to come from boyfriends or girlfriends in a park or by a parent and be resisted using explanations.

As expected, differences in ethnicity were related to several differences in drug experiences, with Latinos/as being placed at greater risk than the other two groups. Latinos/as reported receiving drug offers at a significantly higher rate than either Whites or African-Americans. Latinas (females), in particular, were significantly more likely to be offered drugs in general than other females. These findings are consistent with studies that indicate more drug use among Latino/a adolescents in general: Among inner-city 12-year-olds, use rates were equal or higher for Latinos and African-Americans, and use began earlier (Castro, 1995). Regarding contextual factors, Whites (males in particular) were more likely to be offered drugs in the presence of a less intimate acquaintance than were other groups.

GENDER

Gender adds another dimension to understanding the compliance process. Our findings indicate that there are strong similarities between males and females. Males and females do not differ in their lifetime and last 30-day use rates. In addition, males and females share the overall patterns noted earlier: simple offer, simple no, offers at a friend's house.

Again, some interesting and important gender differences have been observed. Males are more likely to be offered all types of drugs in public (i.e., at the park or on the street) and be offered them by a male acquaintance, parent, brother/male cousin, or male stranger through offers that state the benefits of use and resist by using explanations, especially those involving humor. When females receive offers, they are more likely to be in private (i.e., a friend's home) by a female acquaintance, boyfriend, or sister/female cousin through simple offers or offers that minimize the effects of use.

Gender was also found to have important developmental implications. The drug literature commonly talks about two sets of factors involved in drug use: risk factors and resiliency factors. Risk factors are life experiences that put one at jeopardy for use and abuse. They are characteristics of one's life circumstance over which one often has no control such as the family status (i.e., living in a single-parent household puts one at increase risk of drug use) that make one more likely to use and abuse drugs. In contrast, resiliency or protective factors, allow one to overcome risk or otherwise ameliorate the debilitating effects of risk factors, thereby reducing chances of drug use and abuse. For example, contact with an adult male may reduce the risk of being raised by a single mother. In a recent study, we found different patterns for young males and females (Moon, Jackson, & Hecht, in press). If resiliency factors are not experienced by males prior to experimenting with drugs, they do not reduce their risk of continued use. Thus, interventions designed to decrease drug abuse among males by building resiliency must be targeted early—at least prior to age of initiation. Unfortunately, this age is often quite young. For example, the mean age of initiation for Latinos was in the 11- to 14-year-old range in our research (Moon, Hecht, Jackson, & Spellers, 1998).

Eagly (1983) noted that, in natural settings, men are more influential and women are more easily influenced, which she attributed to the status inequality inherent in such settings. People of higher status, which is usually granted to males, have the right and are expected to make demands on those of lesser status, and people of lower status are expected to comply. Evidence indicates that women tend to respond to noncompliance with more rewarding and more punishing messages than men (deTurck, 1985). As targets of influence, girls are often socialized to care about and for others (Aronson, 1992; Pipher, 1994) and are defined to a greater extent by their relationships with others (Wood, 1994). Baumrind (1987) indicated that girls may be more receptive than boys to interpersonal influences to use drugs, which may partly stem from the fact that girls receive more pressure to use drugs when they initially resist (Hecht et al., 1992). These gender differences in susceptibility to influence may become particularly pronounced in the context of adolescent dating relationships, which are discussed later in this chapter.

Thoughts on Ethnicity and Gender

The differences found for ethnicity and gender were not as strong as might be expected. Although differences in the proportion of offers emerged, there were minimal differences in the social processes of drug offers and resistance strategies. A variety of explanations are plausible (Hecht et al., 1997). First, the findings may represent a true lack of ethnic and gender differences in resistance processes. Although the studies reviewed earlier would argue against such a conclusion, several research programs have found no differences between substance use among various ethnic groups (Flannery et al., 1994; Newcomb & Bentler, 1986; Oetting & Beauvais, 1987). Second, youth culture and perhaps a localized, neighborhood youth culture may be more salient than ethnic or gender group memberships for these students (Kandel, 1995). Third, ethnic and gender identity may require more sophisticated measurement than the use of labels as identifiers (see Collins, 1995; Hecht, 1993; Trimble, 1995, for discussions of these issues). Perhaps measures of degree and/or type of identification would produce stronger results. Fourth, the interview method used in this study may not have effectively elicited differences. For example, Latino/a students may have been more open in recounting their drug experiences than other students, giving the appearance of a higher rate of exposure to drug offers. Fifth, the small sample size may have masked existing differences by reducing the power of the tests. Future research is needed to address the validity of these various explanations.[1]

RESEARCH EVIDENCE REGARDING TYPES OF OFFERS AND REFUSALS BY RELATIONSHIP

As has been argued throughout this book, the degree of relational intimacy between the drug offerer and adolescent should affect the potency of the drug offer. Previous research into compliance gaining in general has shown that close relational partners have a variety of advantages over strangers and acquaintances in making requests: They know which strategies are most likely to work from previous influence attempts, they can draw the offer out over time and use sequential request strategies, they know that the target is motivated to maintain the relationship (Boster, 1990), and they have obligation working in their favor (people go along with intimates' requests because reciprocity is expected). Therefore, the requests of intimates tend to be more straightforward and include fewer explanations, incentives, or apologies (Miller, Boster, Roloff, & Seibold, 1977). Those in long-term, personal relationships are also willing to use threats (Miller et al., 1977), although reward-oriented messages tend to be preferred because they maximize the probability of gaining acquiescence and minimize the amount of damage to the relationship. Threat messages are used only as a last resort with a repeatedly noncompliant target (deTurck, 1985).

It is important to know whether the effectiveness of different types of drug offers and resistance strategies differ depending on the relational connection within the dyad. If they do differ in the drug offer context, then practicing skills to resist a generic peer may result in training ineffective resistance abilities. An analysis of offer and resistance strategies in the middle school survey (Trost et al., 1999) found that, indeed, the relationship between the two interactants matters a great deal in terms of the effectiveness of the offer and resistance strategy. Across the 10 types of offer strategies described, all but two (making a promise and stressing social acceptance) differed in effectiveness depending on the relational tie.

---

[1]This discussion of ethnicity and gender effects is derived from Hecht, Trost, Bator, and MacKinnon (1997). See the full article for a more detailed analysis and discussion.

In examining the percentage of accepted offers for each strategy by relationship type, we found that strangers (particularly male strangers) were easy to refuse regardless of what type of offer strategy they used. However, brothers or male cousins, extended family elders, and romantic partners were particularly difficult to refuse regardless of what offer strategy they used, and they were particularly effective when using the nonverbal pass, simple offer, and threat. Although threats were not frequently reported, they were effective most of the time when used by these partners possibly because they have the ability to follow through on them (Dillard, 1990). The effectiveness of friends' offers tended to fall in the middle; even so, the sheer number of offers from friends still makes them important sources of drugs. As with the middle school students, offers from friends in high school are more likely to be accepted than offers from acquaintances or strangers (Alberts et al., 1991, 1992). Offers from family members such as brothers are also more likely to be accepted (Alberts et al., 1992). In addition, drug offers are more likely to involve pressure when they come from friends or family (Alberts et al., 1992).

In the middle school survey (Trost et al., 1999), students were most likely to resist an offer by either simply saying "no" or leaving the situation. These students had obviously learned the primary resistance script that was taught in the area's most popular drug prevention program. Unfortunately, those two resistance strategies were also the only two to vary depending on who was being refused. Students were significantly more likely to say "no" and still take the drug from family members and romantic partners than from male strangers; leaving was also less effective with loved ones than with friends or strangers. Even so, a simple no and providing an explanation tended to be the most effective for family members, whereas saying "no" and leaving were more effective with friends and strangers. Given that resistance complexity had the strongest effect on drug resistance and resistance abilities differed depending on the relational connection, it is clear that, to refuse competently, students need to learn a wide repertoire of resistance strategies that are personalized for particular relationship partners. As already alluded to, competent interaction management can be especially important when the person who is offering drugs is a romantic partner.

Evidence Regarding Drug Use in Romantic Relationships

We have just started to examine the effects of romantic relationships on susceptibility to drug offers, and our initial investigations indicate that romantic partners have a powerful influence on drug use. At this point, our only information comes from the middle school students (one of the authors has a grant to study drug use in high school dating relationships). Although one might want to discount the seriousness of romantic relationships in middle school, students who had either boyfriends or girlfriends were quick to admit it; several girls at one of our middle school schools already had children. These children, although young in age, were already engaging in serious relationships that aspire to romance. In the survey sample, boys were most likely to be offered drugs by male friends and girls by female friends. However, when boys did make offers to girls, these males were frequently romantic partners (Moon et al., in press; Trost et al., 1999). Romantic partners tended to make a simple offer, and the most common response was to take the drug (Kellar-Guenther et al., 1998). As noted earlier, offers from romantic partners were particularly effective—ranging from 47.6% of students accepting an offer that stressed the benefits of using drugs to 66.3% of students accepting a nonverbal offer (Trost et al., 1999). Trying to resist by avoiding the romantic partner was particularly ineffective (60.9% still took the drug), whereas saying "no" (39.7% accepted) and leaving (43.4% accepted) tended to be more effective. Romantic partners also presented the most complex appeals, using, on average, 3.13 types of appeals in the same offer sequence. These data indicate that, even with middle school students who are just beginning to explore romance, boyfriends and girlfriends wield a great deal of power over drug use behaviors.

We also conducted a more sophisticated path analysis that examined the contributions of individual factors (self-esteem, ability to make negative assertions) and relational factors (importance of having a relational partner, desire for physical intimacy, and willingness to be with a drug user) on susceptibility to drug offers from a romantic partner (Trost et al., 1997). The analyses were conducted separately for boys and girls. For boys, susceptibility to a drug offer from a girlfriend was best predicted by relational factors: Willingness to be with a drug user predicted susceptibility, but was affected by the boys' desire for intimacy and the importance to them of having a partner. For girls, both the relational and individual factors affected their perceived vulnerability to a partner's drug offer. As with boys, those girls who were interested in having a partner felt more vulnerable to their boyfriend's influence. This susceptibility was significantly predicted by their willingness to be involved with a drug user, which was positively predicted by their desire for intimacy and the importance to them of having a partner.

In other words, those girls who wanted to have a boyfriend and were willing to date drug users would also find it difficult to say "no" to offers of drugs from those boyfriends. However, girls' level of self-esteem contributed an independent source of resistance, consistent with previous research. Those girls who had a stronger sense of self-esteem had better negative assertion skills and felt less pressure from boyfriends' drug offers. Although these are interesting results, it is important to note that these models explain little variance (7%–8%) in susceptibility to the drug offers of relational partners. At this developmental stage, it is likely that romantic partners are less important in determining drug use than same-sex friends. Additional studies are being conducted to test these paths on older adolescents.

Although we have focused on the detrimental effects of romantic relationships for adolescent drug use, it is important to note that romantic relationships with nonusers can have positive effects on drug use patterns. Preliminary results from 22 interviews with high school students (Trost, Langan, & Bachman, 1998) indicate that 28% of them had stopped using drugs for a relational partner, 17% of them had asked their partners to stop using for them, and 27% had rejected someone once they found out that they did not approve of the partner's drug use behavior. These results serve as a poignant reminder that the right relationship can enhance resiliency against drug use.

CONCLUSIONS

We started this chapter by claiming that relationships matter, and that the nature of the social context surrounding a drug offer can have an impact on an adolescent's ability to refuse drugs or resist pressure. We have presented findings from a series of studies that support the need to look at drug resistance through the lens of the relational competence model. The relationship between the people in the situation has important implications not only for the type of offer that is made, but the amount of pressure that accompanies the offer, as well as the follow-up pressure exerted by the offerer. When formulating a response to a drug offer, adolescents must weigh who the offer is coming from, the consequences of refusing for themselves and the relationship, and the most appropriate and effective way to frame the response. Our research indicates that this more interactive understanding of drug offer situations can be helpful in explaining drug use patterns and developing interventions.

First, most drug offers are made by same-sex friends, indicating that skills-training scenarios should include both male–male and female–female dyads. In addition, romantic partners who offer drugs can be particularly dangerous: They use the most complex offer scripts and are the most likely to gain acquiescence. Even so, adolescents, particularly middle school students and nonusers, tend to rely on the simple no response to get out of these situations. Unfortunately, our research indicates that simply saying "no" is less effective for more intimate relationships.

The differences found for demographic variables such as ethnicity and gender were not as strong as might be expected (Hecht et al., 1997; Moon, Hecht, Jackson, & Spellers, 1998). Although differences in the proportion of offers emerged, there were minimal differences in the social processes of drug offers and resistance strategies. A variety of explanations are plausible. First, the findings may represent a true lack of ethnic and gender differences in resistance processes. Although other studies would argue against such a conclusion, several research programs have found no differences between substance use among various ethnic groups (Flannery et al., 1994; Newcomb & Bentler, 1986; Oetting & Beauvais, 1987). Second, youth culture and perhaps a localized, neighborhood youth culture may be more salient than ethnic or gender group memberships for these students (Kandel, 1995). Third, ethnic and gender identity may require more sophisticated measurement than the use of labels as identifiers (see Collins, 1995; Hecht, 1993; Trimble, 1995, for discussions of these issues). Perhaps measures of degree and/or type of identification would produce stronger results. Fourth, the interview method used in this study may not have effectively elicited differences. For example, Latino/a students may have been more open in recounting their drug experiences than other students, giving the appearance of a higher rate of exposure to drug offers. Future research is needed to address the validity of these various explanations.

Adolescents seem to be more familiar with alcohol, and they are aware that society sanctions its use by older adults. Therefore, teens see alcohol as less risky than other drugs, perceive more general pressure to use alcohol, and have more difficulty refusing. The respondents in our studies report more use of alcohol, both in the amount consumed and the number of times drunk, than use of other drugs.

Results indicate that, although all sets of factors differentiate alcohol from other drugs, the communication processes involved in offers and resistance provide a stronger effect and more accurate prediction. In fact, the primary differences between alcohol and other drugs are in the refusal process rather than in factors such as attitudes, perceived risk, usage history, availability, and the difficulty resisting. The only noncommunication factor to exert much influence in the overall, combined analysis was perceived pressure, and this also may be a communication variable. Thus, communication factors predict group differences with almost perfect accuracy. If the goal is to explain drug resistance, the communication factors provide a powerful model.

Kline and Floyd (1990) showed that cognitive complexity was related to refusal sensitivity and the number of refusal messages. The present study extended this analysis to refusal complexity and demonstrates greater situational variation in the refusal process. We found that less socially acceptable means (e.g., lies) were used to resist offers of more socially acceptable things (alcohol), and people seem to develop more complex refusal skills for situations they commonly encounter. Further, greater justification is present when less socially acceptable substances are offered. Thus, the process may be more complex for the offerer of socially unacceptable things and the resistor of socially acceptable offers. This suggests the magnitude of the problem with this substance among this age group. We believe it also suggests the need for additional attention to establishing nonuse or moderation norms among this age group.

Norms appear to play a powerful role in adolescent drug use decisions. In fact, some have argued that, without affecting social norms, prevention programs are doomed to failure (Hansen, 1991). However, this literature tends to focus on a single type of norm—descriptive norms—that focuses on perceptions of the prevalence of drug use. Basically, adolescents are more likely to use drugs if they believe that more of their peers use drugs. Because adolescents tend to overestimate the number of peers using drugs, prevention programs have incorporated strategies for reducing these perceptions (Hansen, 1991). Recent theorizing by Cialdini, Reno, and Kallgren (1990) suggested that there are at least two other types of norms. Their norm focus theory expands our consideration to include personal and injunctive norms. Personal norms are an individual's judgments of right and wrong, whereas injunctive norms involve the moral judgments of others (i.e., parents, peers). When we looked at drug norms (Walls & Trost, 1996), we found that there were separate descriptive, injunctive, and personal drug norms for this age group; although all three norms were somewhat important, the largest effects were for descriptive and personal norms.

It is also interesting to note that general assertiveness does not seem to be a key discriminator. We had anticipated that because drugs are less socially acceptable, greater assertiveness would be found in their resistance. Perhaps because teens have received so much assertiveness information regarding drug resistance, those who are capable of being assertive use this tactic regardless of the substance. Others may recognize the dialectic between refusing the offer but not the person making the offer and intuitively realize that assertive individuals are sometimes disliked for their behavior (Wildman, 1986).

One important set of issues that emerged from these studies concerns decision-making and verbal resistance strategies. These findings indicate that if the adolescent has a firm decision and commitment to saying no prior to encountering the offer, he or she is more able to resist the offer, particularly if the offer is for drugs. However, those who have not made a strong commitment or are subject to peer pressure need to develop a repertoire of strategies for saying "no,"—from the simple no to preemptive strategies such as avoidance. A simple no was effective in the majority of cases where respondents ultimately declined the offer. However, in those cases where pressure was applied, more was needed. Thus, "just say no" may be a first response tactic, but it must be followed up with other strategies if additional pressure is applied.

Relational Communication Competence: Implications for Prevention

In an effort to combat the strong pull of peer pressure toward delinquency, school-based prevention programs have traditionally emphasized behavioral skills training (how to resist) and normative retraining (why to resist), with a strong recommendation that peer leaders be involved in disseminating information and modeling successful resistance behavior (Botvin et al., 1995; Hansen, Johnson et al., 1988). In general, effective programs have focused on changing norms about the prevalence of use among students, taught specific resistance skills, and been delivered and reinforced by peers (Tobler, 1989, 1995). Tobler (1995) noted, in fact, that the most successful drug education programs in recent years were those that included training in communicating drug refusal and a participatory delivery method that required interaction between peers. This argues for the importance of positive peer pressure and communication competence in resisting drug use.

The litany of communication (in)abilities associated with drug users is relatively consistent in its extremity. On the one hand, Mayer and Ligman (1989) found heavy marijuana users to be significantly lower on the personality trait of socialization than either moderate users or nonusers; the former were characterized as defensive, demanding, opinionated, stubborn, and deceitful. On the other hand, Allen and Page (1994) found that male cigarette smokers were more shy and unsociable than female smokers (who were overly sociable). Shy males who were high in sociability also tended to use more illicit drugs. The relationship between shyness and heightened sociability presents a particularly unfortunate interpersonal dilemma because the withdrawal attributable to the shyness precludes fulfilling the need to be with others. In fact, for these people, drug use may be a way of coping with their interpersonal difficulties—it provides a shared activity and an opportunity to interact without having to communicate at a deep level. The overly sociable females present a different dilemma, in that social skills training may not only be unnecessary, but may lead to boomerang effects (see Moberg & Piper, 1995).

In effect, the students whose communication abilities are either too much or too little appear to be more susceptible to drug use. This interpretation is supported by research on invulnerable adolescents (those who had never had alcohol, smoked, or tried illicit drugs) who reported better social relationships, better health, and a happier state of mind than users (Marston, Jacobs, Singer, Widaman, & Little, 1988). In other words, adolescents who are able to interact effectively with others may be better able to develop positive social relationships and be less susceptible to drug use.

Finally, these data suggest several important issues for future intervention programs: (a) any scenarios that present drug offer situations must include a variety of relationship types—not just generic peers, but same-sex friends, romantic partners, and family members, as well; (b) adolescents need to be taught a wider range of possible refusal strategies to expand their repertoire and give them more flexibility to counter follow-up peer pressure; and (c) there may be some benefit to working separately with boys and girls to create realistic scenarios that tap into their lived experience.

It is indeed a difficult task to negotiate offers and refusals in an interpersonal interaction. In the end, most people recognize this difficulty. According to a 16-year-old adolescent in our study:

> Anyone who can say, "I don't drink or don't do (other drugs)," I say cool, that's wonderful, I'm proud of you, go for it. I admire that. It's just hard to be friends with people but still be able to hold your ground and not do drugs.

4

Metaphor, Culture, and Action: The Symbolic Construction of Adolescent Drug Use

Membership in adolescent culture is typified by language, language use, and language style. Slang, nicknames, and ingroup phrases used within adolescent groupings provide a sense of membership among members and reflect and construct the norms for the groups' members. Although adolescents may be cognizant of their choice of words and double entendre's and pride themselves in cultural idioms that establish boundaries between the youth and adult worlds, adolescents' use of metaphor in their language is not quite so manifest. Adolescent use of metaphors in their language when they discuss drugs and drug use evokes a powerful representation of narrative knowledge about drugs.

LANGUAGE, CULTURE, AND ACTION

To Gadamer (1982), language is not simply a tool for conveying a person's prior meaning to a receiver, but rather it is the "living ground of all uniquely human existence" (Carr, 1986). According to Carr (1986), we do not have ideas and then decide to verbalize or write them; the ideas and their expression are inextricable. As humans, we do not use language—we live within it. It is through language that we experience and depict our world, and it is through narratives that we organize it.

The intrinsic relationship between everyday language and culture is widely recognized (Garfinkel, 1967; Geertz, 1973; Goffman, 1959, 1967; Goodenough, 1971; Hymes, 1964; Lakoff & Johnson, 1980; Philipsen, 1975, 1976). Burke (1954) claimed that an individual's language and thought are a socialized product of his or her group. "In the profoundest human sense, one communicates by a weighted vocabulary in which the weightings are shared by a group as a whole" (Burke, 1954, p. 162). In general, the vocabulary of a language and, more specifically, the words selected for use by the members of a culture provide us with a catalogue of things considered important to that culture (Saville-Troike, 1989).

This vocabulary can be viewed as an index to the way speakers categorize experience (Blumer, 1969; Carbaugh, 1988, 1989; Hymes, 1972; Katriel & Philipsen, 1981). Burke (1959) further claimed that the words we use function as signposts for how cultural members might act toward these things. Put another way, an individual's use of language is not neutral. To the contrary, the spontaneous speech of a person is loaded with judgments. A given event, object, person, or experience can be at once good, evil, fun, or dangerous depending on the frame of reference by which an individual places it (Burke, 1954).

Therefore, words are not merely signs, but rather names whose attachment to events, objects, persons, expectations, experiences, or institutions advances and advocates an interpretive base. These words, replete with individual meanings, influence what the speaker will do in regard to the bearer of the name (Duncan, 1965). Building on Richards' (1926) conclusions, Burke (1941) extended the relationship even further in stating that an attitude contains an implicit program of action.

If one accepts the arguments of Burke, Duncan, and Richards, then the symbols we use and the names we give to things affect not only our attitudes, but also our actions. Names—the coordinates individuals use to place events, objects, experiences, expectations, and the like—become indicators of possible action to the social scientist.

Three important conclusions regarding the relationship among language, culture, and action necessarily follow. First, language as a product of one's membership in a culture represents a symbolic phase of action. Second, language, culture, and action constitute a continuous process of mutual influence. Membership in a culture shapes an individual's language, the use of which affects his or her attitudes and actions based on the experiential weightings that person assigns to words; completing the circle, an individual's actions help sustain as well as reproduce the culture. Third, by defining and then targeting a specific culture/subculture and analyzing the language of its membership, communication researchers should be able to ascertain implicit plans of action.

We became interested in adolescents' language use only when we began to notice distinctions in the use of metaphors in the narratives that adolescents recounted of their experiences with drugs. We believe analyzing adolescents' language and metaphors contribute to our knowledge about drug use prevention. Based on an analysis of data from Alberts, Miller-Rassulo, and Hecht (1991), we suggest how language and metaphor operate in both drug use and drug prevention.

Consistent with this purpose, this chapter (a) demonstrates a communication strategy for understanding how and what adolescents think about drugs, (b) promotes language/metaphor as a potential factor in the process of identifying at-risk youths, and (c) details a communicative framework for future drug prevention programs designed for adolescents and preadolescents prior to their involvement with drugs. To accomplish these ends, we begin with a discussion of the relationships among language, culture, and action, and provide an overview of our research project.

If adolescents construct stories of drug use as a positive experience, glamorous and mature, it is difficult to persuade them to use resistance strategies when offered these substances. Conversely, if we can alter their language—their narrative knowledge of drugs and drug use—we have a better chance of invoking more conservative norms to motivate them to use their skills and resist offers.

METAPHOR

Perhaps metaphor provides the most substantial and easily recognizable linguistic indicator of possible action. Richards (1926) argued that "all languages contain deeply embedded metaphorical structures which covertly influence overt meaning" (p. 36). "Metaphor," according to Aristotle, "consists in giving the thing a name that belongs to something else" (Sontag, 1989, p.5). This simple definition, however, obscures the force that metaphor historically has had to shape thought and culture. Sontag (1989) argued that we "cannot think without metaphors" (p. 5). In her book *AIDS and Its Metaphors*, Sontag delineated the various competing discourses framing the AIDS issue and revealed how the metaphors of those discourses impact our perceptions and guide our (re)actions to AIDS. In so doing, she highlighted the power of language and metaphor to influence behavior and policy. In fact, in their seminal work, Lakoff and Johnson (1980) claimed that our everyday ways of thinking and acting are fundamentally metaphorical in nature. They concluded that metaphor is not a mere flourish of style, but is pervasive in everyday life; it is not just in language, but in thought and action.

Smircich (1985) suggested that metaphors are generative because they allow one to apprehend the familiar from an unfamiliar vantage point. As Koch and Deetz (1981) demonstrated, however, the form *A is B* is not arbitrary because it evokes a directionality. By shaping the understanding of *A* in terms of *B*, the language of metaphor presents one way to experience the reality of *A*. Metaphor extends a fundamental structure for experience (Koch & Deetz, 1981).

Researchers working in the realm of substance use and misuse have engaged in the examination of metaphor and word associations. For example, Wilhelmsen (1968) found that women who failed in their attempts to quit smoking tended to refer to cigarettes as *companions*. Research on illicit drug use suggests that the story of drug use contains images of the user as mature and unconventional (Jessor, Chase, & Donovan, 1980; Jessor & Jessor, 1977). In addition, Szalay and a variety of co-authors (Szalay, Bovasso, Vilov, & Williams, 1992; Szalay, Canino, & Vilov, 1993; Szalay & Deese, 1978; Szalay, Vilov, & Strohl, 1992) studied representations regarding drug use and abuse. The fundamental premise of these works is that a system of subjective representations exists within individuals that affects their understanding of the environment and provides organization and direction to their behavior.

In addition, the literature in Counseling Education and Counseling Psychology has long recognized the power of metaphor as a means of promoting insight and understanding through therapeutic communication (Erickson, 1948, 1958; Gilligan, 1987; Gordon, 1978; Haley, 1976, 1986; Papp, 1982). Suit and Paradise (1985) suggested that, to achieve desired outcomes, metaphors should be fit to the developmental level of the audience.

These findings regarding language, culture, action, and metaphor have implications for drug prevention and/or drug resistance research. The most significant of these may be that, according to our hypothesis, language can be used as a risk factor to predict high-risk adolescents *before* the onset of drug involvement. We believe that it is important to discover an individual's attitudes concerning drugs and drug usage during those critical periods prior to actual drug involvement. Because attitudes are influenced by language and precede action, persons' words provide meaningful cues as to their implicit plans for action regarding drug usage and/or experimentation.

Thus, identifying those critical periods and analyzing the language (including metaphors) employed by individuals during these periods are valuable. Following such an analysis, individuals should be exposed to one or more relevant tactics/weapons from our arsenal of prevention strategies. Tobler (1989) further argued that prevention programs for at-risk youths should be markedly different from those offered to relatively low-risk adolescents. In addition, messages designed for prevention may be significantly different from those messages fashioned to persuade youths (both preteen and teenage) from continuing or expanding their drug involvements. Finally, social scientists working in the area of drug prevention should be mindful of their younger and less cognitively complex clients when creating their message strategies (including metaphors).

Single risk factors independently do not constitute an etiology for drug use. Nevertheless, it appears that the more risk factors in an adolescent's personal, social, and emotional environment, the higher the probability of that individual becoming a drug user. Newcomb, Maddahian, and Bentler (1986) and Bry (1983) reported the existence of a linear relationship between higher levels of substance use among youth and increased numbers of risk factors. We view language use as an additional, processual, and, as yet, untapped indicator of risk. If we are correct, language adds another weapon to the war on drugs.

RISK FACTORS

As discussed in chapters 2 and 3, in an effort to curb the magnitude of substance use and abuse, numerous factors have been identified as antecedents to adolescent drug use (Catalano, Haggerty, Gainey, & Hoppe, 1997; Gullotta, Adams, & Montemayor, 1995; Hawkins et al., 1992; Kumpfer, 1989; Newcomb, 1992). Language use, however, has not been included as a potential risk or resiliency factor. We argue that if the use of language differs across risk groups of adolescents, perhaps the drug educators may be able to identify at-risk individuals before the onset of substance use. Those individuals could be exposed to a variety of rhetorical strategies designed to dissuade or at least delay them from participating in experimentation with alcohol and other kinds of drugs.

To assess language differences across risk level of adolescents, a number of risk factors other than language use were identified in the substance use prevention literature (Catalano, Haggerty, Gainey, Hoppe, & Brewer, 1994; Hawkins, 1992; Kumpfer, 1989; Newcomb, 1992; Tobler, 1989). The risk scale consisted of several factors: ethnicity (Beauvais, Oetting, & Edwards, 1985; Brannock, Schandler, & Oncley, 1990; Yates, 1987), gender (Brannock et al., 1990; Forney et al., 1989), early use of drugs and alcohol (Forney et al., 1989), and parents' current use and change in use (Baumrind, 1990; Cutter & Fisher, 1980; McLaughlin et al., 1985). Availability was measured by the number of offers and refusals, with the latter weighted based on the answer to the former.

Given those self-reports, individuals were numerically placed along a risk continuum and, following their placement, grouped into high-, medium-, and low-risk subcultures. Our goal was to assess whether the language patterns—themes and metaphors—representative of each subculture would reflect distinguishable differences, at least between the high- and low-risk groups.

AN ANALYSIS OF ADOLESCENT DRUG METAPHORS

Utilizing the data from Alberts et al. (1991), transcripts of oral interviews with 59 teenagers were analyzed for language and metaphor use.[1] Following the recording and transcribing of the interviews, two of the primary researchers independently read and analyzed the transcripts. Each of the two readers performed a qualitative analysis of the individual transcripts. Our examination, broadly reflecting *open coding* as referenced by Glaser and Strauss (1967) and Glaser (1992), resulted in the identification of general categories and their properties. In addition, each researcher recorded the metaphors used by the interviewees when referring to drugs or the use of drugs. The metaphor analysis followed procedures similar to those specified in Smith and Eisenberg (1987). We conducted both the identification of categories and metaphor analysis while naive to the respondents' risk scores.

Next, we calculated risk scores for each individual and placed each respondent into a high-, medium-, or low-risk group. Finally, to determine whether thematic patterns differentiated these groups, we compared the categories, their properties, and the metaphors indigenous to the three risk groups. In the following sections, we summarize these two steps in the research process.

---

[1]See Appendix A for a summary of methods used in all of the studies.

Individual Risk Analysis

After we identified the categories, properties, and metaphors at the
ideographic level, we positioned members of the sample (individuals
within the adolescent culture) along a risk continuum. An adolescent's position on the risk continuum corresponded to the sum of the numbers associated with his or her answers. This placing was necessary for the
subsequent step—to determine whether trends could be distinguished in
the language of three subgroups. For the 11 risk factors used in our study,
adolescents' scores ranged from 9.5 on the low end—the lowest risk—to
19.88 on the high end—the highest risk.[2]

Thematic and Metaphor Analysis at the Group Level

Following the placement of individuals on our risk scale, we arranged these
individuals into high-, medium-, and low-risk groups. We then examined
the individual responses of respondents across each risk group to identify
common themes, metaphor usage, or other distinguishing linguistic patterns at the group level. Baxter (1991) stated that, "Themes are threads of
meaning that recur in domain after domain" (p. 250). To accomplish a thematic analysis, the researcher(s) must execute analyses on more than one
domain (Baxter, 1991). We asked how the meaning domains of the individuals within the different groups were similar and whether differences existed between the groups—particularly between the high- and low-risk
aggregates.

A preliminary examination revealed two areas in which respondents'
language differed: expectations and choice. Participants either described
positive expectations for the drug experience or described negative expectations for the consequences or outcomes of drug use. Further, interviewees
varied across all three risk groups in how they discussed issues of choice:
High-risk group members indicated that they had control over their drug
use choices (internal locus of control), whereas low-risk group members indicated that they believed the issue was beyond their control (external locus
of control). In addition, participants' metaphor usage was consistent with
their negative and positive expectations for drug use. The following details

---

[2]On Questions 9 and 11, it is possible for the respondent to achieve a score of 0. Therefore, although there are 11 questions, a score of 9 is mathematically possible. Refer to Appendix B for a detailed breakdown of the process of assigning numerical values to the 11 risk questions.

a group-by-group description of the patterns of expectations, choice, and metaphor discovered at the group level.

High-Risk Group. The most notable pattern of the high-risk group members was their expectation of a positive experience regarding the consumption of alcohol or other kinds of drugs. From the information disclosed in the interviews, it was apparent that some individuals in this group had already used drugs, others appeared on the verge of using, and one other professed to having never used drugs. Regardless of use history, members of this group anticipated a positive experience from future drug use. The following are typical positive expectation responses in reference to drugs or drug usage uncovered in the language of the high-risk individuals:

* It just gets me, you know, kind of cheery, not as shy.
* It'll make you forget about things and kind of calm you down.
* Things are always a bit funnier.
* I think I'll become more comfortable around people.
* It's a way to ease up on the strain, you know, or it will get me out of a bad mood.
* You don't worry about anything, you just, your troubles are gone and it's almost like having fun, like going through a haunted house or something, you know, just getting that adrenalin flowing.
* I thought something magical was going to happen when I got stoned or when I got drunk and that I actually was doing something really fun and super.
* We were all so sad and for some reason I thought that by drinking I was going to feel better so I decided to drink that night.

Associated with (and technically a subgroup of)[3] expectations and prominently displayed in the language of the high-risk group is the theme of control. High-risk individuals display a tendency for equating taking drugs with an internal locus of control (i.e., they control their own behavior). On the whole, this group frames drugs as a matter of choice over which they

---

[3]Despite its preliminary nature, we felt that this scale, although not recommended in its current form for individual assessment, was effective in assisting the examination of group differences. This conclusion is supported by a .51 correlation between the risk score and self-reported amount of drug use. This is a moderately large correlation.

have complete control. The key, then, for the high-risk individuals is viewing the choice to use drugs as voicing an internal locus of control—as expressing their desire to control their lives. This theme of choice can be discerned readily in the following statements. Note the use of either control or choice in each:

- Things in my mood will trigger and I'll just, if I'll be in a bad mood I'll say … or someone gets me in a bad mood, I'll just be mad that they like can have some control over me and then I'll do it (referring to drugs).
- I just feel like what are the good things, you know, I could try it out, it will be the first time and everything, and it might be as good as they say, and I look at the bad things, I might freak out or something and I was just like … you know, weighing the pros and cons and thought yeah I can handle it. I chose yeah.
- I've been having like problems at home and stuff and so I just decided, and then when I had that beer I just kept wanting more. It just seemed like the better choice because when I'd go home I'd just go to my room and to bed so I don't have to deal with the rest of the household.
- Forget it. I'm just going to do it. You know if I really thought about it I wouldn't have done it, so I was just like, it's my choice, I'm just gonna do it.

Although metaphors for drugs and drug use were not overly abundant, they did surface in the high-risk group language. One high-risk individual used the word *nirvana*, another talked about drugs as *joy*, and another referred to them as *escape*. For the high-risk group, doing drugs is *cool*—it is *takin' a break* or indulging in a *treat*, and pills are *beauties* while alcohol is *adult*. Some equate life with pressure, and drugs become the *release* or an attractive way of *killing time*. The use of metaphor in this group supports the overall pattern of identifying positive outcomes with the use of drugs.

To briefly summarize this section, members of the high-risk group, as reflected in their language, express positive expectations for the experiential outcomes of drug use. The metaphors they choose to represent the drug experience reflect those positive expectations and suggest beneficial associations. In addition, high-risk individuals display a tendency to view drug taking as their choice, thus demonstrating an *internal locus of control*. Clearly, the high-risk individuals in this study have a positive expectation for drug use and believe they exhibit an internal locus of control when they exercise this choice.

Low-Risk Group. Although nothing in their environment or at an individual level explicitly communicates a positive or negative orientation toward drugs, individuals in the low-risk cluster—in contrast to the high-risk group—express a markedly more negative expectation in regard to the consumption of alcohol or other types of drugs. Low-risk individuals generally communicate a negative portrayal of the consequences/outcomes resulting from drug usage.

- It makes me uncomfortable, I mean people who do it make me uncomfortable.
- The smell of it makes me sick.
- It never fails, doin' drugs causes problems and I don't need no more problems.
- Because I knew it would hurt me and I probably, well, something bad would have probably happened.
- Well just, I mean, it doesn't do anything for me ... You know all it's going to do is mess you up.
- I just know the damage it'll do and I don't know, I just, maybe I'm afraid I'll get hooked, you know how they say, "Well, yeah, you do it and you'll get hooked," like that or something and even if you don't ... it just messes you up and right now I want to be healthy.
- I mean because people are stupid when they start drinking, it's just like "okay," you know, they say stupid things, they act stupid, you know, just get themselves into trouble, they start fights.

From our analysis, it was apparent that members of the low-risk group also addressed issues of choice and control in their language. These individuals made choices as well. Their decisions, however, reflected an intent to avoid future involvements with drugs. Many of the interviewees used the phrases *didn't want* or *don't want*, implying a choice had been made (they were not coerced). By making a choice, implicit or otherwise, they too manifested an internal locus of control.

- Because I saw how he was, and he was out of control basically, when he came to school in the morning. For myself, I don't want to be out of control at any time.
- But I really didn't want to because I don't like when you drink too much that you can't control yourself anymore. And they were all so

drunk you know and he was saying come on, you know drink and stuff and I said no …. But you know I don't like drinking too much that you get or that you lose control that's why.

- I see everybody else and like they're gone or something and I don't want to be in that state where I don't have control of myself. That's the only thing I'm really big on. I don't like to be dependent on other people or things and then to see them, they can't even stand up, I wouldn't like to be in that state so I just don't drink.

More fascinating perhaps, these low-risk individuals generally related drugs and those using drugs to a loss or surrendering of control. They believed that those who do elect to use drugs concede their internal locus of control, thereby abdicating to an external locus of control. Because of their disdain for surrendering control to an outside agent, many of the low-risk people went so far as to claim that they saw no real choice. Instead, they chose not to relinquish control. In fact, it is this loss of control that constitutes the primary negative expectation of the outcome of the drug experience—one loses control.

- The dude kept sayin' "Man it's your choice, man. You can do it if you want." Well man, there is no choice is what I felt like sayin.
- I had to keep my sister in control. I do not want to be in that position. It's humiliating, I mean the next day everybody's like oh you did this, you did that, and you don't remember a thing.
- I mean like what's the big decision. I've got a future and don't see drugs even as a choice.

A second interesting subset of the low-risk group's equating drugs with a loss of control is the propensity of these individuals to provide examples of negative role models. In the first three examples of low-risk language, the speaker provides an unsolicited depiction of individuals under the control of alcohol or another kind of drug. In comparison, there were no references within the high-risk members' language to role models, either negative or positive. For example, high-risk individuals did not characterize those who abstain from drugs as people not to model. Although this might be understandable considering they are focusing on their positive expectations for drug use, it may be significant that they advance no instances of other drug users as positive role models worthy of emulation. In contrast to low-risk group members, high-risk individuals provide no role models.

Although low-risk individuals did not incorporate a plethora of rich or graphic metaphors regarding drugs into their language, they did frame drugs as *trouble* and *burn out*. When you *do drugs* and get *messed up*—it's *humiliating* and people have to *babysit* for you because the ability to be in control is gone. Doing drugs and people who do drugs are generally referred to as *dumb*, *stupid*, and *gross*, as well as, more specifically, *chimney's*, *alkies*, or *stoners*, depending on the user's drug of choice. People who frequently take drugs are running the risk of *ruining their family*. Being into drugs causes one to *feel guilty*.

In summary, members of the low-risk group express negative expectations regarding outcomes associated with drug use. Also, the metaphors incorporated into their language reveal negative associations. If metaphors frame the unknown through the known, then for the low-risk individuals in this study, drugs (the relatively unknown) assume extremely negative connotations—drugs are dumb, drugs are trouble, drugs are things that destroy families. They perceive an expected loss of control based on all of these negative associations. Drugs begin to manage the individual and, as a consequence, others must take care of the drug user when he or she is under the influence. According to the perceptions of the low-risk individuals, there is a shift from an internal to an external locus of control. Choice becomes a nonissue due to the magnitude of the negative consequences. Drugs are not an option for a large number of the low-risk individuals.

Medium-Risk Group. We include an examination of the medium-risk group in our descriptive analysis as a quasicontrol factor to discover if any distinguishing characteristics surface in this group that are absent in both the high- and low-risk groups. Due to the nature of any continuum used for measurement of a theoretical construct, we posited that the midrange of our continuum would blur the linguistic differences displayed by the extremes. The data generally support our hypothesis. However, we did perceive a trend to use language expressing a desire *to experiment* or reflecting indecision regarding its effects.

- I wasn't sure. That had been the first time and so I kind of went into it very, you know, not knowing what was going to happen.
- When we did it was this big experimental phase. Yeah, I don't know. I had been so curious. I think my curiosity just got to me because it had been so long and in Junior High it was all such a big scene ... I was really curious and just wanted to get it over with basically.

- Because I had never done it before. I didn't know, you know, there's always that feeling that this is bad and that I shouldn't be doing it but then there's also this, well, I wonder what, I've never done it before so what does it feel like.
- I didn't want to turn it down because I was curious about that stuff.

By focusing on the themes of *experimentation* and *indecision,* we do not mean to diminish the fact that members of this group also use drug metaphors, express expectations for drug usage, and mention issues of control and choice. As opposed to the high- and low-risk groups, however, the medium-risk group displays no discernable trend in its language in regard to any of those linguistic patterns. Those individuals near the center of our risk continuum exhibit characteristics of both extremes to a greater extent than, for example, the high-risk members incorporate the language of the low-risk group or vice versa.

Understanding the Role of Language and Metaphor in Drug Use and Resistance

Our overall goals in this chapter were to (a) call attention to the role of language in drug use narratives, and (b) begin the process of specifying this role in the detection and prevention of future drug use. Although the research detailed in this chapter is preliminary and heuristic, tentative conclusions can be drawn. Through our analysis, we identified basic language as an initial step in this line of research. In place of a restatement of the descriptive analysis of the three risk groups' linguistic trends, Table 4.1 summarizes our findings.

From this table, we can see that: (a) metaphors and language do differentiate between the high- and low-risk groups; (b) high-risk members frame the drug experience positively and imply an association between doing drugs and an internal locus of control; (c) medium-risk individuals exhibit no clear trends in their use of metaphors and framing of the drug experience, but display a greater likelihood of expressing indecision regarding drug experimentation; and, (d) low-risk group members describe the use of drugs as having negative implications, one of which is the creation of an external locus of control, and use negative terms including metaphors to describe drugs and drug use.

One might assume that the valence of expectations would differentiate risk groups. Our findings support this previously untested assumption and

TABLE 4.1
Trends in Language Use

Variable	High-Risk	Medium-Risk	Low-Risk
Expectations	Primarily positive * fun * relax * release	Both positive and negative	Primarily negative * problems * bad * stupid
Choice/control	Individual chooses to do drugs. Choice demonstrates an internal locus of control.	Ambiguous	By choosing not to do drugs, individual also demonstrates an internal locus of control. Sees drug use as a surrender of control. A switch from internal to external control.
Metaphors	Express positive outcome * nirvana * treat * release	Include metaphors of both high- and low-risk groups	Express negative outcomes * trouble * burn out * guilt
Experiment	Some mention but no clear-cut trend	Frequently mentioned along with indecision regarding effects	Some mention but no clear-cut trend

contribute to our understanding of how these expectations are played out in the metaphors of control for teens. Although a more elaborate list of expectations and metaphors may emerge in future research, the current list provides a useful starting point in this pursuit.

Before leaving any discussion of this table, we would be remiss if we did not emphasize that there were no pure groups. As in most analyses accomplished at the group level, there are individuals within those groups who do not reflect the prevalent trend in regard to the highlighted categories. In addition, individuals demonstrate intrasubjective inconsistencies. At times a respondent categorized as a high-risk group member referred to drugs using positive expectations in one statement and negative expectations in the next. This is reflective of the complex nature of thought associated with major lifestyle choices and membership in multiple language and identity communities. We did expect to find some language overlap among groups, and, indeed, there was a degree of overlap. Nevertheless, we do find that the patterns of language use are indicative of group differences. We endeavor to describe trends only at the nomothetic level and make no generalizations at the ideographic level of observation.

FINAL THOUGHTS

Language, as an implicit plan of action, has the ability to provide the drug prevention community with signposts. These signposts are not always accurate or easily read. An individual might be rated as high-risk on a sensation-seeking scale or according to parental income and low-risk in regard to parental alcohol use and gender. That same individual may use high- or low-risk language. Regardless of potential inconsistencies within an individual, we believe that language has the capacity to contribute to the overall notion of risk. Kumpfer (1989) stated that there are no simple solutions in the fight against alcohol and drug abuse. Alcohol and drug abuse is due to long-term, complex causes that begin early in life. Early childhood risk factors put some children on a different developmental path that terminates in alcohol or drug abuse and other problem behaviors. Health care providers need to use their professional training and knowledge to help these children by early intervention and referral efforts.

Kumpfer (1989) detailed an extensive battery of risk factors currently being considered as potential allies for the health providers in the War on Drugs. We are proposing that language be incorporated into that arsenal to aid in the identification of adolescents and preadolescents who may be at high risk with regard to future drug involvement. Beyond its contribution to risk identification, language analysis also may help in the generation of messages targeted for various risk levels in the divergent audiences of intervention and prevention.

The added variable of language use in adolescent narratives can be included when targeting youth of varying risk classifications, thus providing the drug prevention community with one additional indicator of at-risk individuals. It also provides a more efficient vocabulary for communicating with each group.

One additional concern must be considered prior to fully activating language as a force in our War on Drugs. It involves the manner in which we construct our prevention messages. How should the drug prevention community present messages specifically designed for young children and preadolescents? What language and, more specifically, what metaphors should be incorporated into those messages devised to delay the onset of drug involvement? We suggest the language of low- and medium-risk adolescents and preadolescents be used to conceive these messages. In other words, include the metaphors, themes, and other linguistic devices that may help frame the drug experience for the audience we are attempting to reach in prevention—the very young. If language carries an implicit plan for action, exposure to certain language may help promote an acceptance of that plan.

This intervention can be tested in an evaluation study in which youth are exposed to and trained in low-risk language prior to the onset of use. We would hypothesize that, when compared with a control group, high-risk youths who are exposed to this program would exhibit delayed onset or decreased use levels.

We have made reference more than once in this chapter to the War on Drugs—a popular metaphor used to frame the efforts of the prevention community. We have also injected into this chapter's language words associated with the war metaphor, such as *arsenal, tactics,* and *weapons.* In our analysis of the language of the 44 adolescents interviewed during this project, however, we did not find a single reference to wars, tactics, battles, battleplans, weapons, arsenals, campaigns, combat, logistics, batteries, battlefront, recruitment, or any other example of war language. From that we conclude that the war metaphor and its various linguistic extensions held no relevance for this audience.

We are not implying that the war metaphor does not have significance for other audiences. Nevertheless, if our purpose is drug prevention, the audience we must be concerned with is our intended audience—young children and preadolescents. Winner (1988) reminded us that the hearer of the metaphor must discover the intended message. With young children and preadolescents, this would entail comprehending the intended similarity among war, drug prevention, and drug use. Perhaps war does not peacefully coexist with prevention in the mind of this audience. Along with Suit and Paradise (1985), we encourage the use of audience-relevant metaphors. Research has yet to determine how high-risk adolescents and preadolescents perceive messages derived from low- and medium-risk themes, and which risk level messages would be more efficacious in prevention campaigns.

Our analysis now serves a twofold purpose in our war. First, language can help guide us in our effort to determine those youths at risk. Second, language can provide us with the basis for creating meaningful messages, particularly visual metaphors, to be used in ongoing prevention efforts. Prevention campaigns often offer visual metaphors for drugs in a variety of media. The proposal of this chapter is that a more thorough understanding of language and metaphor among adolescents may enable prevention experts to design more salient messages that address these normative conceptions of drugs and drug use.

5

A Narrative and Relational Approach to Drug Prevention in the Drug Resistance Strategies Project

Thus far, this book has discussed adolescent drug use and considered the social and communicative processes involved in drug offers. It is clear from the information presented in the first chapter that adolescent drug use is a problem in the United States. Whatever one's value orientation toward drugs and drug use, and many have argued that the United States has long had a drug culture, we believe that most people would agree that drug addiction is harmful to individuals and society and that individuals should be empowered to resist drugs when that is their choice. Some may choose to extend this argument to claim that all illicit drugs should be avoided and, accordingly, adolescent drug prevention is needed. Regardless of where one stands on this continuum of judgment, drug prevention is a high priority in contemporary U.S. society. The perspective of many in the field of substance abuse prevention is that adolescent use of *any* substance is undesirable (Johnson, Pentz, Weber, Dwyer, Baer, MacKinnon, & Hansen, 1990).

Numerous prevention programs are available in the United States, yet few of these programs consider the myriad of relationships adolescents are involved in on a daily basis. Relationships that adolescents enact and inhabit daily are central to teens' lives, however relational contexts seem to be neglected in many drug prevention programs. This chapter discusses theoretical perspectives on drug prevention and then presents the prevention program derived from a communication and relational perspective.

DRUG PREVENTION PROGRAMS

Anyone who has worked with adolescents in a public school setting can attest that, by the time students reach high school, they have been saturated with antidrug messages. In the last decade, school-based drug prevention programs designed to delay the onset of drug use behavior and decrease current usage have proliferated. Numerous prevention strategies have been developed and used. Most of these programs incorporate three components: information dissemination, affective education, and social skill training (Bukoski, 1985). Meta-analyses of existing prevention programs suggest that exclusive reliance on education or affective (self-esteem) training does not delay the onset of use or affect behavior change (Bukoski, 1985; Nolan, 1990). Bukoski (1985) suggested that the affective strategies fail because they are too focused on vague concepts without providing for actual mastery and competency of skills.

The goals of primary prevention in the substance abuse field are to:

- determine who is at risk for substance use and abuse
- reduce the number of people who abuse substances
- promote behaviors that would protect against the abuse of substances
- encourage healthy behavior that is inconsistent with substance use and abuse. (Meyer, 1995, p. 201)

Resistance skill training is assumed to work by teaching adolescents the competencies they need to avoid drugs. These competencies can protect against the use and abuse of substances and reduce the number of people who use alcohol and other drugs. This model posits that drugs are used due to peer influence and that adolescents who wish to resist drug use lack the skills for doing so.

Recent evidence, however, suggests that this model may be more complicated (i.e., peer pressure may be operating through perceived social norms; MacKinnon et al., 1991). Adolescents believe that many of their peers are using drugs and want to be part of the group. This model is further confounded by attitudes toward risk and beliefs about the consequences of drug use. Adolescents may be more likely to use drugs if they value and engage in risky behavior and if they do not see negative consequences and/or perceive positive consequences attendant to such use. Further, the resistance skill model has not yet dealt theoretically with situations in which drugs are sought. This excludes a large portion of adolescents that must be targeted as at risk. In summary, the motivations to use drugs other than peer pressures have not as yet been addressed.

In addition to these troubling theoretical concerns, prevention programs also suffer from design problems. These programs are often developed and communicated to the student by Euro-American adults with little evidence that these perspectives reflect adolescents' real-life experiences. Students often know more than their teachers about drugs and drug use in the community. By attempting to externally impose the truth about drugs, rather than discover those experiences within the social milieu or the daily practices of the student, prevention programs may be perceived by students as lacking authenticity. This may inhibit the overall impact of the programs. Program content communicates disrespect by denying the adolescents' own experience. This disrespect is compounded by attempting to establish a nonexpert as the conveyor of knowledge. These programs fail to consider the relationship between the adolescents' experience and the message being conveyed by the program's structure and source.

As seen in previous chapters, peer influences are extremely strong among adolescents. The peer group is a strong reference group for most adolescents—modeling drug use and helping to shape the attitudes of the group. Goldstein, Reagles, and Amann (1990) presented findings that indicate that, for adolescents over the age of 12, the peer group substitutes for the family in establishing norms for expectations regarding social behavior. Wilks et al. (1989) found that males, in particular, are strongly influenced by these group norms and social expectations. Chapter 4 discusses the development of a unique adolescent language and communication style salient to youth culture. If peers are the most important sources of norms and behavior and if adolescent culture (in particular, adolescent drug culture) has a unique language system, this group can be most efficaciously reached through the medium of peer messages communicated in their own language.

Considering these conclusions and the differences between adolescents and adults in value systems, norms, experiences, and language, several substance abuse prevention researchers have shifted their emphases to peer-based behavioral skills training, where peers generate program content and provide modeling for desired behavior (Hansen, Johnson et al., 1988; Hecht, Corman, & Miller-Rassulo, 1993). Tobler (1995) reported that peer programs achieve greater change than other programs and produce the only consistent results showing change toward the ultimate aim of reducing drug-abusing behaviors.

Many of the newer peer-based behavioral skills programs are based on Bandura's (1976) social learning theory; they teach adolescents to resist drugs through modeling resistance strategies for specific situations in which adolescents commonly find themselves (Alberts et al., 1991; Polich, Ellickson, Reuter, & Kahan, 1984). Bandura's work acknowledges the importance of the relationship between the model and observer by suggesting that peer modeling of situations from the adolescents' own experience facilitates transference of identification and learning into behavior change.

The theory posits that behavior is a function of social learning and that behavior change occurs when the adolescent is provided with reasons to alter his or her risky behavior and the means to do so (Bandura, 1990). Through modeling other peers' behaviors, adolescents are provided with information, skills, and the self-efficacy to master these skills (Bandura, 1990; Decker & Nathan, 1985). In this manner, an effective relationship is established between model and observer; this relationship facilitates the acquisition of new communication competencies and the confidence or self-efficacy to believe the competencies will work.

Other theoretical models suggest a similar process by which skills can be learned. An interpretive perspective on the social construction of reality (Prus, 1996) suggests that prevention must evolve out of the adolescent social world. Thus, an effective relationship must be established between the change agent and the adolescent in which they jointly construct a system in which drugs are resisted. This can only occur if a number of criteria are met.

First, the interpretations of the adolescent learner must be considered. Rather than externally imposing a new interpretive system, this perspective suggests that we start with the system in place and use the resources of that system as the change agent. Language plays a central role in these interpretive processes and in the social construction of reality. The language used in prevention programs can alienate through tone or identifying the change agent as a member of the outgroup. This may explain the overall ineffectiveness of fear appeals and the utility of peer involvement in prevention work. The interpretive approach and social learning theory both support using models derived from the adolescent world as a means for incorporating the resources of the adolescent world as a change agent. If the content—including language, structure, and peer models—are derived from adolescents' experiences, the program will value the learner while accomplishing the change agent's goal of decreased drug use.

Second, careful attention to social relationships and communication are necessary for change to be learned and then transferred from the classroom environment. If the change agent is outside the peer group, then such transference is unlikely to follow. This implies that the content and delivery of prevention programs can be maximized by peer involvement. In addition, because drugs are a part of the culture of many if not most adolescents, communication abilities and social norms must be considered. These elements are nicely captured in a model of communication competence that includes knowledge, motivation, and skills (Spitzberg & Cupach, 1984). The learner must have enough information to understand the situation, be motivated to act in a certain way, and have the skills to enact these decisions.

Finally, it is important to consider the dialectical tensions that characterize all of social life but seem particularly exacerbated during adolescent years. Adolescents are torn among the pressures of emerging adulthood, the restraints of lingering childhood, and the competing demands of individuality and group pressure. Modern life, with its media infusion and constant change, seems to have heightened the tensions of adolescence. Thus, the dialectical tensions—the pushes and pulls of life—may be extreme for many adolescents. These contradictions can doom prevention work if ignored and provide a path for social change if incorporated. For example, prevention programs that act as if resistance is the only course of action communicate a denial of a dialectic that is real for many adolescents—the group pressure to conform versus the knowledge that drug abuse is dangerous.

Bandura's social learning theory, self-efficacy model, and the interpretivist perspective intersect in a number of areas. These approaches stress developing prevention programs from the adolescent's experience and using peer models that incorporate peer group experiences, language, and interpretations. They also stress the need to understand how the adolescent feels about self and the social world. Bandura's concept of self-efficacy speaks to an important construction of the social world—the belief that one can be successful in managing interaction and events. This combines with the role of social norms inherent in both approaches to account for the motivational component. Finally, these approaches suggest that skills or resources from the social world be used to enact change. Resistance skills are clearly one such resource. Bandura's work and the interpretive perspective provide a frame for understanding drug prevention.

However, prevention must be delivered through a medium or media, and this aspect of prevention is not well understood as of yet.

MODELING, DRUG PREVENTION, AND MEDIA

A variety of communication channels are used to provide prosocial modeling for adolescents in the area of substance abuse prevention. Early on in drug prevention efforts, the use of multimedia resources was recognized as an essential ingredient (Bedworth & D'Elia, 1971). A review of comprehensive prevention efforts reveals that films, videos, and live performances are often combined with other social learning techniques such as role playing, feedback, and group discussion (Ellickson, 1984; Flay, 1985; Hansen, Johnson, Flay, Graham, & Sobel, 1988; National Institute on Alcohol Abuse and Alcoholism, 1986). Currently, a large number of videos are available for program intervention on substance abuse. However, after reviewing 300 such videos, the National Education Association could only recommend 13. Most of the videos were rejected because they contained so much misinformation and distortion that they were practically useless.

In addition to video, live performance of drama is increasingly being used in prevention curricula. The Iowa Department of Substance Abuse trains professional staff to use situational drama as a prevention tool (Palermo & Hetherington, 1985). Several groups across the nation are communicating a substance abuse prevention message via live performance of drama. Arizona's *Positive Force Players*, *Education Through Performance*, New York's *Theaterworks/USA, Theater for a New Audience*, Minnesota's *Small Change Theater*, Chicago's *Music Theater Workshop*, or San Francisco's *Teen's Kick Off* are only a few of the 50-plus national organizations that use live drama to communicate a substance abuse prevention message (Stearns, 1990). *Teens Kick Off,* alone, reached an estimated 89,000 teens in 1989 (Teens Kick Off, 1990).

In terms of empirical evidence, several studies have found drama to be successful in altering target audiences' attitudes toward a variety of topics (Conquergood, 1986; Domino, 1983; Elliot & Byrd, 1983; Gimmestad & Dechiara, 1982; Mann, Hecht, & Valentine, 1988; Metcalf, 1984; Miller-Rassulo & Hecht, 1988; Pelias, 1984; Phillips, Hansen, & Carlson, 1965; Smart, 1986). Dramatic performances have the capacity to persuade and structure the social environment (Capo, 1983; Mann, Hecht, & Valentine, 1988; Mienczakowski, 1996; Mienczakowski, Smith, & Sinclair, 1996; Miller-Rassulo & Hecht, 1988). Drama transforms perceptions and empowers individuals to intervene in their own world (Artaud, 1958). Live dramatic performances communicate peer experiences and provide behavioral modeling. Behavior change can result from the relationship between performance/performer and audience. An individual's identification and involvement with the characters and situations, projection of themselves into the situations, catharsis (purging of emotions), insights into the effects of their decisions, and self-motivation toward action are all crucial in determining the performance's impact. Walter (1976) compared live presentation and video presentation of modeled behavior and found that acted models (live presentation) were more effective in providing concrete cues and promoting behavior change.

Successful live presentations include "The Concept," created and directed by Lawrence Sacharow and performed by recovering addicts from Daytop Village in New York, includes seven Americans—men and women, young and middle-aged, White and Black—who have appeared on several stages including the Moscow Art Theatre to act their own real-life dramas (Smeliansky, 1995). This performance focuses on telling the true stories of how these seven people became drug-addicts, alcoholics, and prostitutes and how they eventually found themselves at Daytop Village, an organization in New York State specializing in treatment of addiction and alcoholism.

"It's My Life," a musical about drug prevention is one of many arts-based interventions included in drug awareness and prevention programs (Antram, 1991). Innovative arts-based modeling programs such as TREND (Turning Recreational Excitement in New Directions) are growing and currently implemented in a variety of settings such as schools, churches, and YMCA's (Librach, 1990). These interventions are based on the assumption that modeling teen experience from teens' points of view is the way to insure young people will listen to drug prevention messages.

Playwrights in general often strive for drama that persuades, moves, and influences others toward action. Yet, whether behavioral modeling occurs during these live presentations or from these videos, Flay (1986) and Botvin (1986) pointed out that few of the programs using these channels of communication conduct evaluations of their efficacy in teaching actual skills or changing behavior. In 1998, the National Institutes on Health issued a special request for scholars to systematically examine media messages and prevention programming messages that address alcohol and other drug use. This section examines the use of live performance and video media presentation as a creative approach to peer-based prevention programming.

PERFORMANCE THEORY

Drama has the potential to be rhetorically aesthete. In addition to being interesting to watch, the use of drama may alter the audience's personal narratives, which in turn mediate perception and behavioral choices. Consequently, drama provides new perceptual frameworks for interpreting phenomena and new models for determining behavior. One way to understand this effect is to conceptualize drama as storytelling. The audience experiences the story and internalizes all or part of its message. This, in turn, changes the audience's own story.

As a communication phenomenon, narratives are expressions of social reality and may be used as an instrument for building and altering the values across communities and cultures (Turner, 1980). Narrative theory conceptualizes human thought and behavior as based in narratives. Narratives are a pervasive, transcultural mode of discourse through which people organize information and experiences of the world. Not only are they one of the primary means for making sense of experience (Cook-Gumperz, 1993) and moral choices (Botvin et al., 1995), but they also serve as an organizing principle for behavior (Howard, 1991). In other words, people use stories or narratives to understand their world and guide their behavior.

Narratives are intimately tied to membership in speech communities and they are highly salient in adolescent communities (Johnson & Ettema, 1982). Adolescents often construct personal narratives that affirm uniqueness and they learn group norms through the exchange of narratives. Indeed, narratives can provide models for adolescent substance use behavior.

In the area of behavioral modeling techniques, dramatic narratives provide a channel through which social reality is expressed, experienced, and potentially altered. To understand how drama works as a medium of persuasion, we must first understand how these stories engage an audience.

Berleant (1991) presented a theory of aesthetic engagement in *Art and Engagement,* which addressed this issue of art *engaging* its audience. This is an audience-centered theory that suggests that spectators develop a closeness—a personal relationship—with a character or situation in the media, yet maintain an awareness of its innate fictionality. Bullough (1912) argued that, although a certain amount of distance is necessary to distinguish fiction from reality, cognitive and emotional distance needs to be reduced in the performance event to facilitate audience identification with characters and help audience members feel emotion pseudovicariously through the characters.

This sense of identification and engagement with the performed message may be heightened by focusing on personalized narrative accounts in the message. Performance, which includes characters, scenarios, strategies, and experiences familiar to the observer, increases identification. Performance of narratives by one's peer group connects the spectator with the event while providing specific awareness of fictionality to allow for insight and cognitive assessment.

Individuals can more easily understand disturbing issues when communicators portray the issues dramatically (i.e., by placing characters in dramatic action with other characters). Shared insights and actual experience from a credible peer constitute a shared fantasy that can alter the social reality of the participants (Bormann, 1983). Thus, it is both the narrative form of information and its performative expression that gives force to the message. Research indicates that these narrative-based performance approaches are an exciting new path to travel in the field of substance abuse prevention.

The next section discusses a project designed to utilize the persuasive properties of performance in drug prevention. During the Drug Resistance Strategies Project, drug prevention performances were developed to establish identification, teach skills, change the story of drugs, modify norms, and decrease use by applying the conceptual position described earlier. This project is presented as an example of how performance can be used in drug prevention and other prosocial influence campaigns.

DRUG RESISTANCE STRATEGIES PROJECT

The Drug Resistance Strategies Project (DRSP) was conducted in a city of 322,000 (Alberts, Miller-Rassulo, & Hecht, 1991; Hecht, Corman, & Miller-Rassulo, 1993; Hecht, Alberts, & Miller-Rassulo, 1992). The preceding chapters discussed the DRSP findings regarding typologies, norms, strategies, risk, and relational variables influencing the social processes of adolescent and young adult drug offers and refusals. This chapter discusses the peer-based model of prevention programming that was developed in this project. The program is sensitive to issues of peer influence and norm setting in the adolescent culture, with a particular emphasis on communication competency.

The DRSP focused on peer modeling of appropriate drug resistance techniques through dramatic videotape and live performances. The project's intent was to: (a) identify the communication strategies actually used by adolescents when resisting offers of drugs and/or alcohol, (b) develop video and live performance media to model the effective resistance strategies, and (c) assess the effectiveness of these communication modalities in behavioral training. The findings from the DRSP support the efficacy of peer modeling of drug resistance situations to transfer identification and learning to behavior change.

The project introduced the concept of *trigger scripting* in substance abuse prevention and the element of postperformance discussion. The term *trigger scripting* refers to the technique of scripting a dramatic performance to kindle responses from a target audience (Miller-Rassulo & Hecht, 1988; Valentine, 1979). The performance is created with a specific audience in mind, and questions are formulated to spark discussion after the performance (Hecht et al., 1993; Valentine & Valentine, 1983). Formal, guided discussion follows the performance to highlight issues and emphasize main points. Group communication literature also supports the persuasiveness of discussion (Clark & Crockett, 1971; Ebbeson & Bowers, 1974). The goals of trigger scripting are to: (a) achieve an open, unforced discussion of salient issues; (b) facilitate communication about these issues; and (c) promote attitude and behavior modification as a result of the trigger-scripted performance experience.

The remainder of this chapter focuses on how the DRSP and prevention messages were developed and implemented. Appendix D includes suggestions for how to develop and implement a similar peer-based prevention program.

DEVELOPMENT AND IMPLEMENTATION OF A PEER-BASED PREVENTION PROGRAM: THE DRUG RESISTANCE STRATEGIES PROJECT

Procedures

Participants and Design.   A large high school in the southwestern United States was selected to participate in this project. A performance-based prevention program was developed, and a pretest, intervention, immediate posttest, and follow-up posttest design was employed to evaluate effectiveness. Cooperation was solicited from administrators, counseling personnel, and teachers. Teachers were asked to volunteer their classes for the project. From the list of volunteers, 21 classes were randomly assigned to one of four intervention conditions and one control condition. Classes were assigned to the various conditions instead of individuals due to the administrative restrictions of the school. Five classes were assigned to the control condition and four classes each were assigned to the intervention conditions. The four conditions included students exposed to peer-based modeling via (a) video only, (b) video plus discussion, (c) live performance only, and (d) live performance plus discussion. Conditions contained an average of 93 participants, ranging from a low of 89 in the control condition to a high of 99 in the film plus discussion condition. Four hundred and sixty-five students were involved in the program implementation phase of the project.

Development of Media. To develop a prevention program based on the insider status of peer experience, interviews and surveys were conducted with students who are members of the target audience. Chapter 3 and Appendix A discuss this process and provide details on the activities of the first phase of this research. Representative narrative accounts from each of the REAL (Refuse, Explain, Avoid, and Leave) strategies were selected from the transcripted interviews and then adapted into two scripted formats: a live performance script and a film performance script (screenplay). Based on the DRSP's theoretical approach, the goal was to create a prevention message that established a relationship. This was accomplished through providing a narrative account derived from peer experiences.

The term *narrative fidelity* in narrative research refers to whether the narratives collected ring true with the stories the target population know to be true in their own lives. To select narratives that accurately reflected the experience of the target population, two teen focus groups consisting of key members of the target audience were established. Specific narrative accounts that were representative of each strategy (Refuse, Explain, Avoid, and Leave) were selected for focus group validation (i.e., member checking). A representative account was selected only if it held together in terms of *clear orientation* (who, what, where, when), a *complicating action* (crisis that complicates action), and *results* (what finally happened; Polkinghorne, 1988). Other criteria suggested in choosing the representative accounts were: (a) Was the story truly representative of the experience? (b) Was the story structured so as to lend itself to performance?

The focus groups were utilized to verify the choices of material in the script and confirm appropriateness of the approach. The focus groups validated the believability of the narrative accounts, brainstormed transitional material, and considered format and structural issues. These groups made specific suggestions for modifications.

During the scripting process, it was necessary to place the representative accounts in the terms of an acronym—REAL. Therefore, the *R*esist account was scripted leading into the *E*xplain account, which led into the *A*void account and concluded with the *L*eave account. It was fortuitous that the account with the most tension and conflict was the Leave scenario. The writer made use of this by gradually heightening the dramatic tension throughout the script until the climax in the last scenario. The final scripts (live and video) utilized the teen's actual accounts, which were couched in a musical docudrama format. The musical numbers bracketed the accounts and functioned as a chorus and transitional mechanism. Two original songs were produced by a professional band for inclusion into the script.[1] Another teen focus group and adult advisory board were utilized to validate and provide feedback on the final draft of the script prior to proceeding into production.

The live performance and screenplay scripts were identical in content and structure. The visual format of the screenplay varied only in terms of including the necessary camera directions. Actors, band members, dialogue, and the musical score were kept consistent across all modalities. The video taped script was initially produced on film and transferred to videotape to reflect a consistency of quality across conditions and to facilitate practical implementation of the program. Both modalities were 34 minutes long and were entitled, "Killing Time." For a more detailed look at this process, see Hecht et al., (1993). See Appendix E for sample scripts.

Discussion Agenda.   Conducting a postperformance discussion may either enhance or distract from the scripted performance. Great care was taken when developing the discussion component of the program. Facilitators for the discussion were chosen carefully and trained in facilitation. The facilitators' primary role was to encourage honest expression of feelings and experiences while establishing a context of acceptance for these expressions. The facilitators guided the discussion along these lines to clarify thoughts and to reinforce content areas of the production's message and plot. A 20-minute discussion agenda based on the script and additional research was developed, and the facilitators

---

[1]The songs written, produced, and performed for this event are entitled "Killing Time" and "Don't Worry We're Only Making a Movie." The artists are Brian Page and the Next, and the songs were produced by Wildwest Productions. A recent release of "Killing Time" can be found on the audiotape *Loud and Proud.*

were trained to use the agenda. Each discussion began with a brief review of the REAL strategies presented in the intervention. The utility of these strategies was then discussed. Discussion concluded with a review of the main points, emphasizing assertiveness, decision-making skills, and suggested resistance strategies. See Appendix F for a sample discussion agenda. An experienced counselor was available at each intervention for any direct needs of referral.

Assessment. Pretest data were collected 1 month prior to the program intervention to minimize testing effects. Follow-up posttests were administered 1 month after the intervention.

The measures used in this study were part of a larger questionnaire and included measures of demographic information, current drug use and amount, use of resistance skills, confidence and difficulty of resistance, attitudes, perceived normative support for use of drugs/alcohol, and the ability to plan for the avoidance of alcohol and other drug offers. The scales were constructed from existing measures (Kumpfer & Turner, 1990; MacKinnon et al., 1991; Zuckerman & Link, 1968) and from content analysis of interview transcripts. Ten teens undergoing drug treatment and 15 teens from the target population were interviewed regarding drug terminology to make the items linguistically correct for this group.

The test instrument was pilot tested on a group of 13 students in the target high school. The students completed the pilot instrument, discussed their answers, and made suggestions. The results of this pilot testing indicate a need to shorten the number of items and alter some of the culturally specific drug terminology (e.g., *blazed* instead of *tripping*). Likert style items were preferred to fill in the blanks, and timing recommendations were made for open-ended or free-response items.

Another independent scale was developed to evaluate the performances in terms of the engaging qualities of the media. This scale was designed to measure *identification, enjoyment, interest, comprehension, realism, personal relevance, and acceptability* (Houlberg & Bishow, 1990; National School Safety Center, 1986). See Miller, Hecht, and Stiff (1998) for a detailed description of these factors. Coefficient alpha reliabilities of these factors in the scale ranged from .79 to .91. Later factor analyses reduced the scales to three dimensions: identification, interest, and realism.

All training interventions were conducted during regularly scheduled class periods on the same day. The two video conditions were administered in two sessions in the school gymnasium and lecture hall on a large, rear projection screen (10 ft. × 15 ft.). The live performance conditions (live performance only, live performance plus discussion) were administered in a single session on the stage in the school auditorium to ensure consistency of content, quality, and performance across conditions. Participants in the discussion conditions spent an additional 20 minutes in classroom discussions of the media led by project personnel and then they completed an immediate posttest. Those participants in the nondiscussion conditions completed the immediate posttest and then spent the remainder of the period in a study hall where they were prevented from interacting with each other. In the control condition, the students were told that the researchers were interested in their opinions concerning drug and alcohol use, and posttest questionnaires were administered concurrently with the experimental group.

FINDINGS AND IMPLICATIONS

The DRSP provides support for increased use of peer-based prevention programming. Dramatizations of narrative accounts generated, validated, and developed into a performance script by adolescents and their peers influenced attitudes and behaviors regarding substance use and abuse.

Statistical analyses of the questionnaire response were used to evaluate the effects of the performances. These responses tapped self-reports of attitudes, norms, behaviors, and so on. Although self-reports are not direct measures of behavior, we have no reason to believe that those who report more drug use do not actually use more drugs than those who report less use. Thus, although the levels of reported use may not be accurate, self-reports are a viable means for program evaluation.[2]

Overall, the results are quite promising. All of the interventions except live performance alone produced significantly less self-reported drug use in the 1-month follow-up than reported for the control group. Only the performance only condition failed to manifest significantly less drug use. Thus, we can conclude that the video, video plus discussion, and live performance plus discussion forms of "Killing Time" were effective in short-term drug prevention.

The utility of the DRSP video was recently tested in an independent study (Polansky, Buki, Horan, Ceperich, & Burows, 1993). In this evaluation study, "Killing Time" was one of three videos shown to 7th, 8th,

---

[2]More detailed reports on the statistical tests may be found in Hecht, Corman, and Miller-Rassulo (1993) and Miller, Hecht, and Stiff (1998).

and 9th graders in a rural southwestern U.S. school with primarily Mexican-American students. Neither of the other videos (including one starring TV star Kirk Cameron) had any significant effects. A single showing of "Killing Time," however, was successful in teaching 9th graders assertive resistance skills, and these effects appear independent of demand characteristics. The video was created for the older audience, therefore failure to find effects between the 7th and 8th graders is not surprising because prevention must be geared to developmental levels (Tobler, 1986). However, none of the prevention videos was successful in producing more negative attitudes or decreasing intended drug use (actual use was not measured). The researchers concluded that this was likely due to ceiling and floor effects (67% indicated a pretest unwillingness to consume alcohol or other drugs) rather than the video's effectiveness.

Other statistical analyses of our own data begin to answer questions about the different media and how they work. Although the discussion component did not have a significant independent effect, its effect did approach statistical significance ($p = .06$). These findings indicate that discussion may increase adolescents' confidence in resisting drugs and decrease the normative beliefs about the prevalence of peer drug usage. These discussions seem to guide adolescents' prevention experience, increase feelings of self-efficacy, and decrease peer pressure by convincing them that their *near peers* (those of their age group and surrounding ages) use less drugs than previously thought.

One may ask, then, why the live performance was more severely inhibited by the absence of discussion? An answer may be provided by comparisons of the engagement scores. Our analyses show that live performance is more engaging on all dimensions (see Table 5.1).

Adolescents identified the live performance medium as more interesting and realistic; the adolescents also identified more with the live performance medium than with the film medium. Live performance elicited a higher

TABLE 5.1
Mean Scores of Engagement by Media Type

Engagement Dimension	Film Medium	Live Medium
Interest	M = 3.55	M = 4.36
Realism	M = 3.47	M = 4.11
Identification	M = 2.43	M = 2.76

level of engagement with the performance event for both males and females. Overall, females were more engaged by both video and live performance.

Further statistical analyses show that the engagement is particularly important when the medium is live performance plus discussion. Only for this intervention and only among males, the amount of engagement played a role in determining drug prevention. In this intervention, males who were more engaged in the performance developed more negative attitudes toward drugs and more conservative drug use norms (i.e., believed that fewer of their near peers used drugs), and this led to less drug usage in the following month.

What does this tell us about how the performances worked? We believe that, because the live performance was more stimulating and involving than the video, the discussion was needed to guide postperformance reactions. Observers at the live performance noted heightened audience response, including calling out performers' names during and after the production; females approached the performers, tried to engage them in conversation, and even offered phone numbers for future interactions. It may be that without discussion to highlight the prevention issues (norms, refusal skills, etc.), these live performance audience members may have focused on the music, attractiveness of the performers, acting, stories, and so on and not the training information. Thus, discussion may be particularly important when the message is highly engaging or involving. Conversely, without discussion, one may be safer using the medium of video.

The work of the DRSP contributes to a growing body of research that emphasizes the role of social norms (MacKinnon et al., 1991). Our analyses suggest that teaching resistance skills may not actually create more competent resistors. Instead, skills training may actually impart a more conservative norm about use (i.e., believe that fewer of their peers and near peers use drugs), especially among males, who are at greater risk demographically.

People who hold more conservative drug norms tend to use fewer drugs, and the goal of this prevention effort is to modify norms to be more conservative. It is clear that drug use is not a simple phenomenon. There are multiple reasons for use, including group norms of use and peer pressure. Thus, future researchers would do well to focus on some of these other processes as well as peer pressure.

Overall, the project was successful. Drug use over a 1-month period was reduced for all performance media except live performance alone. We are beginning to understand the roles of discussion and engagement in these processes. In addition, we are beginning to understand the role of peer pressure and social norms in imparting resistance. Finally, our studies should orient researchers toward the relationship between prevention interventions and their targets. These receivers are not passive in their roles. Rather, they form relationships with the trainers and training. However, focusing on these relationships through concepts of narrative fidelity, norms, engagement, and language prevention can maximize its effectiveness.

Effects of the DRSP intervention were limited to drugs other than alcohol. This effect may be the result of the script itself. Only a single scenario addressed an offer of alcohol and it was, perhaps, less convincing than those for other drugs. Future research needs to be conducted to interpret this finding.

Outside of the realm of research and theory, we find that, although substance abuse prevention and training media on film and video are widely available to schools, organizations, and individuals, live performance media are less accessible. Although there are several theatrical troupes nationwide who perform prevention message scripts in schools, few of these scripts are available nationwide and none includes structured discussion protocols. The National Clearinghouse for Alcohol Information states that there are only six live performance scripts available in contrast with the more than 300 film and video productions available for dissemination to the public. Local and regional troupes have few opportunities for dissemination of their materials to the general public. For the most part, these troupes are dependent on public school donations, private donations, and state grants just to conduct outreach, with little emphasis on dissemination.[3]

It may be beneficial for experts in the area of substance abuse prevention to consider an increased emphasis on peer-based prevention messages communicated through the use of live performance of personal narratives. They should also provide funding for the production costs associated with disseminating these messages.

CONCLUSION

The power of performance to influence thought and behavior has been philosophically and theoretically addressed since classical Greece. Per-

---

[3]In telephone conversations with the Arizona Commission on the Arts and the California Arts Commission, it was discovered that most arts organizations are only partially sponsored by local and state grants. The directors in both organizations expressed an explicit need for more federal corporate support in this area.

haps the latter part of the 20th century and the beginning of the 21st century is timely for exploring other options in empirical research and performance studies. Additional empirical research may corroborate what so many scholars in performance studies intuitively know of the political, social, and personal impact of performance. We all can attest to the value of performance media especially when representing and presenting relationship dynamics. Performance allows for the embodiment of experience and communication of dynamic, interactional situations, such as relational maintenance in drug offers and refusals. Live performance opens up a window of possibilities to represent adolescent relationships. Perhaps it is time to convince funding sources, educators, and community leaders that live performance has not only aesthetic value, but also has "... human value (because) it serves the needs and enhances the life and development of the human organism in coping with her/his environing world."[4]

[4]Richard Shusterman eloquently described the perspective of John Dewey in this quote from *Pragmatist Aesthetics*, p. 9.

6

Conclusions

This book is about the social and relational contexts of drug use and drug prevention. Although most previous drug research has focused on the psychological, demographic, and physiological patterns of use and prevention, ours is one in a growing body of literature that emphasizes the social and relational realms. This approach assumes drug use is a socially constructed phenomenon that depends on such factors as group norms, language, relationships, and message strategies. This approach also focuses attention on prevention messages and their narrative fidelity (ringing true to the audience) and audience engagement (identification with prevention messages and sources). By complementing existing literature, we hope that a fuller understanding of drugs, drug use, and drug prevention emerges.

Adolescent drug use is a highly complex phenomenon that defies easy description and intervention. As adolescents pull away from families and enter the adult world, they become increasingly susceptible to the influences of youth and neighborhood cultures. When this movement away includes heavy and destructive adolescent drug use, its consequences can be particularly dire.

One of the reasons we have difficulty affecting adolescent drug use is that adolescent culture does not consist of one uniform, homogeneous group. In reality, there are as many adolescent cultures as there are divisions within the adult world. Variations exist based on demographic factors such as region, gender, socio-economic status, and ethnicity; psychographic factors such as sensation seeking, attitudes toward society, and self-esteem; and family factors such as family structure, parenting style, and number of siblings. Drug use and its prevention are dependent on understanding nuances within each of the groups—their norms, message styles, language, and so on. Just as advertisers adjust their messages to national cultures and, within nations, population segments (e.g., women, teens, African Americans), so too must prevention be addressed to the specific adolescent cultures within which drugs are used. At the heart of these cultures are the relationships that unite and bind the group and through which group norms, language, and communication competencies are created, reinforced, and changed.

ADOLESCENT RELATIONSHIPS AND DRUG USE

Our work and that of others discussed in this book, such as Harrington, Hansen, Kandel, Hawkins, Reardon, Kumpfer, MacKinnon and others, present an initial understanding of the social and relational processes of adolescent drug use and prevention. It is clear that peer relationships, with their norms and group pressure, play a major role in drug-related decisions and behaviors. We have attempted to summarize the existing knowledge about these processes. Unfortunately, little is known about adolescent romantic relationships and friendships in general, and less is known about the roles these play in drug use and prevention.

We are just beginning to understand how drug norms are created, enacted, and changed in the adolescent social world. Although we know that these norms are important and that their alteration is a key to successful prevention, we know little about the social and relational processes surrounding them. Perhaps drug research can provide a useful context that stimulates the study of adolescent relationships and vice versa.

There is growing evidence that not all drug use and drug offers involve explicit peer pressure. In fact, some may involve drug seeking. It would be fruitful to discover how teens handle denying requests for drugs without jeopardizing the relationship. We also need to focus on the conditions under which peer pressure is operative and how adolescents successfully manage relationships while resisting. We are just beginning to understand the message strategies used in offers and resistance. Clearly, we must continue to examine conversations involving drug offers in greater depth. What happens after an offer is made and refused and continued pressure is applied? It is difficult to legally and ethically capture naturally occurring conversations involving drug offers among adolescents to apply the powerful tools of conversational analysis (Hopper, Koch, & Mandelbaum, 1984). However, utilizing recalled, recent conversations from perceptive and observant teens or, perhaps, teen ethnographers may afford enough detail for more specific extended analyses. These findings can potentially contribute not only to our understanding of drug resistance and prevention, but also to the more general area of influence resistance—an understudied topic.

At a different level of analysis, we need to better understand the processes and contexts of the relationships within which drug offers occur. This work has the potential to further our knowledge of drug use and prevention as well as that of relationships and their development. We can describe stages of relational development for adults (Baxter & Bullis, 1986; Knapp, 1984), but do not have comparable descriptions about such development among adolescents. What role do drugs play in such relationships? Are drugs used to initiate relationships? How do they influence the use of other relational initiation strategies? What role do drugs play in increased relational intimacy? How do adolescents successfully negotiate relationships with others who use drugs without using drugs themselves? Is it possible for one to maintain membership in a group whose members use drugs without using drugs oneself? Is it possible to be the lone user in a group of nonusers? What about the vast majority of users who do not abuse or become addicted? How do drugs affect these relationships? What role do drugs play in relational termination? One of the authors of this book, Melanie Trost, is pursuing answers to these questions in her research.

Early in our studies, Carol Kumpfer of the University of Utah suggested that, because much adolescent drug use is associated with feelings of alienation from the mainstream, perhaps the most important contribution our line of work could make would be to identify ways of refusing drug offers while communicating personal acceptance of the person making the offer. Certainly this model of communication is consistent with Spitzberg and Cupach's (1984) conceptualization of relational competence—a competence that achieves positive outcomes for all communicators and that stresses skills such as other orientation (communicating concern for and interest in the other). If nonusers could find strategies to refuse drugs without rejecting the users, perhaps these users would feel less alienated and develop more conservative use norms, and this might temper their use (and decrease chances of abuse). Of course, the complementary risk is that nonusers may develop fewer conservative norms and be more likely to use/abuse.

One line of relationship research centers on relationship turning points (Baxter & Bullis, 1986; Lloyd & Cate, 1985). These are key moments in a relationship in which intimacy is increased or decreased—actions that bring people closer together or move them further apart. Research shows

that not only do people remember a great deal of the gist of ordinary conversation (Benoit & Benoit, 1990), but moments they define as unusual or significant, such as turning points, are more clearly recalled due to their
salience (Spiro, 1980). It is likely that drugs' use/nonuse will turn up frequently in the turning points of adolescents. Thus, the use of retrospective
interviews (Lloyd & Cate, 1985) may constitute an unobtrusive means for
probing the role of drugs in relationship development.

One key relational moment that we know is influenced by drugs is dating
violence and rape. The evidence is clear that alcohol and other drugs play a
role in these interactions (Muehlenhard & Linton, 1987; Norris & Cubbins,
1992; Schafran, 1996). Drugs also have been linked to abusive relationships (Barnett & Fagan, 1993; Fitch & Papantonio, 1983; Makepeace,
1981). Without implying that the victim is responsible for victimage, we
can still ask if there are communication strategies for dealing with drug use
that might mitigate some of the associated violence in these relationships.

One may also ask about the contexts in which these social relationships
are played out. One of the main themes of our analyses was that drugs were
offered and used while adolescents were *killing time*. In addition, one of the
more sophisticated resistance strategies we identified was the suggestion of
alternative activities—an avoidance strategy. Adolescents who were able to
steer the conversation and attention of the offerer away from drugs were
able to successfully resist without jeopardizing the relationship. This is the
essence of relational competence—a response that reaffirms the relationship ("I want to do things together") while discouraging the other's use and
deflecting the offer. Thus, the leisure world of adolescents, particularly the
discretionary use of time, is certainly salient to drug use and an area worthy
of additional study.

LEISURE ACTIVITIES AND DRUG USE

Social scientists have become increasingly aware that leisure time occupies
a central place in the life of adolescents, rivaling in many ways the importance of family and schools (Adams & Gullotta, 1990; Agnew & Petersen,
1989; Csikszentmihalyi, Larson, & Prescott, 1977; Kleiber & Richards,
1985). Adolescents spend more than 50% of their time in leisure-related activities, many of which take place with peers. Such peer-oriented social activities (e.g., dating, hanging out, cruising) are clearly the most popular
among adolescents (Csikszentmihalyi et al., 1977; Garton & Pratt, 1987).

However, despite the popular notion that leisure is a positive venue for
adolescents to release pent-up energy and emotion, there is an increasing

literature that suggests that certain types of leisure behavior may be dysfunctional and lead to many forms of deviant behavior (Agnew & Petersen, 1989; Csikszentmihalyi & Larson, 1978; Roberts, 1983). For example, Agnew and Petersen (1989) found an inverse relationship among delinquency and participation in organized activities (e.g., school and community programs), passive entertainment (e.g., listening to music, reading), and competitive and noncompetitive sports. The greater the amount of time in these activities, the lower the rate of delinquency. Similarly, they found a positive relationship between delinquency and hanging out and unsupervised peer-oriented social activities. Thus, the greater the level of unstructured peer-oriented activity, the greater the level of delinquency. Certain forms of leisure can be a fruitful way to reduce adolescent drug abuse. Participation in leisure activities, particularly those that are adult supervised, provides an alternative way to *kill time* that is drug free.

Yet simply filling time with recreational activities and/or forcing adolescents to engage in activities in which they have no intrinsic interest is too simplistic a response to a very complex issue. As many scholars have indicated, filling time with forced leisure may serve only to increase adolescent rebelliousness and deviance (Agnew & Petersen, 1989; Hirschi, 1969; Kvaraceus, 1954; Rapaport & Rapaport, 1975). Moreover, boredom and a lack of perceived opportunities for intrinsically rewarding, challenging, and meaningful activities has been shown to be an important source of such deviance (Bernstein, 1975; Csikszentmihalyi & Larson, 1978).

When working with adolescents, it is essential to identify leisure activities that may "engross and involve students to the point where they inhibit concern with and involvement in other activities" such as delinquency (Hirschi, 1969). This perspective is consistent with the work of recent theorists who argue that leisure is a neutral context; leisure time may indeed be boring and unstimulating or it may provide an opportune context for arousal or sensation seeking (Ellis, 1973; Iso-ahola & Weissinger, 1987).

Hence, adolescents have choices to make: They may seek out activities that are functional, intrinsically motivating, and foster growth, or they may choose to engage in activities that, according to societal standards, are dysfunctional (e.g., drinking, drug use, vandalism). With regard to drinking, the difficulty is that the acceptability of the behavior is determined to a great extent by the normative belief system of the reference group involved. For example, with adults, drinking behavior is a legal and acceptable behavior that often takes place during leisure time (e.g., evening cocktails, social events). For adolescents, however, drinking behavior is not only bound up with peer pressure and acceptance, but, because of its illicit nature (for them), it becomes an avenue for risk taking and sensation seeking. The paradox should be obvious. Although adolescent drinking is considered dysfunctional by the society at large, drinking can be perceived by adolescents as a highly functional, leisure-related behavior that helps integrate them into their social reference groups, mirroring its function in the adult world.

An important key to understanding the behavioral choices that adolescents make is to understand the context within which such decisions are made. If much of adolescents' leisure is spent with peers attempting to escape boredom and seek stimulation, positive opportunities for action must be provided. Parents, schools, and community recreation programmers must work closely with adolescents to provide programs that foster the independence adolescents so desire during this period of growth (Kleiber & Richards, 1985). At the same time, they must provide a range of activities that truly engage adolescents in meaningful activities. The point to be underscored is that the activities must be meaningful to the adolescent, not necessarily meaningful to the adults in their own immediate social world.

Thus, it is essential to identify which contexts (e.g., leisure settings, scenarios, and spaces) facilitate drug use among adolescents. It is clear that traditional, conventional, adult-supervised programs (e.g., sport programs, church programs) in the community may be of interest to some adolescent groups at different stages of their development. However, there may be a wide range of opportunities for action that have yet to be identified and/or tapped systematically. What leisure activities are most conducive to drug use? Which are least conducive? Where is resistance the most difficult? Where is it least difficult? Are different resistance strategies needed for different contexts (leisure or otherwise)? What leisure activities facilitate relationships that are instrumental in drug use? Which discourage use? Answers to such questions can allow us to better understand the social processes of drug offers and resistance, as well as design more effective prevention programs.

Much of the preceding discussion has led to a consideration of drug prevention. The design of effective prevention campaigns not only tests theories of social influence and message construction, but has important pragmatic implications for the quality of life in the United States. With teen crime, which often involves gangs, drugs, and guns (an increasing concern in our society), attention to prevention is urgently needed as a piece of the puzzle. What are the implications of our work for drug prevention, and where do we see such campaigns heading?

DRUG PREVENTION

The research described in this book has important implications for prevention campaigns. This emerging body of research stresses the social and relational aspects of drug use and prevention. We have already discussed some of these prevention implications. In addition, we have argued that, as yet, research has not addressed drug use that is not peer pressure based such as drug seeking, and therefore the relevant prevention strategies have not been identified. In the remainder of this chapter, we discuss the implications for drug prevention relevant to relationships (including language and the more sophisticated resistance strategies), ethnicity, and medium of presentation.

ADOLESCENT RELATIONSHIPS
AND DRUG PREVENTION

One of the clear implications of our work and those of other scholars is that effective prevention requires careful consideration of adolescent relationships, with their social properties and implications. Without understanding relationships between adolescents and their norms, rules, communication competencies, and language, we cannot hope to design successful prevention campaigns. Relational context, everyday activities of relational embodiment, and the role of routine communication in relating are all current directions in the area of interpersonal and relational research (Duck, 1994). Perhaps it is time to increase our attention to the role of adolescent relationships in drug interaction. Without understanding adolescent relationships, we cannot maximize prevention campaign effectiveness. It is no coincidence that Nickelodeon made strategic choices to be perceived as on the side of kids—the "kid's network."

We believe that prevention cannot be maximally effective if it does not incorporate the adolescent experience and perspective. Prevention messages designed outside the youth culture are likely to lack narrative fidelity—they will not ring true to members of the group. The stories told by these prevention campaigns may be seen as an adult intrusion on the youth's world and are likely to alienate the adolescents most in need of their messages. Although we believe that the use of focus groups to test the messages is a movement in the right direction, stories that are generated outside of the youth culture are inherently less realistic and engaging and do not maximize persuasive effect. This is not to insinuate the adult direction is absent or unwarranted. Indeed, sensitively designed prevention efforts aspire to have adults provide the direction and encouragement to teens to success-fully reflect on their selves, experiences, and perceptions of norms and to critically look at their relationships. The elicitation of self-reflection and personal narratives is not something that many adolescents can accomplish without guidance and direction. The key is for adults to guide and encour-age self-reflection that results in our learning more about adolescent inter-action and, in turn, assists us in developing prevention messages grounded in adolescents' experiences.

Understanding prevention messages as stories is an important frame-work for predicting their success. What story is being conveyed to adoles-cents by the prevention program? One video shows a young teen drug user transformed into a rat and sinking down into the city sewer system. Does such a message welcome a teen using or even experimenting with drugs by painting such a negative image of the user at a time when self-images are particularly salient? What happens when prevention messages such as the notorious "Reefer Madness" present such unrealistic images of drug use that even the most naive teen knows them to be false? Olson, Horan, and Polansky (1992) argued that the failure of information-based prevention may be because so many curricula are replete with distortions that fuel stu-dent skepticism. Such distortions may communicate unintended messages. Two of the more common may be the relational messages of dishonesty (don't trust adults) and disrespect (did they really think I was stupid enough to believe that?).

Similarly, the language of prevention messages and evaluation studies plays an important role in their impact. Our focus group participants consis-tently repeated one theme—they are not consulted about drug prevention and the messages are wrong as a result. Specifically, they told us that they are never asked about prevention messages and this is disrespectful, the questions on surveys make no sense to them and use the wrong terminology thereby rendering them unanswerable in an honest fashion, and they find some of the messages humorous. For example, the War on Drugs has been trumpeted by the Reagan, Bush, and Clinton administrations as the key metaphor in combating the epidemic of drug abuse. War metaphors are to-tally absent from adolescent talk about drugs in our interviews. Were the metaphor to have penetrated the teen consciousness, one would expect to at least find some evidence of it in teen discussions of drugs and drug use. As a result, the language of these prevention messages alienates the very people it seeks to influence.

Certainly our work on language establishes no definitive and generalizable findings due to its preliminary nature. The findings of our studies can be elaborated using a variety of methods, including the free association technique, in-depth and thematic analysis of cross-sectional interview designs, and longitudinal studies. These contribute to our knowledge of prevention as well as our understanding of youth culture and communication.

Szalay and his colleagues (Szalay & Deese, 1978; Szalay et al., 1992, 1993; Szalay, Vilov, & Strohl, 1992) proposed a free association method to study the meanings that drugs and drug use have for adolescents. A series of word themes (e.g., ME) are presented for free associations and the patterns of response are mapped to uncover the interpretive frameworks of people and allow comparisons such as those between users and nonusers and those before and after therapeutic interventions. Hence, this approach can help us design prevention messages by revealing the cognitive frameworks of message recipients and can provide a means for evaluating program outcomes.

Additional interviews of the type reported in chapter 3 also are needed to explore these issues. Conducted in a conversational style, these interviews can provide a forum for adolescents to express themselves on drugs and drug use. We recommend the inclusion of more topically directive prompts such as: "What do drugs mean to you?" or "Describe the effects alcohol or another kind of drug has on people." In general, discussion guides should be devised to draw the respondent into conversations regarding his or her expectations and attitudes concerning alcohol and other kinds of drugs. However, the interviewer must remain vigilant not to include words or phrases that would suggest or direct the interviewee to a narrow range of responses. Researchers can then perform in-depth thematic and metaphoric analyses to validate and extend our findings. In addition, a cross-sectional design can be used to make worthwhile comparisons between high- and low-risk adolescents and between users and nonusers. One of the weaknesses in our analysis was the confounding of use and risk—most of the high-risk participants had used drugs and the low-risk participants had not. These issues can be separated by comparing the language of youths in each of four cells: high-risk/use, high-risk/nonuse, low-risk/use, low-risk/nonuse). In fact, if the issue is risk, we should observe a main effect such that differences are observed for risk but not for use. Conversely, if use is the salient concern, we would observe the corresponding main effect. Finally, an interaction would demonstrate joint or combined effects.

We would also suggest a longitudinal tracking of youth, their language, and their involvement with drug use. The onset of drug use as well as changes in use could be recognized either through physiological testing or through self-report measures. Researchers would observe children from an early age (prior to the onset of use) and record their language. A change in language (e.g., the incorporation of positive metaphors for drugs, the inclusion of positive expectations for the drug experience, expressions of less control of one's life, reduction in role models) could then be identified as either occurring prior or subsequent to the onset of actual use. This design would allow researchers to identify changes in language and attribute effects to risk, use, or both.

These language analyses would accomplish three purposes. First, language can be used as a risk factor to identify adolescents and children likely to use drugs. If adequately developed, the system could be taught to parents, teachers, nurses, doctors, and youth workers to help them identify children and adolescents who may be experimenting with or using drugs.

Second, the language and metaphors identified by these methods can be incorporated into prevention messages. Perhaps the use of low- and medium-risk language and metaphors can help decrease drug abuse among the high-risk group. Social judgment theory suggests that presenting a position somewhat near the targeted position or at least not in the latitude of rejection is an effective influence strategy (Littlejohn, 1996). For example, one might approach an antigun control advocate with a message that is only slightly more progun control to begin movement in the desired direction. Similarly, one may be able to use the language of medium-risk/experimental or light users to decrease the abuse of heavy users and the language of low-risk/nonusers to influence the medium-risk/experimental user group.

One implication of our findings is that high-risk adolescents feel less in control in most areas of their life and use drugs as a means for taking control. Would an intervention that increases their sense of control in other areas of their life (school, future jobs, leisure choices) decrease their use and abuse of drugs? Another finding suggests that high-risk adolescents may not have role models in their lives—at least there is no one to model a drug-free life. Perhaps there is a way to reach these people through potential role models. Many existing media figures from this age group model just the opposite behaviors.

Finally, language analysis may be used as a means to assess the impact of prevention and treatment programs. Certainly the ultimate goal is to eliminate drug abuse and dependency. One indicator of this is nonuse. However, if the linguistic/interpretive framework of the user remains in place, such behavioral change may be short lived. Thus, in some cases, language analysis may be a more powerful tool for assessment than behavior change.

Our language analysis is one way to describe the social properties of drug resistance. We can also examine the messages strategies used to resist drugs that are presented in refusal skills prevention campaigns. We propose a four-part system under the acronym REAL: Refuse, Explain, Avoid, and Leave. We believe that, by teaching these strategies, we impart a more conservative norm for drug use and provide some adolescents with the tools needed for resistance.

Our research demonstrates that the more sophisticated uses of these strategies are not common. One characteristic of successful use is planning: successful resistors plan their strategy prior to entering a context in which drugs are offered. This is consistent with our argument that refusal complexity (e.g., being able to plan) and perspective taking (e.g., being able to predict where drugs will be and how to resist) are key skills. Recently, Berger and colleagues articulated an approach to the study of communication plans (Berger & DiBattista, 1993). For example, they have asked how college students plan dates and other activities. Not only does this provide an indirect method of measuring drug prevention strategies by asking about plans for settings in which drugs are likely to be offered (e.g., parties, bars, dates), but it also provides us with a useful training module to teach adolescents how to anticipate drug offers and plan resistance. Like the general refusal skills approach, which not only teaches adolescents to resist drugs but also how to assertively say "no" to other influence attempts, planning training would provide drug refusal skills as well as more general life skills training. If we can encourage more sophisticated plans that include anticipation of obstacles and branching logic (if X happens, I do Y; if A happens, I do B), adolescents should be more successful across a wide range of contexts. We may also be able to teach adolescents to identify the psychological states that may trigger drug use (e.g., boredom, restlessness), thereby helping them develop an awareness and knowledge of other behavioral options available in the community.

A recent finding of the planning research is that when plans fail people do not adopt more sophisticated strategies for achieving their goals (Berger & DiBattista, 1993). Instead they use lower level tactics such as increased volume and decreased rate. This is consistent with our finding that few adolescents employ the more sophisticated strategies such as suggesting alternative activities. If our suggestion for research in leisure activities is successful, we can teach adolescents where to go to decrease drug involvement and provide a repertoire of alternative activities to suggest if drugs are offered.

The conversations in which drugs are offered occur within the context of a relationship. Our work shows that few offers are made by strangers and most recipients know the offerer well. Thus, a relationship exists that may make it difficult to say "no" to drug offers. Duck (1994) suggested that researchers examine the everyday interactions of people to understand their relationships. Perhaps by examining relationship rituals that involve drugs—having morning coffee with one's parent(s), drinking wine in religious rituals, having a beer after work—we can help adolescents come to grips with and differentiate between acceptable and unacceptable forms of drug use in our society without falling into the trap of abuse and dependency. As suggested earlier, we also need greater knowledge of the role of drugs in relational initiation, maintenance, and termination. By teaching adolescents about these findings, they can be better prepared to deal with these situations. If a person becomes drunk on a first date, what does this communicate about the future of the relationship? If a person smokes marijuana prior to every sexual act, what does this reveal? Although information is not a cure all, greater sophistication in managing relationships may allow adolescents to handle the peer pressure and avoid drugs.

This section has discussed relational and social implications for drug prevention campaigns. However, relationships and social interaction take place within a larger context and are not the only salient characteristics of youth culture. Ethnic group membership also plays an important role in drug use.

ETHNICITY AND DRUG PREVENTION

Research shows that members of certain ethnic groups are more at risk for use than others (Bachman et al., 1991; Botvin et al., 1995; Dryfoos, 1987; Kumpfer, 1989; Kumpfer & Turner, 1990; Newcomb & Bentler, 1986; Pentz, Dwyer, MacKinnon, Flay, Hansen, Wang, & Johnson, 1989) and that members of various groups hold different attitudes toward drugs (Korzenny, McClure, & Rzyttki, 1990). Most studies of drug use suggest that alcohol and other drug use are more prevalent among Native Americans and European Americans than among African-American adolescents (Allen & Page, 1994; Bass, 1993; Harford, 1986; Johnston, O'Malley, & Bachman, 1989, 1993, 1996, 1998; NIDA, 1996; Oetting & Beauvais, 1987;

Parker, 1995a, 1995b; Wallace, Bachman, O'Malley, & Johnston, 1995; Secretary's Task Force on Black and Minority Health, 1986).

Evidence of ethnic differences surface in the types of drugs most commonly used (Kandel, 1995) and the degree of health risk associated with drug use (Maddahian, Newcomb, & Bentler, 1985). Various ethnic groups also hold different drug-related attitudes and behaviors (Hecht, Trost, Bator, & MacKinnon, 1997; Korzenny, McClure, & Rzyttki, 1990). European Americans have been found to perceive the least amount of risk in drug use and the least amount of friends' disapproval of drug use (Wallace & Bachman, 1993). They also tend to be higher sensation seekers (Kalichman, Tannenbaum, & Nachimson, 1998; Lawrence, 1998), are at greatest risk when they have lower levels of family pride and involvement (Vega, Zimmerman, Warheit, Apospori, & Gil, 1993; William & Smith, 1993), and/or have peer models for beer and wine use (Newcomb & Bentler, 1986). African Americans report the highest levels of perceived risk and friends' disapproval of substance use (Wallace & Bachman, 1993) but also tend to have peer models for beer and wine use (Newcomb & Bentler, 1986). Latinos/as fell between the European Americans and African Americans with regard to amount of perceived risk of use and friends' disapproval of use (Wallace & Bachman, 1993) and have more peer models for using pills like "uppers" (Newcomb & Bentler, 1986).

For youth ages 12 to 17, the percentage reporting that smoking marijuana once a month constitutes a great risk varies by racial/ethnic group (Marsiglia, Kulos, & Hecht, 1999). Among Whites, 29.3% report perceptions of great risk compared to 35.3% of Blacks and 35.2% of Hispanics (SAMHSA, 1998). Perceptions of risk associated with using cocaine once a month also varies by racial/ethnic group with 64.8% of Black youth, 53.0% of Whites, and 52.6% of Hispanics perceiving this behavior to be a great risk.

Research has also demonstrated that members of various ethnic groups differ in their general communication competencies and norms (Collier, Ribeau, & Hecht, 1986; Hecht, Andersen, & Ribeau, 1989; Hecht, Collier, & Ribeau, 1993; Hecht, Larkey, & Johnson, 1992; Hecht & Ribeau, 1991; Hecht, Ribeau, & Alberts, 1989; Hecht, Ribeau, & Sedano, 1990) and communication styles (Kochman, 1982; Moore, 1976). These studies suggest, for example, that Latino/a culture is more concerned with relational solidarity, African-American culture is more focused on power relationships and assertiveness, and Euro-American culture is more future oriented and focused on external rewards. In addition, Latino/a norms are more focused on family and the immediate circle of friends. Although there was some evidence of these differences in the DRSP, there were not as many differences as would be expected given the research literature. Thus, the communication, relational, and normative processes that underlie teen drug use need to be examined more closely across ethnic groups, particularly because targeting media messages to specific audiences (e.g., different ethnic communities) is a key to their success (Wartella & Middlestadt, 1991).

Rather than pursue a demographic approach to ethnic group differences (ancestry, place of origin), a more promising approach is to examine relationships and ethnic identity. Ethnic identity involves perceived membership in a group (Hecht, Collier, & Ribeau, 1993). Specifically, ethnic identity is a person's view of self as group member as well as his or her interpersonal relationship and communication within and between groups (Hecht, 1993). Ethnic identities situationally recede and emerge in importance. We argue that the type of ethnic identity a person adopts in a situation as well as the degree of identification with that version of group membership are more salient concerns than skin color or racial background. A particular Chinese American may not see his ethnicity as a salient identity. An African American may not see her ethnic identity as salient to her drug choices.

This perspective has important implications for drug prevention. First, culturally sensitive drug interventions are needed to maximize their effectiveness. Showing a Euro-American prevention video in an inner city, Japanese-American classroom may communicate an invisibility to the students that increases alienation and presents messages not designed for the audience. Merely putting faces of color (*others*) in a video that is written by Euro-Americans and *sounds White* is equally ineffective. Prevention must consider culture as a primary factor in development. Culturally derived narratives can give voice to the community, and the intervention must incorporate cultural practices.

However, our approach to ethnic identity indicates that this is a more complicated process than first thought. Prevention campaigns must consider identity, not demographic group membership. Take the example of a person who is racially classified as Euro-American but is reared in a Mexican-American community and sees this as an important part of his or her identity. Exposing that person to a Euro-American-based prevention message may be just as ineffective as exposing his or her close friends who are Mexican American through race and ethnic identity. It may be similarly ineffectual to present an African-American-based prevention message to a person who is racially African American but does not identify strongly with that ethnic group. Further, a large number of our adolescents are racially mixed and their identities may reflect this. Thus, the goal of cultural sensitivity is not easily met.

FAMILY-BASED PREVENTION

The recommendations for effective or competent family communication in prevention programs have exceeded the science of examining actual family communication regarding drug use. Most investigations of family communication have relied on self-report, used mostly White samples, and focused only on tobacco (Durlack, 1995). Among the breadth of information on parent–child communication, there seems to be a gap in the research literature on the role of parent–child communication regarding drug use. In particular, there seems to be a lack of focus on culturally sensitive family research and drug prevention.

Many substance abuse prevention programs tend to bypass the family as a major target audience for alcohol and other drug prevention messages. As noted by Bush and Ionnotti (1985), large sample surveys have been successful in identifying key family risk factors (such as nonintact families), but have been less successful in identifying the more complex family processes that would make youth more vulnerable to drug use. We suggest that communication skill and competence may be seen as a protective factor to counter these risk factors and develop resilient youth.

The family communication of normative messages and perceptions of these norms may be an important factor in the understanding of drug use and prevention. Although we know that parental norms influence decisions to try different types of drugs (Hansen, 1991), most of the normative research centers on perceived prevalence of drug use between peers and friends (Hansen, 1991). In addition to the application of the focus theory of norms in peer interaction, an examination of family norms, personal norms, and how these are constructed in a family communicatively may be useful in understanding family norms regarding drug use.

PREVENTION MEDIA

The final area we wish to discuss under prevention concerns the media of presentation. We have addressed two important domains: live performance versus video and the role of aesthetic engagement. We briefly revisit some of these issues.

Video is clearly the preferred medium for presentation of prevention materials if one judges by the sheer number of programs available in this format. Clearly video has an advantage over live performance in its *transportability*—the same video can be shown over and over again, whereas performances have to be re-created and vary in quality. Video costs more to produce initially, but is less expensive to use thereafter. Our research suggests that video has no advantage in comparative effectiveness. Although limited to one video and one live performance, our results show that each can be effective, although live performance should be accompanied by a postperformance discussion. The validity of our results is bolstered by the fact that the same basic script, actors, and band were used in each format to control for performance differences.

We also know that the live performance was the more engaging medium, manifesting greater identification, interest, and realism. Although engagement is likely to be an issue for the audience, prevention professionals may want to utilize this medium. In addition, it may be important that live performances maximize their engaging qualities. This can be accomplished through techniques such as breaking the fourth wall (performers talking directly to the audience) and scripting indigenous narratives. Future research should assess whether there is a maximum amount of engagement beyond which effectiveness decreases and it should understand the role of engagement in the effectiveness of film.

CONCLUSIONS

This book has described a line of research in which we have been engaged for a number of years. We have attempted to link this work to that of others operating from a similar perspective. No attempt has been made to provide an inclusive review of drug use and prevention. Instead, we chose to focus on the social and relational aspects of drug use and prevention. We believe that this communicative and relational approach has much to recommend it and hope that, after completing this book, the reader agrees. As indicated in this chapter, much work is left to be done. If this book encourages some relationship and communication researchers to explore their ideas in the context of drug offers, resistance, and prevention, we consider our efforts successful. If the book encourages drug researchers to consider the social, relational, and cultural aspects of their work, we are gratified. If the work described in the book has helped some adolescents avoid drug abuse or taught general life skills, we feel fulfilled.

APPENDIX A:
Methods

Alberts, J. K., Miller-Rassulo, M., & Hecht, M. L. (1991). A typology of drug resistance strategies. *Journal of Applied Communication Research, 19,* 129–151.

RESPONDENTS

Respondents were 33 community college and high school students (18 males, 15 females) from a metropolitan area in the southwestern United States. The age range was from 14 to 23 years, with an average age of 17. The subjects were White and Hispanic and were reared in working- and middle-class families. Volunteers were recruited from college and high school classrooms and were selected based on their ability to comment on their drug experiences. Three respondents from their early 20s were allowed to participate in the belief that their experiences were sufficiently similar to those of late adolescents' experiences and that they may be somewhat more sophisticated or skilled in their refusal skills.

PROCEDURES

Respondents were interviewed by three trained interviewers—two graduate students and a therapist who specializes in treating adolescents. Training consisted of a discussion of interviewing techniques, interview questions, procedures, as well as repeated practice and feedback sessions. The interviews were based on two open-ended, nondirective questions:

1. Would you tell me about a time when you were offered drugs or alcohol and you turned that offer down?
2. Would you tell me about a time when you were offered drugs or alcohol and you wanted to say no but didn't?

The opposing questions were asked to collect information about both successful and unsuccessful resistance strategies.

To improve the validity of the interviews, we assured respondents of confidentiality, carefully established rapport, asked respondents to focus on recent events, and framed the questions in a general fashion (Nurco, 1987). All interviews were tape recorded and transcribed.[1] The transcriptions ranged from 10 to 25 pages.

ANALYSIS

The data were content analyzed separately by two of the investigators, and the results were combined into a single category system. As a preliminary to the analysis, one of the investigators read through the transcripts while listening to the tape recordings to verify the accuracy of the transcripts as well as note the influence of paraverbals such as vocal tone and stress on the meaning of the utterances. Then the narratives for each successful and unsuccessful resistance attempt were read by two investigators, the location of specific resistance stories were determined, and the essential narrative features were identified. A fully developed narrative includes an abstract (a summary telling what the story is all about), an orientation (who, what, where, when), a complicating action (then what happened), and the results (what finally occurred and the evaluation). Reflective of these elements, the following types of information were identified and a category or coding system developed for each:

1. Who made the drug/alcohol offer
2. What was offered (alcohol or controlled substance)
3. Where the offer was made
4. How the offer was made
5. How the narrator responded to the offer
6. Why the narrator made the choice (acceptance/refusal)

---

[1] Special thanks to Marian Buckley, Fran Mularski, and Tammy Stein of the Auxiliary Resource Center for transcribing the tapes.

The elements were sorted into categories by the investigators, and the sorts of each investigator were combined. For unitizing, the investigators reached 75% agreement; for the six categories, agreement ranged from 90% (where) to 78% (why).

Krizek, R. L., Hecht, M. L., & Miller, M. (1993). Language as an indicator of risk in the prevention of drug use. *Journal of Applied Communication Research, 21*, 245–262.

Following the recording and transcribing of the interviews by Alberts et al. (1991), two of the primary researchers independently read and analyzed the transcripts. Each of the two readers performed a qualitative analysis of the individual transcripts. Our examination, broadly reflecting open coding as referenced by Glaser and Strauss (1967) and Glaser (1992), resulted in the identification of general categories and their properties. In addition, each researcher recorded the metaphors used by the interviewees when referring to drugs or the use of drugs. The metaphor analysis followed procedures similar to those specified in Smith and Eisenberg (1987). We conducted both the identification of categories and metaphor analysis while naive to the risk scores of the respondents.

Next, we calculated risk scores for each individual and placed each respondent into a high-, medium-, or low-risk group. Finally, to determine whether thematic patterns differentiated these groups, we compared the categories, their properties, and the metaphors indigenous to the three risk groups. In the following sections, we summarize these two steps in the research process.

RISK

After we identified the categories, properties, and metaphors at the idiographic level, we positioned members of the sample (individuals within the adolescent culture) along a risk continuum. An adolescent's position on the risk continuum corresponded to the sum of the numbers associated with his or her answers. This placing was necessary for our subsequent step—to determine whether trends could be distinguished in the language of three subgroups.

For the 11 risk factors used in our study, a subject's score had a potential range of 9 on the low end—the lowest risk—and 33 on the high end—the highest risk.[2] The scores for the respondents interviewed during this study ranged from 9.5 to 19.88. Those individuals representing the highest 9 scores and the lowest 10 scores (of the 59 adolescents interviewed, only 44 successfully completed the demographic information sheet) were combined into distinct subcultures for the purpose of group level analysis of language. We incorporated the top 9 scores into the high-risk group due to a natural break in the numbers (16.13 and over) and, by the logic of the same reasoning, included the bottom 10 scores into the low-risk group (12.75 and under). Therefore, the medium-risk group was composed of 25 individuals with scores ranging from 13 to 16. Risk was assigned relative to the variance in this sample.

The factors we selected are by no means comprehensive; in a later version of the scale, we incorporated additional factors (Alberts, Hecht, Miller-Rassulo, & Krizek, 1992). Furthermore, due to the scarcity of risk information, we weighted individual factors equally and employed a somewhat arbitrary assignment of numerical values to their various levels to standardize these scores for each factor between one and three. For example, from the literature, we knew that members of certain ethnic groups (e.g., Native Americans and Hispanics) are more at risk for drug use than others (e.g., African-Americans, Asian Americans) and assigned values between one and three based on this ranking.[3]

THEMATIC AND METAPHOR ANALYSIS AT THE GROUP LEVEL

Following the placement of individuals on our risk scale, we arranged these individuals into high-, medium-, and low-risk groups. We then examined the individual responses of respondents across each risk group to identify common themes, metaphor usage, or other distinguishing linguistic patterns at the group level. Baxter (1991) stated that, "Themes are threads of meaning that recur in domain after domain" (p. 250). To accomplish a thematic analysis, the researcher(s) must execute analyses on more than one domain (Baxter, 1991). We asked how the meaning domains of the individuals within

---

[2]On Questions 9 and 11, it is possible for the respondent to achieve a score of zero. Therefore, although there are 11 questions, a score of 9 is mathematically possible. Refer to Appendix B for a detailed breakdown of the process of assigning numerical values to the subjects' responses to the 11 risk questions.

[3]Despite its preliminary nature, we felt that this scale, although not recommended in its current form for individual assessment, was effective in assisting the examination of group differences. This conclusion is supported by a .51 correlation between the risk score and self-reported amount of drug use. This is a moderately large correlation.

the different groups were similar and whether differences existed between the groups—particularly between the high- and low-risk aggregates.

Alberts, J. K., Hecht, M. L., Miller-Rassulo, M., & Krizek, R. L. (1992). The communicative process of drug resistance among high school students. *Journal of Adolescence, 27*, 203–226.

RESPONDENTS

Respondents were 69 high school students from a lower middle-class high school in a metropolitan area in the southwestern United States. Thirty-five percent of the subjects were male and 65% female. Whites comprised 74% of the population, Hispanics 12%, African-Americans and Asians each represented 6%, and Other accounted for 2%. The age range of the students was from 11 to 17 years; 6% were between the ages of 11 and 13, 29% were 14 or 15, and 65% were 16 or 17. Median income of their families was between $30,000 and $40,000, and the mode was between $20,000 and $30,000. Thirty-three percent of the families represented had an income under $20,000, whereas 20% had an income over $40,000.

PROCEDURE

Respondents were interviewed by four trained interviewers—three graduate students and a therapist who specializes in treating adolescents. Training consisted of a discussion of interviewing techniques, interview questions, procedures, as well as repeated practice and feedback sessions. The interviews were based on five open-ended, nondirective questions. (The first question was used to acquaint the subjects with the procedures and make them more comfortable.) The five questions were:

1. Would you tell me about a time when someone tried to persuade you to do something you did not want to do?
2. Would you tell me about a time when someone offered you alcohol and you turned that offer down?
3. Could you tell me about a time when someone offered you alcohol and you wanted to turn it down but didn't?
4. Could you tell me about a time when someone offered you drugs and you turned that offer down?
5. Could you tell me about a time when someone offered you drugs and you wanted to turn that offer down but didn't?

The opposing questions were asked to collect information about both successful and unsuccessful resistance strategies.

A series of follow-up questions were used to probe the subjects' responses and obtain additional information in an effort to understand the entire drug offer experience, such as participants, location, and phrasing of the offer and response. To elicit this information, specific questions were designed and used when necessary.

To improve the validity of the interviews, we ensured respondents of confidentiality, carefully established rapport, asked respondents to focus on recent events, and framed the questions in a general fashion (Nurco, 1987). All interviews were tape recorded and transcribed. The transcriptions ranged from 15 to 30 pages.

ANALYSIS

The data were content analyzed using a category system developed in an earlier study (Alberts et al., 1991). Preliminary to the analysis, one of the investigators read through the transcripts and noted such factors as vocal tone and stress in the meaning of the utterances. Then the narrative for each successful and unsuccessful resistance attempt was read by an investigator and the elements were sorted into the established categories: (a) who made the drug/alcohol offer, (b) what was offered (alcohol or other substances), (c) where the offer was made, (d) how the offer was made, (e) how the narrator responded to the offer, (f) why the narrator made the choice (acceptance/refusal), and (g) how the offerer responded to the narrator's choice.

As a reliability check, a second investigator coded 25% of the data; the investigators reached between 88% and 100% agreement and 95% unitizing agreement. Intercoder reliabilities were calculated and ranged from .88 to 1.00.

Next a risk scale was constructed from previous research to measure the degree to which individuals are at risk for drug and alcohol use. The scale initially consisted of ethnicity (Beauvais et al., 1985; Brannock et al., 1990; Yates, 1987), gender (Brannock et al., 1990; Forney et al., 1989), early use of drugs and alcohol (Forney et al., 1989), and parents' current use and change in use (Baumrind, 1990; Cutter & Fisher, 1980; McLaughlin et al., 1985). Availability consisted of number of offers and refusals, with the latter weighted based on the answer to the former. Risk was calculated by converting all items into scores ranging from 1 to 3, taking their mean, and multiplying by 10 to create a range of 1 to 30. Reliability analysis resulted in the exclusion of gender, which was then treated as a separate variable.

Reliability for the remaining items was .71, and validity was supported by a .55 correlation with self-reported use. Because use was measured on a single-item scale, this correlation may be even higher when corrected for attenuation. Even assuming perfect reliability for the use scale, the correlation between risk and use was .65 when corrected for attenuation.

Hecht, M. L., Alberts, J. K., & Miller-Rassulo, M. (1992). Resistance to drug offers among college students. *The International Journal of the Addictions, 27*, 995–1017.

RESPONDENTS

Respondents were 452 students from a large university in the southwestern United States. Four hundred seventy-five students were administered a questionnaire in an introductory communication lecture classes over a 1-year period (March 1989–March 1990), with 11 students leaving before completing the questionnaire and 12 students turning in blank forms. The age ranged from 17 to 42 years, with a median age of 19. The respondents were 44% females and 56% males, of whom 86% were White. Average family income was $44,700. The respondents represented a variety of majors, such as business, architecture, education, and communication.

PROCEDURES

Respondents were administered a three-page questionnaire requesting a description of a drug offer that they had refused. Respondents were asked to describe a personal account of a specific time that they were offered drugs. The request was then followed by questions designed to elicit more specific data. Demographic information (gender, ethnicity, family income) and current drug use information were also requested.

Based on the Alberts, Miller-Rassulo, and Hecht (1991) and Alberts, Hecht, Miller-Rassulo, and Krizek (1992) studies, which indicated that alcohol differed from offers of other drugs, two separate questionnaires were distributed in the classes. Half the respondents (randomly chosen) described a situation in which they turned down alcohol; the other half described a situation in which they turned down other drugs. (A copy of the alcohol questionnaire is provided in Appendix B.) For purposes of clarity in the remainder of this chapter, these are referred to as *alcohol* and *drug* offers, respectively.

The requests were followed by 13 follow-up questions designed to elicit more specific information concerning who, what, where, how, age, gender, dialogue, and behavior of the offerer and refuser. Scales were used to measure amount of drug and alcohol use, frequency of offers, and change in consumption during the past 30 days. Closed-ended questions asked about gender, ethnicity, and family income of respondent.

To encourage participation, researchers said, "Thank you for your time and cooperation. The information you provide today will be very useful in helping us understand how offers of drugs and alcohol occur and will allow researchers to develop more effective training programs." To improve the validity of the data, respondents were ensured of confidentiality. No names were associated with the questionnaires, which respondents placed in ballot-type boxes as they exited the rooms. Respondents were told their participation was strictly voluntary and they could turn in a blank questionnaire if they wished without penalty. Those responding were asked to provide as much detail as possible, including exact quotes. The questionnaires took approximately 25 minutes to complete. We wanted the students to offer a specific account of a drug or alcohol offer so that we could examine their subjective experience as portrayed in their own experience-near concepts (Geertz, 1973; Hecht et al., 1989).

A coding system was developed from previous research to analyze the accounts (Alberts, Miller-Rassulo, & Hecht, 1991). Two coders naive to the purposes of the study were trained on the coding system. The coders were a male graduate and a female undergraduate student in communication. The graduate student had taken four graduate research methods courses and had participated in numerous research projects. The undergraduate student had taken two research methods courses and served as a classroom apprentice supervising student research projects. First the coders read the original article (Alberts, Miller-Rassulo, & Hecht, 1991), and the categories were verbally explained and discussed. Then each practiced coding, and the results were compared and discussed. Next reliability was calculated. After reliability was established, one coder coded the remaining alcohol questionnaires and the other coded the remaining drug questionnaires.

Hecht, M. L. & Driscoll, G. (1994). A comparison of the communication, social, situational, and individual factors associated with alcohol and other drugs. *The International Journal of the Addictions.*

PARTICIPANTS AND DESIGN

One of six high schools in a southwestern United States city was selected to participate in the Drug Resistance Strategies Project. As part of a larger project, a questionnaire was administered. Cooperation was solicited from administrators, counseling personnel, and teachers. Teachers were asked to volunteer their classes for the project. From the list of volunteers, 21 classes were randomly selected to participate. These classes represented a variety of subjects (e.g., Shop, Home Economics, Spanish, English) and varied in size from 8 to 27 students. The questionnaires were administered during regularly scheduled classes by research assistants. Students were told that we were interested in understanding how people responded when offered drugs as well as their attitudes toward drugs and drug use. They were ensured of confidentiality (a certificate of confidentiality had been obtained from the U.S. government) and asked not to write their names on the questionnaires.

Students absent on the administration day were surveyed on the second or third day following to decrease attrition. Two hundred and seventy-seven students participated with gender relatively equally represented (52% females and 48% males). Approximately 75% of the respondents were White, 12% Hispanic, and 13% Other/Unknown. Participants were primarily of middle- and working-class families and, judging from attire and talking with school administration/counselors, appeared to be within the norm of high school students in the area.

MEASURES

A paper-and-pencil questionnaire was developed from previous research, including measures of demographic information and scale measures of:

1. communication processes in drug offers and resistance (i.e., how drugs are typically offered, how they are typically refused);
2. social factors (i.e., perceived pressure and difficulty refusing);
3. situational factors (i.e., availability);
4. individual factors including usage history (i.e., current use and amount, age of first use) and attitudes (i.e., overall attitudes, perceived risk, perceived positive consequences of use).

Open-ended items were used to measure the remaining communication processes (i.e., number of strategies, perspective taking, assertiveness). As a one-time measure of publicly expressed intended behavior, responses to these open-ended items may not be isomorphic to actual behaviors. However, these open-ended questions were used to establish the repertoires of possible behaviors and not to predict how people would behave in any one situation.

The scale items were constructed from existing measures (Kumpfer & Turner, 1991; MacKinnon et al., 1991) and content analyses of interview transcripts (Alberts, Hecht, Miller-Rassulo, & Krizek, 1992; Alberts, Miller-Rassulo, & Hecht, 1991). These included measures of how often they face six types of offers—simple offer, minimization (e.g., minimizing the effects), availability (e.g., drugs just there), appeal to group norms (e.g., everyone does it), statement of benefits (e.g., you'll like it), and strong persuasion (e.g., use of mockery)—and five types of refusal strategies—refuse (e.g., simple no), explain (e.g., provide a justification), avoid (e.g., walk to the other side of the room when an offer is coming), leave (e.g., leave the place where drugs are used), and lie (e.g., make up a false explanation; Alberts, Miller-Rassulo & Hecht, 1991; Alberts, Hecht, Miller-Rassulo, & Krizek, 1992; Hecht et al., 1992). Separate sets of scale items were constructed for alcohol and other drugs.

There were two open-ended items. One described an alcohol offer by a friend in a social situation and asked respondents how they would refuse. The other asked about how they would refuse an offer of drugs other than alcohol. Order of presentation was randomly determined. Respondents were asked to list all of the ways they could think of to refuse the offer and circle the one they would be most likely to use. Following the procedure developed by Delia et al. (1979), each item on the list was considered a refusal strategy, and the number of different strategies was calculated as a measure of their refusal complexity. A greater number of strategies is indicative of a larger repertoire of potential behaviors and thus greater complexity in approaching any drug offer. At the very least, differences in the number of reported strategies for refusing alcohol and other drugs references the ease of retrieval. The chosen strategy was then rated on a 5-point scale measuring assertiveness and coded on a 9-point scale for its level of perspective taking (the degree to which the selected refusal message reflected an understanding of the perspective of the person making the offer). This was done using a modification of the coding system presented in Delia et al. (1979). The perspective-taking coding system is similar to that used by Kline and Floyd (1990), which was not available when these data were analyzed.

PILOT TESTS

Ten teens undergoing drug treatment and 15 teens from the respondent pool were interviewed regarding drug terminology (e.g., descriptions of the highs experienced with various drugs) to make the items linguistically correct for this group. The instrument was then pilot tested on a focus group of 13 students in the target high school. These students were selected by school counselors from a variety of classes and skills levels so that they would represent a range of conceptual and educational abilities. The students completed the pilot instrument, discussed their answers, and made suggestions. The results of this pilot testing indicate a need to shorten the number of items and alter some of the wording, including culturally specific drug terminology (e.g, *frying* instead of *tripping*). Scaled items were preferred over fill-in-the-blank items and timing recommendations were made for open-ended or free-response items. The questionnaire appeared to require no more than minimal reading and conceptual skills and was well within the abilities of all in the pilot group.

Hecht, M. L., Corman, S., & Miller-Rassulo, M. (1993). Evaluation of the drug resistance project: A comparison of film vs. live performance. *Health Communication, 5,* 75–88.
Miller, M., Hecht, M. L., & Stiff, J. B. (1998). An exploratory measure of engagement with film and live media. *Journal of Illinois Speech and Theater, 56,* 69–86.

PARTICIPANTS AND EXPERIMENTAL DESIGN

One of six high schools in a southwestern U.S. community was selected to participate in the DRSP. A pretest, intervention, immediate posttest, and follow-up posttest design were employed. Cooperation was solicited from administrators, counseling personnel, and teachers. Teachers were asked to volunteer their classes for the project. From the list of volunteers, 21 classes were randomly assigned to one of four intervention conditions and one control condition. Classes were assigned rather than individuals due to the administrative restrictions of the school. Five classes were assigned to the control condition; four to each of the others. Conditions contained an average of 93 participants ranging from a low of 89 in the control condition to a high of 99 in the film plus discussion condition. Four hundred and sixty-five students were involved in this study. Gender was relatively equally represented in this study, with 52% females and 48% males. Approximately 75% of subjects were White, 12% Hispanic, and 13% Other/Unknown.

MODALITY DEVELOPMENT

Two performance modalities and one discussion agenda were created from two sets of intensive interviews. Alberts, Miller-Rassulo, and Hecht (1991) interviewed 33 respondents, ages 14 to 23, about situations in which drugs were successfully and unsuccessfully resisted. Content analyses identified four primary resistance strategies effectively used in response to offers of drugs and alcohol: Refuse, Explain, Avoid, and Leave. These were categorized into the REAL system. In a pretest for the present study, an additional 59 narrative accounts of personal resistance experiences were collected and categorized into the REAL system (reliability = .88). Representative accounts of each strategy were selected from these sources and adapted into two scripted formats: a live performance script and a film performance script (screenplay).

The script writer was instructed to minimize any alterations in the actual teen dialogue or teen experience to retain the realism of the personal accounts. The writer developed the screenplay based on the REAL system, narrative accounts of experience, interview segments, and prevention education curriculum information. After developing the structure and content of the messages, two teen focus groups were utilized to validate the materials and approach. The resulting training curriculum utilized actual narrative accounts that were performed by actors and couched in a musical docudrama format. The film curriculum was produced on film and transferred to videotape to reflect a consistency of quality across conditions, maintain credibility among the adolescent target audience, and facilitate practical application of the program. Film provides the rich look that teens have come to expect from music videos. The screenplay was then adapted into a live performance format that utilized the same content in a live, multimedia approach, including a live band, rear-screen projection, lighting, and sound design. All actors, band members, dialogue, and the musical score were kept consistent across conditions. Both performances were 34 minutes long and entitled "Killing Time."

The discussion agenda was developed to support the content and follow each performance intervention. An adolescent substance abuse specialist in conjunction with the researchers and scriptwriter developed a 20-minute discussion agenda based on the script and past prevention research. Discussion leaders were trained to use the agenda. The length of the discussion was set at 20 minutes to minimize boredom and fit within a single class period.

Each discussion began with a brief review of the strategies presented in the intervention: Refuse, Explain, Avoid, and Leave. The utility of these strategies was then discussed. Each group explored the realism of the accounts, personal strategies used, perception of peer strategy use, alternative strategies, and reaction to the media. Discussion concluded with a review of the main points, emphasis on assertiveness and decision-making skills, and a final review of suggested resistance strategies.

MEASURES

A paper-and-pencil questionnaire was used in a pretest/posttest design. As part of a longer questionnaire, the pretest included measures of demographic information, current use and amount, use of resistance skills, confidence and difficulty of resistance, attitudes, perceived normative support for use of drugs/alcohol, and use of planning to avoid drug/alcohol. These items were constructed from existing scales (Kumpfer, 1989; Kumpfer & Turner, 1990; MacKinnon et al., 1990; Zuckerman & Link, 1968) and content analysis of interview transcripts (Alberts, Hecht, Miller-Rassulo, & Krizek, 1992; Alberts, Miller-Rassulo, & Hecht, 1991; Hecht, Alberts, & Miller-Rassulo, 1992). Ten teens undergoing drug treatment and 15 teens from the target population were interviewed regarding drug terminology to make the items linguistically correct for this group. Because the immediate posttest was administered 1 day after the intervention, likelihood of use ratings were substituted for self-reported use at that time.

The test instrument was pilot tested on a focus group of 13 students in the target high school. This validation phase was completed based on information from Alberts, Miller-Rassulo, and Hecht (1991) stating that teens believe that they are too often left out of the development process of packaged programs (i.e., surveys, videos, tasks, literature). The students completed the pilot instrument, discussed their answers, and made suggestions. The results of this pilot testing indicate a need to shorten the number of items and alter some of the culturally specific drug terminology (e.g., *blazed* instead of *tripping*). Scaled items were preferred over fill-in-the-blank items and timing recommendations were made for open-ended or free-response items.

PROCEDURES

Pretest data were collected 1 month prior to the program intervention to minimize testing effects. Posttests were administered 1 month after the intervention (follow-up posttest). Students absent on the administration day were surveyed on the second or third day following to decrease attrition.

136

APPENDIX A

All training interventions were conducted during regularly scheduled class periods on the same day. The two film conditions (film only, film plus discussion) were administered in two sessions in the school gymnasium and lecture hall on a large rear projected screen (10 ft. by 15 ft.). The live performance conditions (live performance only, live performance plus discussion) were also administered in a single session on the stage in the school to ensure consistency of content, quality, and performance across conditions. Subjects in discussion conditions spent an additional 20 minutes in classroom discussions of the media led by project personnel. Those in the nondiscussion conditions spent the remainder of the period in a study hall working individually.

In the control condition, the students were told that the researchers were interested in their opinions concerning drug and alcohol use. Immediate posttest questionnaires were administered concurrently with the experimental group on the day following the performances.

Hecht, M. L., Trost, M. R., Bator, R. J., & MacKinnon, D. (1997). Ethnicity and sex similarities and differences in drug resistance. *Journal of Applied Communication Research, 25*, 75–97.
Miller, M. (1998).The social process of drug resistance in a relational context. *Communication Studies, 49*, 358–375.

These studies were conducted in two urban geographic locations. Interviews (30–45 minutes) were conducted with 158 middle school students from five schools in the 1997 study and with 83 middle school students from four sites in another geographic location in the 1998 study. After parental consent was obtained, student volunteers were solicited, paid $5, and provided with a movie pass or food certificate. Young adult students ages 18 to 23 were trained to use a structured interview protocol. Interviews were conducted individually and began with a warmup period. Respondents were asked if they had ever been offered drugs. Those who replied affirmatively were asked to describe the event in detail, including who made the offer, where, any others present, and what was said. The interview went on to ask about leisure activities, ethnic identity, norms, family communication, neighborhood perceptions, and risk factors. The respondents provided their age, sex, and ethnicity. The interviews were tape recorded and transcribed. Coders read the transcripts and developed preliminary categories. These were discussed and a coding system was developed. Four coders were trained and the mean agreement for placing items into categories was 94% in the 1997 study and 89% in the 1998 study.

RECRUITMENT

Students were recruited with a message that stated that the project intended to learn about the students' experiences with alcohol and other drugs. Permission slips were then distributed for students to take home. These permission slips described the project more thoroughly, explaining that the student would receive $5 and a movie ticket (Arizona sites) or a McDonald's food coupon (Tennessee sites) for their participation and guaranteeing the students' confidentiality. Only those returning permission slips were eligible to participate in the studies. The sites where recruitment occurred varied in size: When possible, interview participants were randomly selected from those who had returned the consent slips. In smaller locations, all available children were interviewed.

Procedures

Twenty-one Arizona State University (ASU) undergraduates were trained to conduct the interviews in the 1997 study. Twenty-three University of Memphis undergraduates were trained to conduct the interviews in the 1998 study. Interviewers participated in an 8-hour training session in which interviewing was described in general (e.g., establishing rapport, using open- and closed-ended questions and probes, eliciting complete answers); the interviews for this study were explained and practiced. They were given a packet of questions that included four discussion topics, with a variety of subtopics within each of the four. Each interviewer was instructed to cover the first topic, participants' drug offer experiences, and continue onto as many of the other three topics as time permitted. After the training session, each interviewer conducted a practice interview and returned for a debriefing session with the trainers for further training as needed.

Participants were escorted or directed to interview rooms by the organization's staff, where they were left alone with the interviewer for a private 30- to 40-minute interview. The interviewer asked the participant's permission to tape record the interview and reminded the participant that all responses were confidential. No student refused to be tape recorded. The interviewer recorded his or her interviewer number, the participant number, and the school number. The participant filled out a demographic sheet describing age, sex, and ethnicity in response to open-ended questions.

After a short getting acquainted period, the interviewer told the respondent, "I'd like to talk with you about a time when you were offered drugs—including not only drugs like marijuana and crack, but also glue or paint. Can you remember a time when someone offered you drugs?" Respondents who answered "yes" were asked to describe the episode in detail. Prompts ensured that they described where they were when the offer occurred, who made the offer, what type of drug was offered, what was said in the offer, how they responded, who else was present, how many people in the setting were using drugs, the relationships among the people present, and whether the offer was repeated, including the nature of this repeat offer and the response to it. Participants who refused the offer were asked to describe the refusal verbatim and the reason for it. Respondents were also asked to describe other activities they could have done to resist. If participants were never offered drugs, they were asked to describe why they thought they had not been offered. All participants responded to these core questions and their replies are the basis for the current analyses.

In the 1997 study, the 158 audible interview tapes were transcribed verbatim for content only, resulting in approximately 1,230 pages of transcription—an average of 7.8 pages per interview. In the 1998 study, the 83 audible interview tapes were transcribed verbatim for content only. Open coding of responses to all questions was conducted by three graduate research assistants who read the transcripts, made theoretical memos, and noted specific examples using the coding and inductive processes suggested by Strauss and Corbin (1990). These preliminary codes were then subjected to a process of constant comparison across the data set by which semantic relationships were observed and compared. These methods were used to generate a codebook of categories for 245 items that addressed the primary questions in the study. Most of these categories consisted of dichotomous, yes/no classifications (e.g., "Has the student indicated that he or she was ever offered a drug, yes or no?"). Next, three coders were trained and given the same three interviews to read and code. The mean agreement among the coders for coding these three interviews was 94% in the 1997 study and 90% in the 1998 study. The data from the codebooks were used for the analyses.

APPENDIX B:
Decision-Making
Questionnaire

Do not put your name on this questionnaire. Your responses are confidential and will not be revealed to anyone outside of the project staff.

Please answer the following questions, providing as much detail as you can. Also, if possible, try to remember exactly what was said. Use the back of the pages if you need more room.

We would like for you to tell us about a time you were offered alcohol and you turned it down.

1. What type of alcohol was it?

2. Did you want to turn it down? [Why/why not?]

3. Where were you when this offer was made?

4. Who was there?

5. Who offered the alcohol to you? [What was his or her relationship to you?]

6. How old were you?

7. Was this the first time you were offered alcohol?

8. Exactly what did the other person say when he or she offered it to you?

9. Exactly what did you say?

10. Why did you say it this way?

11. How did the other person respond?

12. What else was said or done?

13. Did you feel comfortable saying no?
[If yes, why?]

[If no, what would have had to be different for you to feel comfortable?]

14. How often are you offered drugs?

15. How often do you turn drugs down when they are offered?

DECISION-MAKING INTERVIEW SCHEDULE

I.   Has there been a time when someone tried to persuade you to do something you didn't want to do? Could you tell me about that time?

Prompts for Question 1

(Check off the question as it is answered during the narrative. If it is not answered during the narrative, ask the question *before* moving onto the next set of questions.)

_____ **1.** How long ago did this happen? Do you remember the conversation clearly?

_____ **2.** When did this happen?

_____ **3.** Where did this happen?

_____ **4.** What was his or her relationship to you?

_____ **5.** What did he or she try to talk you into?

_____ **6.** Why didn't you want to do it?

_____ **7.** Exactly what did the person say?

_____ **8.** Exactly what did you say?

_____ **9.** Why did you say it this way?

_____ **10.** How did the other person respond?

_____ **11.** What else was said or done?

_____ **12.** Do you wish you had handled it differently?

_____ **13.** What would you like to have done differently?

Now, I'd like to ask you some questions about times you've been offered drugs.

II.   Could you tell me about a time you were offered drugs or alcohol and you turned it down?

(Prompts for Question 2. Check off the question as it is answered during the narrative. If it is not answered during the narrative, ask the question *before* moving onto the next set of questions.)

_____ **1.** How long ago did this happen? Do you remember the conversation clearly?

_____ **2.** What type of drugs/alcohol was it?

_____ **3.** Did you want to turn it down? [Why/why not?]

_____ 4. Where were you when this offer was made?

_____ 5. Who was there?

_____ 6. Who offered it to you? What was his or her relationship to you?

_____ 7. How old were you?

_____ 8. Exactly what did the other person say when he or she offered it to you?

_____ 9. Exactly what did you say?

_____ 10. Why did you say it this way?

_____ 11. How did the other person respond?

_____ 12. What else was said or done?

_____ 13. Why did you say no?

_____ 14. Did you feel comfortable saying no?

[If yes, why?]

[If no, what would have had to be different for you to feel comfortable?]

III.   Now, could you tell me about a time you were offered drugs or alcohol and you wanted to turn it down, but didn't?

(Prompts for Question 3. Check off the question as it is answered during the narrative. If it is not answered during the narrative, ask the question *before* moving onto the next set of questions.)

_____ 1. How long ago did this happen? Do you remember the conversation clearly?

_____ 2. What type of drugs/alcohol was it?

_____ **3.** Did you want to turn it down? [Why/why not?]

_____ **4.** Where were you when this offer was made?

_____ **5.** Who was there?

_____ **6.** Who offered it to you? What was his or her relationship to you?

_____ **7.** How old were you?

_____ **8.** Was this the first time you were offered drugs?

_____ **9.** Exactly what did the other person say when he or she offered it to you?

_____ **10.** Exactly what did you say?

_____ **11.** Why did you say it this way?

_____ **12.** How did the other person respond?

_____ **13.** What else was said or done?

_____ **14.** Why did you want to turn the offer down?

_____ **15.** Why didn't you refuse?

_____ **16.** How would the situation have needed to be different for you to have refused?_____

APPENDIX C:
Formula for Determining
Risk Factors

1. Ethnicity
    Native American. 3
    Hispanic 2
    White or African American. 1.5
    Asian 1

2. Gender
    Male 3
    Female 1

3. Frequency of alcohol offers
    Almost every day 3
    2–3 times per week 2.5
    Once per week 2
    Once per month. 1.5
    Never 1

NOTE: If the answer to Question 3 is NEVER (#1), the answer to this
next Question 4 must also be NEVER. That subject gets a total of

two points for Questions 3 and 4. If Question 3 is answered NEVER and Question 4 is answered anything else but NEVER, the data must be discarded—the subject has made an error.

If the answer to Question 3 is anything else but NEVER, the scale to Question 4 is reversed.

4. Frequency of refusals for alcohol
   Never 1
   (provided the answer to Question 3 was also NEVER)

   Never 3
   Once per month. 2.5
   Once per week 2
   2–3 times per week 1.5
   Almost every day 1

NOTE: If the subject answers Question 3 as once per week and Question 4 as almost every day, the refusals exceed the offers and the data must be thrown out. Refusals CANNOT exceed offers.

There is one more exception. If the answers to Questions 3 & 4 are more than NEVER but the same for each question, then Question 3 is given the correct amount of points in the Question 3 formula, but Question 4 is assigned a value of 1 because the subject did turn down the offer every time it was made.

The highest risk (pointwise) combining Questions 3 and 4 would be a subject who answers ALMOST EVERY DAY for Question 3 and answers NEVER for Question 4. That combination would earn the subject 6 risk points.

If a subject answered 2–3 TIMES PER WEEK for Question 3 and ONCE PER MONTH for Question 4, he or she would receive 2.5 and 2.5 points, respectively, for a total of 5 points for Questions 3 and 4.

5. Frequency of drug offers (other than alcohol)
   Almost every day 3

2–3 times per week 2.5
Once per week 2
Once per month. 1.5
Never 1

6. Frequency of refusals for drugs (other than alcohol)
    Never 1
    (provided the answer to Question 5 was also NEVER)

NOTE: Follow same criteria as described above for Question 4.

Never 3
Once per month. 2.5
Once per week 2
2–3 times per week 1.5
Almost every day 1

REMEMBER: Exceptions apply as they did in Questions 3 and 4.

7. Parents income
    Under $10,000 3
    $10–$20,000. 2
    $20–$30,000. 1
    $30–$40,000. 2
    Over $40,000 3

8. Perceived parents' alcohol use in the past 30 days
    Almost every day 3
    2–3 times per week 2.5
    Once per week 2
    Once per month. 1.5
    Never 1

The answers to the next question are affected by the answers to Question 8.
Therefore, the best way to demonstrate how we score this question is to
place it in a matrix.

9. Perceived change in parental use of alcohol over the past 3 years.

ANSWER TO QUESTION 9

	good			bad	
QUESTION 8 ANSWER	MUCH MORE	MORE	SAME	LESS	MUCH LESS
NEVER (1)	.75	.375	0	XXXX	XXXX
1 MO. (1.5)	1.125	.75	.375	1.5	1.875
1 WEEK (2)	1.5	1.125	.75	1.875	2.25
2–3 WK (2.5)	1.875	1.5	1.125	2.25	2.625
ALWAYS (3)	2.25	1.875	1.5	2.625	3

10. Perceived parents' drug use in the past 30 days
     Almost every day 3
     2–3 times per week 2.5
     Once per week 2
     Once per month. 1.5
     Never 1

11. Perceived change in parental use of drugs over the past 3 years.

NOTE: The schedule for this answer is the same as Question 9.

The possible range of scores is 9 on the low end and 33 on the high end.

APPENDIX D:
Development and Implementation of a Peer-Based Prevention Program

Live dramatic performances of narrative accounts communicate peer experiences and provide behavioral modeling. The peer model is based on an insider status that increases the realism of the message and viewer identification with situations and characters. In the area of substance abuse prevention, professionals seek to develop adolescent prevention programs that will affect both attitudes and behavior. In these performances teens face personal issues encountered in their own lives and actively engage in decision-making along with the teen actors. Using this peer-based model, behavior change is possible through the youth's identification and involvement with the characters and situations, projection of themselves into the situations, catharsis (purging of emotions), and gaining insight and self-motivation toward action and change.

Decker and Nathan (1985) stressed that modeling is facilitated when the model: (a) is of the same age and race as the target, (b) has high competence, (c) is in control of the resources, and (d) exhibits to the target rewards for positive behavior. In addition, the modeled behavior must be: (a) distinctive, (b) meaningful to the observer, (c) not too complex, and (d) observable. The challenge of developing this type of program is to present modeled behavior that meets these criteria while remaining salient to the

148

youth issues at hand. Communication research shows that, to be maximally effective, messages must be adapted to the specific audience.

Chapter 4 described the creation of a school and communication-based prevention program. This program was predicated on certain principals: (a) teaching resistance skills will reduce drug use, and (b) any prevention message must be tailored to the audience. This can be accomplished for adolescent audiences through peer models, developing prevention materials from the target group's experience, and using members of the group in the development of the prevention program. This appendix provides additional pragmatic hints on how to create successful adolescent school-based prevention programs. The following suggestions for developing this type of program are not written in stone. However, they are suggestions based on previous programmatic research evidence. For the purposes of this how-to guide, the focus is on a peer-based prevention program designed to model effective resistance skills. For more information on these steps, see Alberts, Miller-Rassulo, and Hecht (1991) and Hecht, Corman, and Miller-Rassulo (1993).

OBTAIN PERMISSION AND GATHER SUPPORT

Support of the administration, staff, teachers, and community is essential prior to embarking on developing a prevention program. Local educational systems often resist intrusiveness from outsiders (i.e., university personnel, state workers) because of past negative experiences and uncertainty about potential benefits based on their involvement. Active support from key personnel inside the educational system will facilitate the process of gaining entre into organizations. Teachers and other key players within a school system often need the additional support of their administration to institute any type of prevention program, thus all parties should be informed of the proposed program, convinced of its worth, and assured that they will benefit from involvement in the project. The benefits of involvement must be clearly articulated to insure a win–win partnership among all participating agencies.

Most new or innovative programs are given approval contingent on a trial basis. Thus, presenting your program for the first time as a pilot program may elicit greater acceptance within a school or community. Cite specific programs to strengthen the credibility of your choices. Key programs to refer to are Glicksman, Douglas, and Smythe (1983), Hecht, Corman, and Miller-Rassulo (1993), Johnson (1987), and Kumpfer, Molgaard, and Spoth (1996).

Interviews

To develop a prevention program based on the insider status of peer experience, experiences must be gathered from students who are members of the target audience. Interviews, open-ended questionnaires, and ethnographic observations can accomplish this purpose. Interviews may be conducted in various forms—from informal focus group settings to face-to-face open-ended interviews. Open-ended questionnaires can complement the interviews, and the written form allows for greater anonymity. Although ethnographic observation of actual resistance to drug offers raises serious moral questions, one can observe resistance in other health-related areas.

Adolescents who have been in situations where they have been offered substances and successfully resisted and those who have been offered substances and have not successfully resisted all need to be a part of the data-collection process.

The interviewers who conduct the interviews or facilitate the focus groups need to be matched for gender and ethnicity to the population of youth participants. They must also be trained in the basic interviewing skills of a qualitative researcher. At a minimum, the interviewers should attend a 4 to 8 hour training program where they are trained in general interviewing techniques, observation of nonverbal cues, and practicing the actual project interview in role-playing scenarios. All interviewers must have an opportunity to practice their interviewing skills and receive feedback on their performance from a qualified trainer. Validity of the interviews can be enhanced if the interviewer (Nurco, 1987):

1. Ensures respondents of confidentiality. Depending on the context of this program, there may be certain limitations to confidentiality and anonymity issues. To make disclosures anonymous means that the researcher does not even know the identity of the interviewee. The interview process would be blind. Confidentiality refers to the assurance that disclosures will be respected and not divulged outside of the research objectives nor linked to any one individual. Your school may have specific guidelines and state laws pertaining to disclosures of abuse, illegal activities, and other issues pertaining to minors. Become aware of these limitations prior to developing the interview schedule.

2. Carefully establishes rapport with the group members or individual.

3. Asks respondents to focus on recent events.

4. Frames the questions in a general fashion.

Open-ended questions are used to elicit stories and narrative accounts from the respondents. Obtaining adolescents' subjective experience of the situation is essential to this process. As Rawlins and Holl (1987) stated, adolescents' stories of their own experience are an important resource that young people use to both reflect and constitute their social world. This approach allows an account to be developed and allows you to capture more of the adolescents' world than that of the adult culture (Geertz, 1973; Rawlins & Holl, 1987).

Two open-ended, nondirective questions that may be used are:

1. Would you tell me about a time when you were offered drugs or alcohol and you turned that offer down?
2. Would you tell me about a time when you were offered drugs or alcohol and you wanted to say no, but didn't?

The interviewer should be prepared with follow-up prompts that encourage the student to tell a story. If brief answers are the response style of the respondent, the interviewer may want to prompt a more thorough account with suggestions to identify the who (characters), what (action), when (temporal frame), where (setting), and how (internal states/feelings) of the situation.

A copy of a suggested interview schedule is located in Appendix F. All interviews should be tape recorded and transcribed. Interviews must remember to obtain permission/consent to tape record, and it is wise to record the agreement on tape.

SCRIPTING

Keep in mind, when scripting dramatic scenarios for intervention or prevention, many mainstream depictions of "what it is like" for youth, African-Americans, Hispanics, and so on are considered inauthentic. Co-opting counterculture messages in an attempt at overt persuasion may be considered offensive to many youth especially if the message is delivered by a mainstream adult authority figure (i.e., Partnership for a Drug Free America campaign). Urban youth, in particular, tend to be highly suspicious of mainstream culture.

If students have a chance to design their own messages, with no sanctions from parents or institutions, this message will have an inherent strength to prompt attitude modification and compliance with the message.

The bottom-line advice for scripting prevention scenarios is to avoid giving too much information, preaching a moral, or presenting an obvious resolution. Gathering narrative accounts from the peer group allows for a variety of responses and interpretations from the audience. This is not to say that salient issues and conflicts should not be identified. In fact, this takes us to the first stage of scripting—identifying the major themes.

Action is given more attention when the spectator can identify with the theme and it is salient to his or her life. The theme must be engaging. To ascertain some of the major themes of your target population, a focus group should be established, consisting of key members of your target audience. If your audience will eventually be Hispanic fifth and sixth graders, avoid focus groups consisting of eighth-grade White students. Central themes and values of a group are often sociocultural. Take extra pains to make your focus groups representative of the larger target population.

With your focus group of 8 to 10 students, brainstorm the major concerns facing them regarding substance use and abuse. Some themes that may emerge are: peer pressure to drink, gender-role differences in drinking behavior, and lack of other leisure time activities. The strongest themes that emerge from this group should then be categorized among the many narrative accounts gathered in the interview process. For example, Alberts, Miller-Rassulo, and Hecht (1991) found resisting substance offers centered around the dramatic elements of who made the offer, what was offered, how the offer was made, where the offer occurred, how the recipient responded, and if in the story the person accepted or refused the offer. Four themes were identified in this study as ways that students realistically resist offers of drugs or alcohol: Refuse, Explain, Avoid, and Leave. Each theme had representative accounts in the transcriptions. The information generated by the focus group may be matched with the findings from the interview transcripts. This process ensures that the script accurately reflects the lived experiences of the target group.

When targeting your message to an intended audience, research indicates you should consider gender and ethnicity in addition to age differences. Research on gender differences indicates that women are more persuaded by characters who convey the message through relational terms, whereas men are more persuaded by issues of power and control.

Ethnicity may play a factor in persuasion as well. One study suggested that African-Americans (males and females) find scenes promoting male values more persuasive than those that focus on women characters' values. The key is to avoid stereotyping while maintaining group identification.

One method for accomplishing this is to appeal to cultural core values. For example, African-American culture frequently stresses sharing, individuality, realism, and assertiveness (Hecht, Collier, & Ribeau, 1993).

Once you have established major themes, you need to categorize each account from your transcripts into one of the themes. A cut-and-stack method often works well. This method necessitates that you make a copy of all transcripted accounts, cut out each account separately, and place in a specific thematic pile. If an account does not fit into any of the identified themes, you may start an *Other* pile. Eventually you may want to reanalyze the Other pile if it is large to determine whether additional themes have been overlooked.

After perusing each pile, specific narrative accounts should be chosen that represent the theme; these accounts hold together in terms of clear orientation (who, what, where, when), a complicating action (crisis that complicates action), and results (what finally happened);(Polkinghorne, 1988). The results need not articulate a clear resolution. It is strongly suggested that you avoid revealing too much in a scene. The script must allow for postperformance discussion. Other criteria suggested in choosing the representative accounts are: (a) Is the story truly representative of the experience? (b) Is the story realistic to other youth? (c) Is the story structured so as to lend itself to performance?

To obtain feedback and validate the first two criteria, additional peer focus groups may be used to verify the choices of material in the script, confirm appropriateness of the approach, and brainstorm transitional material. These groups may provide specific suggestions for modifications. The third criterion may be satisfied by preliminary readings of the stories by teen performers who assess the performability of each story.

The Alberts et al. (1991) study resulted in a training script that utilized actual accounts performed by peer actors; it was couched in a musical docudrama format. The musical numbers bracketed the accounts and functioned as a chorus and transitional mechanism. Two original songs were produced by Page (1990a, b) for inclusion into the scripts. Additional suggestions include:

- Use repetition and restatement. Simplicity is key.
- Engage the audience through realism. One study found that rap songs that were lyrical or used unfamiliar metaphors were considered too deep and were not considered as seriously as those party songs that were easily identifiable.

- Touch on content areas often eschewed by institutionalized prevention materials (e.g., motivation to use, financial benefits of selling and encouraging others to use, distinction between use and abuse).
- Portray settings of teens hanging out as a context for action.
- Adolescents often respond to action revolving around characters who are romantically involved.
- Many prevention messages focus on what the youth should *not* do. Perhaps a focus on alternative success scenarios or alternative activities are warranted (i.e., what *can* they do?).
- Keep the length of the script to less than 35 minutes. This allows for performance and postperformance discussion to be completed within a 50-minute class period. You may even want to consider shorter segments, which can be administered over many class periods rather than as a single-shot intervention.

IMPLEMENTATION

After the script is drafted, another focus group session may be warranted to obtain feedback. If possible, a staged reading is a good idea so the focus group members can hear the script performed. Then a final script can be completed. The casting of the characters is the next crucial step.

Casting actors to portray the various characters in your script is a challenging task. The selection of actors is crucial to the success of the program. It is not necessary for the actors to be professional actors, yet they must meet two minimum criteria: (a) be a peer or near-peer of the target group, and (b) be believable in the role. Depending on the comprehensiveness of the program, you may want to employ local professional actors or you may want to recruit talent from the target audience. Professional teen actors can be obtained via local talent agencies, drama clubs, and community theaters or by holding auditions for the program. No matter how simple or complex the role, each actor should sign a contract obligating him or her to attend rehearsals and performances.

Rehearsals should take place after the final script has been approved and all revisions completed. Allocate at least 1 month or 40 hours of rehearsal time. During the rehearsal period, the coordinator of the prevention program should have the schools, classrooms, teachers, and schedule of performances arranged. All arrangements for vehicles to transport actors and set objects should be made at this time as well.

The style of the peer-based dramatic performance is contingent on the script and the targeted audience. Lack of resources may necessitate a production with minimal extras such as lighting, costuming, props, or music. Several effective programs have not used a set at all, some have used a few stools, while others have utilized a complete set that is easily dismantled after each performance.

The performance in the Hecht et al. (1993) study utilized several elements to heighten the sense of style:

- Live music
- Actors directly addressing the audience (eliminating fourth wall)
- Use of graphics (in the film) and rear-screen projection (in the live performance)
- Oral introductions to highlight pedagogical concepts
- Emphasis of story over character

Music is integral to the youth culture's value system; it seems to influence the listener to be increasingly receptive to the message embedded in the music (Irvine & Kirkpatrick, 1972). The band may function as a Greek chorus restating the strategy and commenting on the action.

DISCUSSION

Conducting a postperformance discussion may either enhance or detract from the scripted performance. Great care should be taken when developing the discussion component of the program. Discussion allows the spectators of the presentation to talk openly about their lives and feelings, gain personal insight, and direct these in a productive way. Discussion may present new information that can alter attitudes and generate alternative behaviors not previously addressed in the script. Guided discussion is what is triggered by the script.

Facilitators for the discussion should be chosen carefully and trained in facilitation. The facilitators' primary role is to encourage honest expression of feelings and experiences while establishing a context of acceptance for these expressions. Facilitators guide the discussion along these lines to clarify thoughts and reinforce content areas of the production's message. Discussion of plot may be pursued to discuss what happened in the performance. This avoids the pedantic frame of discussing their understanding of an educational message.

Overall, facilitators should positively reinforce responses, summarize content, and end on a positive note. Facilitators should also have credibility within the group and function as a positive role model for the teens. If possible, it is recommended that an experienced counselor be available at each intervention for any direct needs for referral. The Hecht et al. (1993) postperformance discussion agenda was developed to support the content and follow the performances. A specialist in adolescent substance abuse, researchers, and the scriptwriter developed a 20-minute discussion agenda based on the script content and prevention research. Discussion leaders were trained to use the agenda.

During this stage of program development, it is a good idea to conduct a training session with the teachers from the classrooms involved in the program. A written memo may be thrown away, so it is suggested that a brief training session be conducted at a convenient time. This training session provides general drug education, rationale for your program, and information on how to handle and refer questions on individual cases.

ASSESSMENT

Program evaluation is one of those activities that many would dispense with, yet assessment of the program is essential to evaluate the efficacy and ultimate impact on attitudes and behavior and provide information on how to improve the program. There are two levels of objectives you want to evaluate—process and outcome.

Process objectives of your program can be evaluated in terms of the day-to-day activities of your particular program. Is the timeline being adhered to? How many performances are scheduled? What was the attendance at each performance? Save any press items that may pertain to the program. What was the feedback you received from your focus groups?

Of more concern to many program coordinators are the bottomline effects of the performance—the outcome. In most cases, this outcome would be the attitude and behavior change that occurred as a result of the program. What are the overall goals of your program and what are the smaller objectives that must be met to achieve those goals? These questions must be asked and answered before any evaluation effort can begin. Some examples of a program's goals are:

- Stop or delay experimentation with alcohol or other substances.
- Promote the acceptability of the nondrinker/nonuser.

- Encourage health-enhancing behavior.
- Improve the willingness and ability of the target audience to resist alcohol and other substances.
- Stop or decrease current alcohol or other drug use.

To evaluate whether you have met your objectives and achieved your goal(s), the following experimental design procedures are suggested:

- Divide your audience into at least two groups: those who are exposed to the performance and those who were not (control group). If you want to control for effects of the discussion, you may want an additional group to separate out those students exposed to (a) performance plus discussion, (b) performance only, and (c) control group.
- Measure attitudes and behaviors prior to the intervention. Attitudes that you may want to assess are attitudes toward substance use and abuse, abstinence, family, self-risky behaviors, norms, consequences or drug use, and social pressure. You may want to measure drug use in the past 30 days, including the number of times, quantity, and substance used. Separate measures are needed for each substance (e.g. alcohol, marijuana, cocaine).

Design the form on colored paper using graphics and/or illustrations. These design options decrease the feel of taking a test. You may want to administer the survey a few days prior to the intervention to avoid testing effects.

- Measure the same attitudes and behaviors after the intervention, perhaps at different time intervals (e.g., immediately after the intervention, 1 week later, 1 month later). This measurement assesses the difference scores between the time prior to the intervention and the point after the intervention.
- Assess the performance itself by administering a *Perception of Performance* scale (included in Appendix H). This scale was developed in the Miller, Stiff, and Hecht (1999); it evaluates the performance in terms of the engaging qualities of the performance: identification, enjoyment, interest, comprehension, realism, personal relevance, and acceptability.

Identification with characters and events may be an important component of engagement. Feeling at one with both the characters and action should lead to the unity of experience indicated by aesthetic engagement. Identification of the audience member is a prerequisite to gaining insight. Audience activity research by Perse and Ruben (1988) also linked identification with program satisfaction. In the interpersonal domain, Bogardus (1983) argued that the stronger the identification of one person with another, the less the social distance.

Interest is defined as the degree of attention to the media. Audience members are unlikely to feel close to a performance that bores them. Interest should bring the audience closer to engagement with the performance, or at least invite them closer. Immanuel Kant emphasized interest as an ever-present variable in aesthetic judgment.

Comprehension is defined as the understanding of content. It was felt that a lack of comprehension would disengage the spectator from the performance event. *Realism* is defined as the audience's experience of the situation as authentic. Establishing a perception of realism should be necessary for engagement. As related by J.R. Tolkien (1983):

> ... when a world can become real or believable on all levels of consciousness, the (receiver) can experience that world fully as a human being with all the emotions and feeling with which he can experience the world.

If a performance is perceived as unrealistic, the audience member should experience increased disengagement from the event.

Relevance refers to the degree to which the performance was important to the spectator. As with realism, a performance must be relevant to the audience member to be identified with. Finally, *acceptability* is whether elements of the performance were perceived as offensive. Offending an audience member should weaken engagement, whereas acceptable content should strengthen engagement. For additional information of attitude and behavioral items that can be used in assessment, see Appendix H.

STEPS AT A GLANCE FOR PROGRAM PLANNING

1. *Achieve community and school acceptance of the program.* Whether the program developed reaches one class or entire schools within a community, the first step is to gather support for your ideas so that the paths

are cleared, the waters are smoothed, and everyone necessary is kept informed. Become an expert at updating individuals with memorandums.

2. *Develop the goals and objectives for the program.*

3. *Obtain interviews from representative peer group members.* Conduct one-on-one or focus group interviews with students from the target population.

4. *Content analyze the transcribed narrative accounts generated from the interviews.* Categorize and select representative accounts that can be used in the scripted performance.

5. *Script the narratives into a performance.* Using the peer-based narratives, creatively develop a script to be performed for the target audience.

6. *Validate the script with focus group representatives.*

7. *Cast and rehearse the script with actors.* Stage the script with the resources available. Allow for flexibility in the staging to adapt to a myriad of playing spaces.

8. *Arrange all performance dates and transportation needs, and confirm all details.*

9. *Develop discussion agenda and protocol.*

10. *Select and train discussion facilitators. Conduct teacher training.*

11. *Administer pretest instruments for evaluation.*

12. *Perform, conduct discussions, and make referrals.*

13. *Administer posttest instruments for evaluation.*

14. *Conduct any follow-up activities.* Referrals, follow-up discussions, guest speakers, or additional classroom assignments occur in addition to the performance program.

15. *Save all press clippings, correspondence from schools, students, parents, or administration.* Often the press reports, thank you notes, and anecdotal reports that result from this kind of a program may provide fuel for future funding of the program. In addition, they are fun to read.

16. *Provide control schools with the intervention* in order to ensure they gain a benefit from participation.

17. *Disseminate summary reports to participating organizations.*

APPENDIX E: Killing Time

A Film Script[*]
By
Joe Rassulo

I INT. MOVIE THEATRE-DAY [COLOR]

On a large movie screen, we see the beginning logo of a movie chain, followed by the graphic signaling the "feature presentation". A series of fast clips from REFER MADNESS, the 193Os horrific campy tale of pot and its bizarre after affects begin. As this slowly fades to black...

DISSOLVE TO:

2 EXT. RAILROAD PARK-DAY [COLOR]

Teenagers—Victoria, Kris, Mario, and Dan-are sitting on and around the front of an old steam engine. They are talking to the camera. They are laughing.

---

[*]Drug Resistance Strategies Project, Phoenix, AZ. Sponsored by the National Institute on Drug Abuse. Finalist in the *1990 International Film and Television Festival of New York.* Copyright 1990. Based on the Collected Stories of Teenagers talking about how they say "no" to drugs and alcohol. February 20, 1990.

VICTORIA
Just say no!

KRIS
Just do it!

DAN
Just shut up!
Don't worry, we told'em, we're only making a movie.

VICTORIA
But they kept asking us ... why do we like these kids? We don't feel we
know them. And, really, why are they making this movie? We need to root
for them ... to see them overcome the odds!

KRIS
What do they think our life is all about?

MARIO
Try ... overcoming the odds, you know what I mean?

VICTORIA
So we write the movie our way and they say..."it sounds too
preachy"..."there's no plot". Hell, sometimes life's like that.

DAN
Plotless?

VICTORIA
Craziness. No logic to it.

KRIS
But movies can't be like that.

MARIO
Didja like the film "Election?"

KRIS
Weird.

VICTORIA
I liked it.

KRIS
I rest my case.

MARIO
How about "Breakfast Club?"

VICTORIA
Contrived.

KRIS
I liked it.

MARIO
How about "The Phantom Menace?"

VICTORIA
How about it?

DAN
What's real to you?

VICTORIA
My life ... and your life ... and your life... and ... you know.

DAN
Come on.

VICTORIA
I mean it ... (to Dan) like you're rich so your parents buy you a camera ... and they don't even know what you do with it.

MARIO
He doesn't even use it. I use it.

VICTORIA
(to Mario) you used to be a stoner-now you can't handle anybody who does dope...

MARIO
But I can handle a camera.

DAN
But you can't hit from the outside.

VICTORIA
(to Kris) and your parents are divorced...

KRIS
Big deal ... so are yours.

VICTORIA
I try to forget about that ... so we have 4 mothers, 5 stepbrothers, assorted grandparents, and too many phone numbers to remember. Why are we friends?

KRIS
'Cause we hang together.

MARIO
And cause we decided to make this movie together.

VICTORIA
But why?

DAN
Because we need to show what's real.

VICTORIA
Thank you.

DAN
So what do *WE* do?

KRIS
We don't show fried eggs, football heroes, or needles ... or football heroes sticking needles into fried eggs... or bacon and eggs frying on the brains of a football hero ... Here's your brain ... here's your eggs... here's your brain on eggs!

DAN
Ok. Ok. We get the picture.

MARIO
That's what this is all about then. Making sure we all *get the picture*. So we make this movie. We get the stories straight. We tell it our way ... in our own words.

VICTORIA
Can we say anything we want?
Mario turns to the director.

RYAN
Well?
A voice from behind the real camera speaks.

DIRECTOR
You know the rules. No brand names. No four letter words. No nudity.

KRIS
With this body ... no chance.

DIRECTOR
No real violence.

DAN
That's ok ... I bruise easy.

DIRECTOR
Other than that, you can do pretty much anything you want.
Victoria talks to the director.

VICTORIA
But will you respect us in the morning?

They all laugh as Mario picks up his camera and points it directly at the REAL CAMERA. He walks right at it until the frame is filled with the lens of his camera lens.

CUT TO:

3 TITLE

The title song-DON'T WORRY, WE'RE ONLY MAKING A MOVIE-is heard through the credits.

They are.-

THE NATIONAL INSTITUTE OF DRUG ABUSE AND ARIZONA STATE UNIVERSITY DEPARTMENT OF COMMUNICATION AND 300 TEENAGERS

presents
"don't worry ... we're only making a movie!"

[As each individual teen is seen, their name is flashed along side the home movie screen.]

4 EXT. ARCADIA INTERVIEWS-DAY [Color]

Victoria holds the microphone. She is asking a female teenager a question. The REAL CAMERA moves in on VICTORIA.

TITLE-.

VICTORIA

5 EXT. MOVIE THEATRE DEAD POETS SOCIETY-IN DAY [Color]

The 4 teens are rushing into a movie theatre. Mario has no money. Victoria gives him 5 dollars and they go in. Dan and Kris stare, then follow them.

CUT TO:

6 EXT. SHANA'S STORY INTRO-AT LUNCH-DAY [B & W]

Victoria, Kris, and Dan are eating at an outdoor table. Mario is moving his camera around them.

CUT TO:

7 EXT. MOVIE THEATRE-DEAD POETS-OUT AS SCENE 5-DAY [Color]

Mario, Kris, Dan, and Victoria leave the movie theatre. They walk quietly and together. Kris is crying.

CUT TO:

8 INT. VICKY'S PROJ. SCENE DAY [Color]

The four teens are sitting in the living room. Kris is teasing Vicky's hair. Mario is piercing Danny's ear.

CUT TO:

9 EXT. ARCADIA INTERVIEWS DAY [Color]

Mario holds the microphone. He is asking a male teenager a question. The REAL CAMERA moves in on MARIO.

CUT TO:

10 EXT. MOVIE THEATRE-PREDATOR-IN DAY   10

The three teens are trying to push Vicky into the movie theatre. Mario finally shoves her in.

CUT TO:

11 EXT. DESERT-NIGHT [B & W]

Mario and Dan are scuffling near the edge of a desert cliff.
Kris is holding the mike. Victoria is filming.

CUT TO:

12 EXT. MOVIE THEATRE-PREDATOR-OUT DAY [Color]

Mario, Dan, and Kris exit the theatre together. They walk one way as Vicky goes the other way. When they realize she is walking the other way, they turn and walk toward her.

CUT TO:

13 INT. MARIO PROJ. SCENE-DAY [Color]

Mario and Dan are practicing the fight. The two girls are shaking their heads and trying to hide from what they see.

CUT TO:

14 EXT. ARCADIA INTERVIEWS-DAY [Color]

Kris is holding the microphone. Kris is asking a female teenager a question. The REAL CAMERA moves in on KRIS.

CUT TO:

15 EXT. MOVIE THEATRE-SEX, LIES, VIDEO-IN DAY [Color] 15

Mario, Dan, Kris, and Victoria are walking up to the Theatre. Vicky pushes Mario-who is walking slowly.

CUT TO:

16 EXT. A JUNKYARD-DAY [B & W]

Kris is sitting in the bed of a pickup truck. Victoria is filming. Mario and Dan are sitting in the cab of the truck, looking through the window at Victoria.

CUT TO:

17 EXT. MOVIE THEATRE-SEX, LIES, VIDEO-OUT DAY [Color]

Mario, Dan, and Kris come through the doors and stare in bewilderment at Vicky who is taking notes.

CUT TO:

18 INT. KRIS'S PROJ. SCENE-DAY [Color]

Kris is rehearsing the boys on chairs in the middle of the living room. Victoria is smacking some sense into them.

CUT TO:

19 EXT. ARCADIA INTERVIEWS-DAY [Color]

Dan is holding the microphone. He is asking a male teenager a question. The REAL CAMERA moves in on DAN.

CUT TO:

20 EXT. MOVIE THEATRE-BILL & TED'S-DAY [Color]

The four teens are at the movie theatre. They are buying tickets. Dan buys Vicky's ticket.

CUT TO:

21 EXT. DAN'S BASKETBALL INTRO-DAY [B & W]

Victoria is filming. Mario and Dan are playing basketball. Kris runs and picks up the ball throws it to Mario, who misses. They all laugh.

CUT TO:

22 EXT. MOVIE THEATRE-BILL & TED'S-OUT DAY [Color]

The four teens walk out of the theatre. Kris is laughing. The others look at her and walk away.

CUT TO:

29 DAN'S PROJ. SCENE-NIGHT [Color]

Dan is up late looking at the video screen. The other are sacked out around him. He gets an idea and wakes them all up.

CUT TO:

23 INT. MOVIE PROJECTION BOOTH-DAY [Color]

The four teens are preparing the projector. They are sitting around it. They are talking to the REAL CAMERA.

VICTORIA
Pot, marijuana, weed, smoke... stuff like that.

DAN
Beer, booze, kegs that, too.

KRIS
It's about all that the movie is, I mean.

DAN
And us ... how we handle it ... or don't.

VICTORIA
Just stories ... true stories...what it's like for us...

MARIO
Where ... what came down...why ... You know, the kind of stuff that happens when you're just killing time.

DISSOLVE TO:

27 INT. MUSIC SEGUE-SHANA-DAY [Color]

Vocalist runway singing a verse of KILLING TIME that relates to this story. The camera is in close on him. His shadow is cast against the giant screen behind.

BRIAN (SINGING)
"It's ok
t's alright
If the only way out is a little lie
Make up a story
They'll never know

So you tried to trick 'em
That's how you said no...

Find better ways of Killing Time..."

CUT TO:

25 TITLE

Against a white screen, the following words are handwritten in black

**DECEIT
SHANA'S STORY**

DISSOLVE TO:

26 EXT. SHANA'S STORY-LUNCH TABLE-DAY [B & W]

Victoria, Kris, and Dan are walking down the slatted walkway. It is brisk. A battered mural is on the wall behind them. Mario is filming. It is his voice we hear off-camera.

MARIO (VO)
What exactly did they say to you when they wanted you to drink?

VICTORIA
"Our parents aren't home; come on, let's do it" ...I can't do this. I can't play this person.

26 CONTINUED

MARIO
Come on, Victoria. We need to act it out like it happened. Remember, you're the one who wanted real.

DAN
Just do it.

MARIO (VO)
What exactly did they say to you when they wanted you to drink?

VICTORIA
"Our parents aren't home; come on, let's do it"

DAN
"They'll never find out."

VICTORIA
I said, "That was ok, but I didn't want to do it right now." I just asked for something else ... I don't know ... water or a pepsi ... something.

KRIS
Games, Shana.

VICTORIA
Yeah, well, at the time, just taking it, but then not drinking it, was ok. They still thought you were cool.

KRIS
Still, lying pretty much always works. Tell'em about the bathroom.

VICTORIA
My parents ... all of us ... were out of town on a class reunion, my Dad's 25th class reunion. We were at a hotel in Indiana and ... I walked into the bathroom ... no, I walked into our hotel room and there was my sister and my cousin watching TV and so I walked in and needed to use the bathroom and the door was locked.

VICTORIA
And I'm like knocking on the door and some people are saying... "aauugh" and so I can hear them and it's like "what's going on, I've got to use the bathroom, you know, this is my place, too". And they open the door and they were doing lines ... I don't know if it was coke, crystal, crack, whatever, but I went in. They said, like, well, I had a choice, you can either do a line or you can wait in line. They thought that was pretty funny. I said ... no ... neither. I gotta use the bathroom. One of the guys, who knows who he was, maybe a friend of my cousin's ... says ... I know you do lines.

DAN
No ... you "look" like you do lines.

VICTORIA
Yea ... another guy says ... let her go to the bathroom, you know. But the other guy looks kinds scared and said he was afraid I was gonna say something and they started getting into it ... so, like I really had to go to the bathroom, so I said... "ok, ok ... just let me go to the bathroom first." So they walked out ... and when I was done I just pushed it around ... you know, a line ... to make it look like I did it, you know ... sol they wouldn't bug me anymore. Turns out they were relatives ... 2nd cousins or something.

MARIO
How did they look at you when you came out of the bathroom?

VICTORIA
I don't know... I was more worried about the look on my face, you know, because it was like, did I look like I did it, you know, and would my sister figure I did anything wrong.

MARIO (VO)
So you tried to trick'em. Is that how you said no?

VICTORIA
I suppose. Pretty lame, actually. I mean, who were they anyway.

DAN
Exactly.

MARIO
Does she, you sister, judge you because of the way you look or dress?

VICTORIA
Yea, Yea..

DAN
They think we deal drugs ... or do drugs.

KRIS
Yea ... it's the earring.

VICTORIA

Yea ... with Sam it's the earring. With me it's the hair. You know, basic stuff, little stuff, you know, like you wake up and it's just like, you know, you have zits on your face, and she'll say... "what's that? don't you wash?" ...you know, that kind of stuff. "Do something with your hair ... you look like..." I mean I like my hair ... the way I look at it ... it's my head, you know, as long as it's clean, why should anyone care. I mean come on ... why does she think it has anything to do with zits...

DAN
Or drugs...

VICTORIA
You can't judge anybody anymore by the way they look because every-body's got their own style, everybody.

They all start to laugh. Dan looks at the camera.

DAN
Well, how were we? Didja get that?

KRIS
You know, Danny, your hair looks good that way.

DAN
Maybe it's the real me.
Kris and Dan start fooling around, laughing at one another. Victoria speaks to them and then looks at the camera.

VICTORIA
Are we done ... I mean are you still rolling, Mario?

CUT TO:

32 INT. MUSIC SEGUE-JORDAN-DAY [B & W]

Brian Page is on the runway singing another verse of KILLING TIME that relates to this story.

BRIAN (SINGING)
"You could just leave

Walk away
They can think what they want
Say what they wanna say...

Find better ways of Killing Time..."

                                                        DISSOLVE TO:

30 TITLE
Against another white screen, the following words are written in black.

LEAVE JORDAN'S STORY

                                                        DISSOLVE TO:

31 EXT. A DESERT NIGHT [B & W]

The camera swoops out of a burning fire. There are a bunch of teens surrounding the fire. Most have beer cans in their hands. Mario and Dan are standing behind the fire, talking. Victoria is filming. Kris walks up to the two boys. They stop talking.

KRIS
Ok, so play it out ... like it happened. Mario, you be Jordan. Dan, you be Bert.

MARIO
Yea, well, Bert got a little rough with Jordan that night.

VICTORIA
Mario ... get real!

KRIS
It doesn't matter. Just do the best you can.

DAN
What do ya mean, it doesn't matter?

KRIS
Don't worry, wimp, Mario won't hurt you. You ready, Victoria?

VICTORIA (VO)
I've been ready. Action.

Kris runs out of frame. Mario and Dan talk to the camera at first.

MARIO
Ok, ok. Jordan ... a friend of mine was at this party. Bert got a keg and all, cans, you know. They all drove out to the desert. Jordan's brother dropped him off 'cause he didn't have any wheels.

DAN
See, Jordan and Bert are friends ... not best friends ... but good friends. I'm Bert.

Mario and Dan take on the personas of different characters now. Mario joins the crowd by the fire. Everyone's loud. Music starts playing. Someone offers Mario a beer. He refuses. They offer it again. Mario nods, no thank you, stands, and walks away from the fire. Dan has been watching this. He chugs his beer, grabs another, and walks quickly after Mario.

BERT
Hey, come on, drink a beer.

JORDAN
No, I don't want to.

BERT
Eh, you want a beer!

JORDAN
No. I don't

BERT
Hey, you gonna be at my party ... if you're gonna stay here, you gotta drink something!

JORDAN
I don't know, man. No, I don't want it.

BERT
Hey, if you're not gonna drink nothing, I don't want you around here.

JORDAN
I don't have no way home. I don't want to drink anything.

Bert shoves a beer can into Jordan's chest, knocking him over.

BERT
Here, take it! It's your beer!

JORDAN
No, I don't want any. Just go back to your party, go have fun, you've had enough yourself, you know.

BERT
You don't have to care what I do. You don't have to boss me. You don't control me. I could go out and kill myself, you wouldn't care.

JORDAN
Hey, you're a nice guy. I like being around you. Just don't push on my line. I don't want it.

BERT
Hey, if you're gonna stay here, drink. If not, leave.
Bert grabs Jordan by the collar forcibly and starts to push him backwards, too near the edge of the high drop.

BERT
If you're not going to drink, you're getting out of here.

JORDAN
Enough of this. I'm leaving.

BERT AND JORDAN are facing each other off. Jordan/Mario walks off into the darkness. Bert/Dan runs after him, pulling at him. Jordan/Mario turns on him. Their tempers are hot. Kris runs over to them and pulls them apart.

KRIS
Whoa, you guys. Let's stop it, ok.

They both break apart. And look at each other. They are both breathing hard. They take some time to recover.

MARIO
You know, I don't know if I could have handled it that way. I would never put myself in that spot.

DAN
Ok, that's cool. I would never go to that guy's party either if that's how he reacts.

MARIO
I'd leave. I'd say... "Hey, I don't want any"... and I'm outa there.

Ryan and Pete are still worked up.

MARIO
Let's walk a little.

DAN
Yeah. Cool it with the camera, ok?

Kris looks toward the camera and Victoria and signals to stop filming. Mario and Dan walk away from the camera and the screen goes to white.

                                                        DISSOLVE TO:

37 INT. MUSIC SEGUE-SARA-DAY [B & W]

Brian Page is on the runway singing the next verse of KILLING TIME..

BRIAN (SINGING)
"Stay in control
all the time
gotta be thinkin about it
such a fine line

Find better ways of killing time..."

DISSOLVE TO:

35 TITLE

Against a white screen, the following words are handwritten in black.

SAY NO
SARA'S STORY

DISSOLVE TO:

36 EXT. A JUNKYARD-DAY [B & W]

The camera swoops down from the sky. KRIS is sitting in the bed of a pickup truck in a junkyard near the Salt River Flats. She is talking directly to the camera and laughing.

KRIS
What a jerk! You know, I thought ... when I first went into high school I thought ... I had this like image that people were going to nab me in the bathroom and say... "Here, do you want to do these drugs? ... and I was just like freaked out so I didn't go to the bathroom for like my whole freshman year! I didn't. I was so afraid that they were going to like try to ... get me to use drugs ... so I told my brother ... and he just laughed....

Kris stands up in the bed of the pickup truck, jumps down, and gets into the cab of the truck as she continues talking.

KRIS
Only on Geraldo Rivera ... nobody's doin it except on TV ... you know movies and stuff. He really fooled me, you know ... my brother.

Kris positions herself in the passenger side of the front seat.

KRIS
About a month later we were going along. My brother was behind the wheel, his best friend in the middle, and I was on the passenger side. I had my window down. They asked me to roll it up ... you know ... roll up the

window. I wasn't sure what was going on ... this was the first time I was really, you know, around them, saw it.

The camera gets in the front seat with Kris. The perspective is now from the driver's side, looking at Kris. [From here on, through the rest of the scene, the camera will alternate from the driver's perspective to Kris's perspective accordingly]

A little pipe, whatever. They each took it about three or four times. It kinda stunk. It was gross ... so I started to roll down the window. NO! NO! Don't do that. They got kinda mad, you know. Then we got down there a ways ... they started getting it ... more ... you know, whatever.

Suddenly, whenever the camera turns to Kris' perspective, Mario and Dan are in the car as if they are Kris', brother and his best friend.

KRIS
Then my brother says...

MARIO
"Hey, Sara, you want some?"

KRIS
We were getting about half way there. My brother's best friend starting getting really messed up because he wasn't driving. My brother, he was, he was fine. He only had a couple. And I say... "No".
My first thought ... you know, hey, I've never tried it before. I don't know what happens. It's bad stuff. Everybody says it's bad. Everybody. Don't do it. You get bad stuff from it, you know. But my brother and ... they're like sitting there going...

MARIO
It's good.

DAN
It's good. Yeah.

KRIS
So, I kinda go ... 1-1-1 don't know".

MARIO

"We're not gonna push her. Nothing."

DAN

"Come on, come on ... you ... it's not gonna do nothin,"

KRIS

"I don't think I want it." I decided and he wasn't gonna convince me.

DAN

"You can do it. No problem. Hey, it's not gonna kill you, ya know. Look at us! Hey!"

KRIS

"No, I don't want it. No, thank you." ...but he kept on pushing me ... until my brother stopped the truck ... took him out, pulled him out and said...

MARIO

"That's enough of that. Get in the back of the truck. Until you cool off and quit pushing, you ride in the back!"

Kris gets out of the truck and walks around to the back of it. She stands, leaning against the tailgate.

KRIS

My brother and me got back in the front of the truck and kept driving. I don't know if it was the wind blowing at him in the back or what, but his friend seemed to straighten out. Drove all the way back like that. No more ... never pushed it again ... never even asked. No more pushes after that. My brother stood behind me. What it could do for me, I have no idea. I just decided to say no.

Kris starts to walk past the camera, then she stops.

KRIS

'Course I don't know what would of happened if my brother had been the one tryin' to get me to, you know, do it. Don't know what I'd of decided then.

DISSOLVE TO:

42 INT. MUSIC SEGUE-JIM-DAY [B & W]

Brian Page is on the runway singing the next verse of KILLING TIME.

BRIAN (SINGING)
"Whatcha gonna do?
How will you play?
Situations are comin'
What will you say?

Find better ways of killing time..."

DISSOLVE TO:

40 TITLE

Against a white screen the following words are handwritten in black.

NO ... WITH AN EXPLANATION JIM'S STORY

DISSOLVE TO:

41 EXT. BASKETBALL COURT-DAY [B & W]

The camera swoops down from the sky and onto the court. Mario and Dan
are playing one-on-one at one end of the court. The camera walks toward
them as Dan fakes past Mario and goes in for a sure lay up. Mario sees the
camera coming by him and looks right at it.

MARIO
Jim knows drugs...
Dan turns toward the camera and Mario quickly.

DAN
Make that basketball!

MARIO
Not any more.

Dan takes a jump shot and misses.

MARIO
Nice touch. you been drinking?

DAN
Not funny.

Mario retrieves the ball and tosses it to Dan.

DAN
The next game, it's the district championship.

MARIO
Which is about 2 days away... Saturday.

DAN
It's Thursday night. We won two games that week to qualify. We get back late. We go to somebody's house.

MARIO
You and the guys on the team.

DAN
Yeah. There's gonna be a few girls there, but it's gonna be pretty much a guy's party.

Dan quickly tosses the ball to Mario, catching him unprepared and hitting him square in the gut.
He starts to laugh.

DAN
Gotcha!

MARIO
Not as bad as they got you that night.

DAN
So we party. They had a keg and they want a buck for a glass. Drink all you want-all night long. They finally get to me. I go... "Uh, no, I don't want any"...just straight out.

MARIO
Everybody you knew ... everybody around you ... was drinking. And you
thought... ?
Mario throws the ball back to Dan. He starts to dribble. Mario tries to guard
him. He talks as he plays.

DAN
Is this the thing to do? I don't know. I was happy. The game was won. Don't
got another game for two days. These guys are doin it. They're gonna have
to get up on Saturday and play that game, too. It all went through my head.

Dan tried to fake Mario, but this time Mario knocks the ball out of his hands.
It goes across the court. Mario smiles and goes after it.

DAN
I wasn't drinking... I still wasn't ... I told 'em I didn't want to yet 'cause one
of us has to be excellent to play in that game, you know?

MARIO
The other team ... they're not gonna be a piece of cake. They didn't get there
easily, either.

Mario dribbles behind Dan and Harmlessly puts up a layup.

DAN
I sat back and thought about it, you know.

MARIO
Yeah ... I know.

DAN
I don't want any, but, eh, if we're gonna win this district championship,
we're gonna do it by all sticking together as a team ... doing what other guys
do and just stick with each other.

MARIO
Aw, Jim wants to be part of the team.

DAN

Hey, they tell me, you are not part of it no more. You don't know. If there's a spot at the end of the game, you know. These four guys are together, and I'm the only one open, and they got to throw me the ball, and I get to shoot it.

Dan plays the perimeter. Mario plays the key, holding the ball, looking everywhere but in Dan's direction.

DAN

One, are they gonna throw me the ball? Two, are they gonna be really mad at me if I miss?

Suddenly Dan stops and the camera comes walking directly at him, quickly.

DAN

Hey, if we're a team, I want to be acceptable when we win this thing. I don't want to just win it and then everybody leaves and I'm still left there... so I said ... Well, hey, they're doing it, I'm gonna do it.

Mario walks into camera frame and looks directly into the camera.

MARIO

Hey, we're a team. Let's stick together. Let's do it right.

Mario looks at Dan.

And you said ... ?

DAN

All right, I will. No problem. I went over and got my glass, started drinking, and everybody's having fun. The next thing you know, there's a knock on the door. Everyone's bugged. It was our city cop, a sheriff, and a state trooper.

MARIO

That trooper was ready to handcuff everybody and haul 'em away. But our buddy, our own city cop that knows everybody in town ... he looks around and sees the TEAM. So he takes our boys to the city jail and doesn't call any parents. Guess who he does call?

Mario takes the ball and shoves it into Dan's gut. Dan is caught unaware and it briefly knocks the wind out of him.

DAN
He called the coach. He looks at us. Two guys passed out on the floor. A couple can't even sit straight on the chairs. I wasn't bad.

Dan turns and heaves the basketball at the backboard. It bangs against it and ricochets across the gym.

DAN
He didn't say much right away. He just looked at us.

The camera, which is se on Dan, slowly pulls far away, leaving him alone on the court. Mario is no longer around.

DAN
"You would put the district championship on the line? Have a beer? You worked since November 11th as a team together, and you put the district championship on the line for one beer? Two days before it? After being together all this time?

Mario's voice is heard from off-camera. It has a hollow echo to it.

MARIO (VO)
How would you have handled it differently than the way you did?

DAN
I wouldn't have gone to the party ... but not only would I have not gone to the party, I would have tried my hardest to get the other guys I knew were gonna play and that were on my team to go, too.

MARIO (VO)
Oh, yeah?

DAN
Yeah. I would have tried to influence 'em.

Mario tosses the basketball at Dan from off-camera. Dan just lets it roll by him. He is like a solitary speck on the court now.

DISSOLVE TO:

44 INT. MOVIE PROJECTION BOOTH DAY [Color]
The projector is off. The four teens are cleaning up, getting ready to leave the booth. Mario picks up his camera one more time.

MARIO
Come on. Once more. Let 'em know how we feel ... I mean ... now ... at the end of everything.

Victoria looks at him.

VICTORIA
It's overkill, Mario. We made the point.

DAN
He's right, Victoria ... no big deal ... let's finish it.

KRIS
Go ahead, Mario, I'll start.

Kris and Dan settle in and stop what they are doing. Reluctantly, Victoria joins them. Mario begins filming.

KRIS
Before we made this movie, I gotta admit ... most things I've seen and stuff, I mean with my friends and stuff .. if you say no, most people will leave you alone.

DAN
You always hear a lot about peer pressure and it's always there and, yeah, it is at times, but most people I have been around it's like there's no peer pressure because they know if you don't want to do it you don't have to...

KRIS
They won't force you. I mean, it's still available and all ... but it's up to you if you want it or not.

VICTORIA
But a lot of the stories we heard weren't like that. I guess people are just exposed to different things. The stories we told in this film were the ones that made us think twice ... about our own lives. Who knows what goes on in other lives.

KRIS
This whole drug thing, you know. You gotta be in control all the time ... you gotta be thinking about it all figuring what you're gonna do in a situation. What your options are.

DAN
Yea ... like...if you're going to a party after a game or whatever ... and you know there's gonna be a keg, or we , or stuff there ... think about what you'll do.

KRIS
And then ... just do it.

VICTORIA
Like this movie. Maybe we didn't follow all the rules ... but I'll tell you one thing ... there can't be too many better ways to kill some time!

24 INT. MOVIE THEATRE DAY [Color/B & W]

Brian Page and the Next are playing on the runway of the Valley Art theatre. Behind them is a beautifully lit movie screen, casting shadows across the band. The camera swoops down from above and settles in quickly on Brian as he sings, KILLING TIME, the main theme of the teens' movie.

As he sings this song, we SEE FACES of teens. We LOOK into their eyes as we cut back and forth between Brian and them.

As the song progresses, we see groups of teens in the theatre seats below the runway.

Gradually, through a series, the group that is in the seats below, is discovered on the runway, surrounding Brian as he continues to sing KILLING TIME.

Eventually, the teens join Brian in singing the chorus. He leaves the band and joins the teens, leading them through the lyrics.
The camera rises from his eye level, in the middle of the crowd, and swoops back up to the overhead shot. The runway is now jammed with teens.

WE SEE BRIAN PAGE AND THE NEXT IN THE MIDDLE OF THE SCREEN. HE IS FINISHING THE LAST CHORUS OF "KILLING TIME".

THE FOLLOWING GRAPHIC COME UP.

"don't worry
we're only making a movie!"

THE CREDITS ROLL THROUGH "KILLING TIME".

FADE OUT.

APPENDIX F:
Discussion Guide

In general, we want to stick with their opinions—what they have to say about drug resistance. We want to avoid preaching or talking at them as much as possible. However, there are certain topics that need to be covered and some information we want to come out in either discussion or through your summaries. This information is highlighted in **BOLD** below.

1. Review strategies. **REAL**
As you've just heard in the presentation today, the strategies that you told us that you use, that work, are:
Resist ... saying a simple no.
Explain ... give an explanation of why you won't use.
Avoid ... don't go where drugs will be offered or avoid confrontation by pretending.
Leave ... or you could leave.
One way to remember this is REAL ... Resist, Explain, Avoid, Leave.

2. Ask open-ended, probing questions.
Does this seem realistic to you?
Is this how you would deal with some of these situations?
While you were watching, did you think of a strategy that you use that wasn't presented?
What was it?

Did anyone see something that they think they could use to avoid using drugs or alcohol?

Which one seemed most useful? (If discussion is dragging, having them take a vote.)

Do you think that you or your friends would handle drug situations differently having seen this?

Does it make a difference how well you know the person offering the drugs as to which strategy you would choose? Would you say something different to someone you knew really well?

3. Summary.

I'm really impressed by your honesty and willingness to share your ideas with us. One of the points that I found very interesting in this presentation was that sometimes it really helps if you let the other person know you **understand their thoughts and feelings**. Like you might tell a friend that you can't drink because you know that he wants to go dancing in a little while and you're driving. (If there is time, ask for examples.)

Another of the points I found interesting was how important it is to be **assertive** in refusing. Sometimes *how* you say no is more important than *what* you say. Can someone give me an example of an assertive way of saying no? A nonassertive way? (Be careful to separate aggressiveness from assertiveness.) (If there is time, ask for examples.)

Something else that came out when we were reading the interviews was the idea of **planning and decision making**. People said they planned beforehand how to avoid drugs or how to say no if they are offered. Today we've reviewed a few of the strategies that they used. The important point is that they thought about it beforehand and made a decision, so that they were ready. Sometimes that can mean a lot of things to think about—where you're going, who will be there, what to say, how to leave if you need to.

APPENDIX G:
Perception
of Performance Scale

Items retained for use in the *Perception of Performance* scale after completion of factor analyses.

INTEREST and REALISM were measured on the following scale:

1	2	3	4	5
Strongly Agree	Agree	Neither Agree Nor Disagree	Strongly Disagree	Disagree

INTEREST

1. The play/film was boring.
2. The play/film held my attention.
3. I was interested in what was happening in the play/film.

REALISM

1. The characters in the play/film were very realistic.
2. The characters in the play/film were not believable.

3. The content of the play/film was very realistic.

4. The content of the play/film was not believable.

5. Some of the characters in the play/film were not very realistic.

6. Some of the stories (accounts) in the play/film were not believable.

Identification was measured on the following scale:
Please rate how much the main character(s) in the play/film is like each of
the following people. Use the main character who is most like the people in
each of the questions.

1	2	3	4	5
Very Much Like	Somewhat Like	Moderately Like	Very Little Like	Not At All Like

IDENTIFICATION

1. My close friends

2. My other friends

3. My girlfriend/boyfriend

4. Me

References

Agnew, R., & Petersen, D. (1989). Leisure and delinquency. *Social Problems, 36,* 332–350.

Aktan, G., Kumpfer, K. L., & Turner, C. (1996). Effectiveness of a family skills training program for substance abuse prevention with inner-city African-American families. *International Journal of Additions, 31,* 158–175.

Alberts, J. K., Hecht, M. L., Miller-Rassulo, M., & Krizek, R. L. (1992). The communicative process of drug resistance among high school students. *Journal of Adolescents, 27,* 203–226.

Alberts, J. K., Miller-Rassulo, M., & Hecht, M. L. (1991). A typology of drug resistance strategies. *Journal of Applied Communication Research, 19,* 129–151.

Allen, O., & Page, R. M. (1994). Variance in substance use between rural black and white Mississippi high school students. *Adolescence, 29,* 401–424.

Amey, C. H., & Albrecht, S. L. (1998). Race and ethnic differences in adolescent drug use: The impact of family structure and the quantity and quality of parental interaction. *Journal of Drug Issues, 28,* 283–298.

Andrews, J. A., Hops, H., Ary, D., Lichtenstein, E., & Tildesley, E. (1991). The construction, validation, and use of the Guttman scale of adolescent substance use: An investigation of family relationships. *Journal of Drug Issues, 21,* 557–572.

Andrews, J. A., Hops, H., Ary, D., Tildesley, E., & Harris, J. (1993). Parental influence on early adolescent substance use: Specific and nonspecific effects. *Journal of Early Adolescence, 13,* 285–310.

Anglin, M. D., Hser, Y., & McGlothlin, W. H. (1987). Sex differences in addict careers: 2. Becoming addicted. *American Journal of Drug and Alcohol Abuse, 13,* 59–71.

Antram, J. C. (1991, January 26). Anti-drug musical to be staged. *Los Angeles Times* p. 7.

Apter, T. (1993). Altered views: Father's closeness to teenage daughters. In R. Josselson & A. Lieblich (Eds.), *The narrative study of lives* (Vol. 1, pp. 163–190). Newbury Park, CA: Sage.

Arizona Criminal Justice Commission. (1994). *Substance abuse and public school students: 1993 Arizona public schools substance abuse survey.* Phoenix, AZ: Author.

Aronson, J. (1992). Women's sense of responsibility for the care of old people: But who else is going to do it? *Gender and Society, 6,* 8–29.

Artaud, A. (1958). *The theatre and its double.* New York: Grove.

Ashery, R., Kumpfer, K. L., & Robertson, E. (1999). *Drug abuse prevention through family interventions* (National Institute on Drug Abuse Research Monograph 177). U.S. Department of Health and Human Services, National Institutes of Health, NIDA.

Bachman, J. G., Wadsworth, K. N., O'Malley, P. M., Schulenberg, J., & Johnston, L. D. (1997). Marriage, divorce, and parenthood during the transition to young adulthood: Impacts on drug use and abuse. In J. Schulenberg, J. Maggs, & K. Hurrelmann (Eds.), *Health risks and developmental transitions during adolescence* (pp. 246–279). New York: Cambridge University Press.

Bachman, J. G., Wallace, J. M., O'Malley, P. M. (1991). Racial/ethnic differences in smoking, drinking, and elicit drug use among American high school seniors, 1976–1989. *American Journal of Public Health, 82,* 372–377.

Bailey, S. L., Flewelling, R. L., & Rachal, J. V. (1992). Predicting the use of marijuana among adolescents: The relative influence of drug-specific and social context factors. *Journal of Health and Social Behavior, 33,* 51–66.

Bandura, A. (1976). Self-reinforcement: Theoretical and methodological considerations. *Behaviorism, 4,* 135–155.

Bandura, A. (1986). *Social foundations of thought and action: A social cognitive theory.* Englewood Cliffs, NJ: Prentice-Hall.

Bandura, A. (1990). Perceived self-efficacy in the exercise of control over AIDS infection. *Evaluation and Program Planning, 13,* 9–17.

Barber, J. G., & Gritching, W. L. (1987). The assessment of drug attitudes among university students using the short form of the drug attitude scale. *International Journal of the Addictions, 22*(10), 1033–1039.

Barnett, O. W., & Fagan, R. W. (1993). Alcohol use in male spouse abusers and their female partners. *Journal of Family Violence, 8*(1), 1–25.

Bass, L. (1993). Stereotype or reality: Another look at alcohol and drug use among African American children. *Public Health Reports Annual, 108,* 78–85.

Baumrind, D. (1966). Effects of authoritative control on child behavior. *Child Development, 37,* 887–907.

Baumrind, D. (1978). Parental disciplinary patterns and social competence in children. *Youth and Society, 9,* 239–276.

Baumrind, D. (1983). Rejoinder to Lewis' reinterpretation of parental firm control effects: Are authoritative families really harmonious? *Psychological Bulletin, 94,* 132–142.

Baumrind, D. (1989). Rearing competent children. In W. Damon (Ed.), *Child development today and tomorrow* (pp. 349–378). San Francisco, CA: Jossey-Bass.

Baumrind, D. (1990). *Types of adolescent substance users: Antecedent and concurrent family personality influences.* Paper presented for the Department of Psychology, Arizona State University.

Baumrind, D. (1991a). *Types of middle-class adolescent substance users: Concurrent family and personality influences.* Unpublished manuscript, University of California, Berkeley, CA.

Baumrind, D. (1991b). The influence of parenting style on adolescent competence and substance use. *Journal of Early Adolescence, 11,* 56–95.

Baxter, L. A. (1991). Content analysis. In B. M. Montgomery & S. Duck (Eds.), *Studying interpersonal interaction* (pp. 239–254). NY: Guilford Press.

Baxter, L. A., & Bullis, C. (1986). Turning points in developing relationships. *Human Communication Research, 12,* 469–493.

Beauvais, F., Oetting, E. R., & Edwards, R. W. (1985). Trends in drug use of Indian adolescents living on reservations: 1975–1983. *The American Journal of Drug and Alcohol Abuse, 11,* 209–230.

Beauvais, F., Chavez, E. L., Oetting, E. R., Deffenbacher, J. L., & Cornell, G. R. (1996). Drug use, violence, and victimization among white American, Mexican American, and American Indian dropouts, students with academic problems, and students in good academic standing. *Journal of Counseling Psychology, 43,* 292–315.

Beck, K. H., & Lockhart, S. J. (1992). A model of parental involvement in adolescent drinking and driving. *Journal of Youth and Adolescence, 21,* 35–51.

Bedworth, A. E., & D'Elia, J. A. (1971). Multi-media resources for drug education. *Journal of Drug Education, 3*, 293–303.

Behnke, M., Eyler, F. D., Woods, N. S., Wobie, K., & Conlon, M. (1997). Rural pregnant cocaine users: An in-depth sociodemographic comparison. *Journal of Drug Issues, 27*, 501–524.

Benoit, W. L., & Benoit, P. J. (1990). Memory for conversational behavior. *Southern Communication Journal, 37*, 24–34.

Berger, C. R., & DiBattista, P. (1993). Communication failure and plan adaptation: If at first you don't succeed, say it louder and lower. *Communication Monographs, 60*, 220–238.

Berkowitz, A., & Perkins, H. W. (1988). Personality characteristics of children of alcoholics. *Journal of Consulting Clinical Psychology, 56*, 206–226.

Berleant, A. (1991). *Art and engagement.* Philadelphia: Temple University Press.

Berndt, D. J., & Zinn, D. (1988) Stressful life events and adolescent depressive symptomatology. In A. E. James & C. Chiland (Eds.), *Perilous development: Child raising and identity formation under stress. Yearbook of the International Association for Child Adolescent Psychiatry and Allied Professions* (pp. 353–362). New York, NY: Wiley.

Berndt, T. J. (1996). Friendships in adolescence. In N.A. Vanzetti & S. Duck (Eds.), *A lifetime of relationships* (pp. 181–212). Pacific Grove, CA: Brooks/Cole.

Bernstein, H. (1975). Boredom and the ready-made life. *Social Research, 42*, 512–537.

Biglan, A., McConnell, S., Severson, H. H., Barry, J., & Ary, D. (1984). A situational analysis of adolescent smoking. *Journal of Behavioral Medicine, 7*, 109–114.

Bloodworth, J. (1975). Communication in the youth counter-culture: Music as expression. *Central States Speech Journal, 26*, 304–309.

Blumer, H. (1969). *Symbolic interactionism.* Englewood Cliffs, NJ: Prentice-Hall.

Bogardus, E. (1983). Citation of scale for measuring social distances. *Sociology and Social Research, 17*, 48–49.

Bormann, E. G. (1982). Fantasy and rhetorical vision: Ten years later. *Quarterly Journal of Speech, 68*, 288–305.

Boster, F. J. (1988). Comments on the utility of compliance-gaining message selection tasks. *Human Communication Research, 15*, 169–177.

Boster, F. J. (1990). Commentary on compliance-gaining message behavior research. In J. P. Dillard (Ed.), *Seeking compliance: The production of interpersonal influence messages* (pp. 41–56). Scottsdale, AZ: Gorsuch Scarisbrick.

Botvin, G. J. (1986). Substance abuse prevention research: Recent developments and future directions. *Journal of School Health, 56*(9), 369–374.

Botvin, G. J., Schinke, S., & Orlandi, M. A. (Ed.). (1995). *Drug abuse prevention with multiethnic youth.* Thousand Oaks, CA: Sage.

Botvin, G. J., & Schinke, S. (Eds.) (1997). *The etiology and prevention of drug abuse among minority youth.* New York: Haworth.

Brannock, J. C., Schandler, S. L., & Oncley, P. R. Jr. (1990). Cross-cultural and cognitive factors examined in groups of adolescent drinkers. *Journal of Drug Issues, 20*(3), 427–442.

Brasch, P. (1990, February 26). Many local groups are helping to spread anti-drug messages. *St. Louis Post-Dispatch,* p. 1.

Braucht, G. N. (1978). Psycho-social correlates of empirical types of multiple drug abusers. *Journal of Consulting and Clinical Psychology, 46*(6), 1463–1475.

Brody, G. H., Flor, D. L., Hollett-Wright, N., & McCoy, J. K. (1998). Children's development of alcohol use norms: Contributions of parent and sibling norms, children's temperaments, and parent–child discussions. *Journal of Family Psychology, 12*, 209–219.

Brook, J. S., Brook, D. W., Gordon, A. S., Whiteman, M., & Cohen, P. (1990). The psychosocial etiology of adolescent drug use: A family interactional approach. *Genetic, Social, and General Psychology Monographs, 116*(2), 111–267.

Brown, B. B., Lohr, M. J., & McClenahan, E. L. (1986). Early adolescents' perceptions of peer pressure. *Journal of Early Adolescence, 6*(2), 139–154.

Brown, S. A., Goldman, N. S., Inn, A., & Anderson, L. R. (1980). Expectations of reinforcement from alcohol: Their domain and relation to drinking patterns. *Journal of Consulting and Clinical Psychology, 48*, 419–426.

Bruner, J. (1990). *Acts of meaning.* Cambridge, MA: Harvard University Press.

Bry, B. (1983). Predicting drug use: Review and reformulation. *The International Journal of the Addictions, 18*, 223–233.

Bry, B., Catalano, R. F., Kumpfer, K. L., Lochman., J. E., & Szapocznik, J. (1999). Scientific findings from family prevention intervention research. In R. Ashery, K. Kumpfer, & E. Robertson (Eds.), *Drug abuse prevention through family interventions* (NIDA Monograph 177). Rockville, MD: U.S. Department of Health and Human Services, NIH.

Bukoski, W. J. (1985). School-based substance abuse prevention: A review of program research. Special Issue: Childhood chemical abuse, prevention and intervention. *Journal of Children in Contemporary Society, 18*, 95–115.

Bullough, E. (1912). "Physical distance" as a factor in art on aesthetic principle. *British Journal of Psychology, 5*, 87–118.

Burke, K. (1941). *The philosophy of literary form.* Berkeley, CA: University of California Press.

Burke, K. (1954). *Permanence and change* (2nd ed.). Berkeley, CA: University of California Press.

Burke, K. (1959). *Attitudes towards history* (3rd ed.). Berkeley, CA: University of California Press.

Burleson, B. R., Wilson, S. R., Waltman, M. S., Goering, E. M., Ely, T. K., & Whaley, B. B. (1988). Item desirability effects in compliance-gaining research: Seven studies documenting artifacts in strategy selection and procedure. *Human Communication Research, 14*, 429–486.

Bush, P. J., & Ionnotti, R. J. (1985). The development of children's health orientations and behaviors: Lessons for substance abuse prevention. *National Institute on Drug Abuse: Research Monographs Series, 56*, 45–74.

Caetano, R. (1985). Drinking patterns and alcohol problems among Hispanics in the U.S.: A review. *Drug and Alcohol Dependence, 12*, 37–49.

Califano, J. A. (1997). *National Center on Addiction and Substance Abuse Report III.* Washington, DC: National Center on Addiction and Substance Abuse.

Camarena, P. M., Sarigiani, P. A., & Petersen, A. C. (1990). Gender-specific pathways to intimacy in early adolescence. *Journal of Youth and Adolescence, 19*, 19–44.

Capo, K. E. (1983). Performance as social dialect. *Literature in Performance, 4*, 31–36.

Carbaugh, D. (1988). *Talking American.* Norwood, NJ: Ablex.

Carbaugh, D. (1989). Fifty terms for talk: A cross-cultural study. *International and Intercultural Communication Annual, 13*, 93–120.

Carr, D. (1986). *Time, narrative, and history.* Bloomington, IN: Indiana University Press.

Castro, F. G. (1995). Drug use and drug-related issues. In C. Molina & M. Aguirre-Molina (Eds.), *Latino health in the US: A growing challenge* (pp. 425–446). Washington, DC: American Public Health Association.

Castro, F. G., & Booth, M. W. (1992). Drug use and related drug problems among Latinos. In C. Molina, P. Lecca, & M. Aguire (Eds.), *Latino health: American's growing challenge.* Washington, DC: American Public Health Association.

Castro, F., Sharp, E., Barrington, E. H., & Walton, M. (1991). Drug abuse and identity in Mexican Americans: Theoretical and empirical considerations. *Hispanic Journal of Behavioral Sciences, 13*, 209–225.

Catalano, R. F., Gainey, R. R., Fleming, C. B., Haggerty, K. P., & Johnson, N. O. (1999). An experimental intervention with families of substance abusers: One-year follow-up of the focus on families project. *Addiction, 94*, 241–254.

Catalano, R. F., Haggerty, K. P., Fleming, C. B., & Brewer, D. D. (1997). Focus on families: Scientific findings from family prevention intervention research (NIDA Research Monograph).

Catalano, R. F., Haggerty, K. P., Gainey, R. R., & Hoppe, M. J. (1997). Reducing parental risk factors for children's substance misuse: Preliminary outcomes with opiate-addicted parents. *Substance Use and Misuse, 32,* 699–721.

Catalano, R. F., Haggerty, K. P., Gainey, R. R., & Hoppe, M. J. (1995). *Reducing parental risk factors for children's substance abuse: Preliminary outcomes with opiate-addicted parents.* Seattle, WA: Social Development Research Group.

Catalano, R. F., Morrison, D. M., Wells, E. A., Gillmore, M. R., Iritani, B., & Hawkins, J. D. (1992). Ethnic differences in family factors related to early drug initiation. *Journal of Studies on Alcohol, 53,* 208–217.

Center for Substance Abuse Prevention (1998). *Prevention enhancement protocol system (PEPS).* DHHS Pub. No. (SMA) 3224-FY98. U.S. Department of Health and Human Services, Substance Abuse and Mental Health Services Administration.

Children's Defense Fund. (1994). *The state of America's children yearbook.* Washington, DC: CDF Publications.

Christopher, F. S. (1994). Adolescent sexuality: Trying to explain the magic and the mystery. In N. A. Vanzetti & S. Duck (Eds.), *A lifetime of relationships* (pp. 213–242). Pacific Grove, CA: Brooks/Cole.

Cialdini, R., Reno, R., & Kallgren, C. (1990). A focus theory on normative conduct: Recycling the concept of norms of reduced littering in public places. *Journal of Personality and Social Psychology, 58*(6), 1015–1026.

Clark, R., & Crockett, W. H. (1971). Subjects' initial positions, exposure to varying positions, and the risky shift. *Psychonomic Science, 23,* 277–279.

Clark, R. A., & Delia, J. G. (1977). Cognitive complexity, social perspective taking, and functional persuasive skills in second- to ninth-grade children. *Human Communication Research, 3,* 128–134.

Clark, R. A., & Delia, J. G. (1979). Topoi and rhetorical competence. *The Quarterly Journal of Speech, 65,* 187–206.

Clark, R. A., O'Dell, L. L., & Willinganz, S. (1986). The development of compromising as an alternative to persuasion. *Central States Speech Journal, 37,* 220–224.

Cohn, D. A., Patterson, C. J., & Christopoulos, C. (1991). The family and children's peer relations. *Journal of Social and Personal Relationships, 8,* 315–346.

Coie, J. S., Dodge, K. A., & Coppotelli, H. (1982). A behavioral analysis of emerging social status in boys' groups. *Child Development, 54,* 1400–1416.

Collier, M. J., Ribeau, S., & Hecht, M. L. (1986). Intracultural rules and outcomes within three domestic cultural groups. *International Journal of Intercultural Relations, 10,* 439–457.

Collins, R. L. (1995). Issues of ethnicity in research on the prevention of substance abuse. In G. J. Botvin, S. Schinke, & M. A. Orlandi (Eds.), *Drug abuse prevention with multiethnic youth* (pp. 28–45). Thousand Oaks, CA: Sage.

Collins, W. A., & Repinski, D. J. (1994). Relationships during adolescence: Continuity and change in interpersonal perspective. In R. Montemayor & G. R. Adams (Eds.), *Personal relationships during adolescence: Advances in adolescent development* (pp. 7–36). Thousand Oaks, CA: Sage.

Conger, R. D., & Elder, G. H. Jr. (1994). *Families in troubled times: Adapting to change in rural America.* New York: Aldine de Gruyter.

Conquergood, D. (1986). *Between experience and meaning: Performance as a paradigm for meaningful action.* A paper presented at the Speech Communication Association Convention, Dallas, TX.

Cook-Gumperz, J. (1993). The relevant text: Narrative, storytelling, and children's understanding of genre: Response to Egan. *Linguistics and Education, 5,* 155–165.

Coombs, R. H., Paulson, M. J., & Richardson, M. A. (1991). Peer vs. parental influence in substance use among Hispanic and Anglo children and adolescents. *Journal of Youth and Adolescence, 20,* 73–88.

Coventry Drug and Alcohol Council. (1987). *Summary of study on drug and alcohol use by students in Coventry schools.* Unpublished report.

Craig, M. E., Kalichman, S. C., & Follingstad, D. R. (1989). Verbal coercive sexual behavior among college students. *Archives of Sexual Behavior, 18,* 421–434.

Csikszentmihalyi, M., & Larson, R. (1978). Intrinsic rewards and school crime. *Crime and Delinquency, 24,* 322–330.

Csikszentmihalyi, M., Larson, R., & Prescott, S. (1977). The ecology of adolescent activity. *Journal of Youth and Adolescence, 6,* 281–294.

Cutter, H. S. C., & Fisher, J. C. (1980). Family experience and the motives for drinking. *International Journal of Addictions, 18,* 223–233.

Daly, J. A., Bell, R. A., Glenn, P. J., & Lawrence, S. (1985). Conceptualizing conversational complexity. *Human Communication Research, 12,* 30–53.

Decker, P. J., & Nathan, B. R. (1985). *Behavior modeling training: Principles and applications.* New York: Praeger.

Delia, J. G., Kline, S. L., & Burleson, B. R. (1979). The development of persuasive communication strategies in kindergartners through twelfth graders. *Communication Monographs, 46,* 241–256.

deTurk, M. A., (1985). A transactional analysis of compliance-gaining behavior: Effects of noncompliance, relational contexts, and actors' gender. *Human Communication Research, 12,* 54–78.

Dielman, T., Butchart, A., & Shope, J. (1993). Structural equation model test of patterns in family interaction, peer alcohol use, and intrapersonal predictors of adolescent alcohol use and misuse. *Journal of Drug Education, 23*(3), 273–316.

Dillard, J. P. (1990). A goal-driven model of interpersonal influence. In J. P. Dillard (Ed.), *Seeking compliance: The production of interpersonal influence messages* (pp. 41–56). Scottsdale, AZ: Gorsuch Scarisbrick.

Dishion, T. J. (1997, September). *Advances in family-based interventions to adolescent drug abuse prevention.* Paper presented at the National Conference on Drug Abuse Prevention Research, Washington, DC.

Dishion, T. J., French D., & Patterson, G. R. (1995). The development and ecology of antisocial behavior. In D. Cicchetti & D. Cohen (Eds.) *Manual of developmental psychopathology: Vol. 2. Risk, disorder, and adaptation* (pp. 421–471). New York: Wiley.

Dishion, T. J., & Kavanagh, K. (1999). *Adolescent problem behavior: Theory and intervention.* New York, NY: Guilford Press

Dixson, M. D. (1995). Models and perspectives of parent–child communication. In T. J. Socha & G. H. Stamp (Eds.), *Parents, children, and communication* (pp. 43–62). Mahwah, NJ: Lawrence Erlbaum Associates.

Dodge, K. A. (1991). The structure and function of reactive and proactive aggression. In D. J. Pepler & K. H. Rubin (Eds.), *The development and treatment of childhood aggression* (pp. 201–218). Hillsdale, NJ: Lawrence Erlbaum Associates.

Domino, G. (1983). Impact of the film "One Flew Over the Cuckoo's Nest" on attitudes toward mental illness. *Psychological Reports, 53,* 179–182.

Donovan, J. E., & Jessor, R. (1985). Structure of problem behavior in adolescence and young adulthood. *Journal of Consulting and Clinical Psychology, 53,* 890–904.

Douvan, E., & Adelson, J. (1966). *The adolescent experience.* New York: Wiley.

Downs, W. R., & Robertson, J. F. (1987/1988). Family dynamics and adolescent alcohol use: A path analysis with a treatment sample. *Journal of Applied Social Sciences, 12,* 24–25.

Downs, W. R., & Rose, S. R. (1991). The relationship of adolescent peer groups to the incidence of psychosocial problems. *Adolescence, 26*(102), 472–492.

Dryfoos, J. G. (1987). *Youth at risk: One in four in jeopardy.* Report submitted to the Carnegie Corporation. Available from author, 20 Circle Drive, Hastings-on-Hudson, NY, 10706.

Dryfoos, J. G. (1990). *Adolescents at risk.* New York: Oxford University Press.

Duck, S. (1994). *Meaningful relationships: Talking, sense, and relating.* Thousand Oaks, CA: Sage.

Duncan, H. (1965). *Introduction in Kenneth Burke Permanence and Change* (2nd ed.). Berkeley, CA: University of California Press.

Duncan, T. E., Duncan, S. C., & Hops, H. (1994). The effects of family cohesiveness and peer encouragement on the development of adolescent alcohol use: A cohort-sequential analysis approach to the analysis of longitudinal data. *Journal of Studies of Alcohol, 55,* 588–599.

Duncan, D. F., & Petosa, R. (1995). Social and community factors associated with drug use and abuse among adolescents. In T. P. Gullota, G. R. Adams, & R. Montemayor (Eds.), *Substance misuse in adolescence.* Thousand Oaks, CA: Sage.

Dunphy, D. C. (1963). The social structure of urban adolescent peer groups. *Sociometry, 26,* 230–246.

Durlack, J. A. (1995). *School-based prevention programs for children and adolescents* (Vol. 34). Thousand Oaks, CA: Sage.

Eagly, A. H. (1983). Gender and social influence: A social psychological analysis. *American Psychologist, 38,* 971–981.

Eagly, A. H. (1987). *Sex differences in social behavior: A social-role interpretation.* Hillsdale, NJ: Lawrence Erlbaum Associates.

Ebbeson, E., & Bowers, R. (1974). Proportion of risky to conservative arguments in a group discussion and choice shift. *Journal of Personality and Social Psychology, 29,* 316–327.

Eldred, C. A., & Washington, M. N. (1976). Interpersonal relationships in heroin use men and women and their role in treatment outcome. *International Journal of the Addictions, 11,* 117–130.

Ellickson, P. L. (1984). *Project alert: A smoking and drug prevention experiment.* Santa Monica, CA: Rand.

Ellickson, P. L, Hays, R. D, & Bell, R. M. (1992). Stepping through the drug use sequence: Longitudinal scalogram analysis of initiation and regular use. *Journal of Abnormal Psychology, 101,* 441–451.

Elliot, T. R., & Byrd, E. K. (1983). Attitude change toward disability through television portrayal. *Journal of Applied Rehabilitation Counseling, 14,* 35–37.

Elliott, D. S., & Morse, B. J. (1989). Delinquency and drug use as risk factors in teenage sexual activity. *Youth and Society, 21,* 32–60.

Ellis, M. (1973). *Why people play.* Englewood Cliffs, NJ: Prentice-Hall.

Erickson, M. H. (1948). Hypnotic psychotherapy. In *The medical clinics of North America, 32,* 571–583.

Erickson, M. H. (1958). Pediatric hypnotherapy. *American Journal of Clinical Hypnosis, 1,* 25–29.

Erikson, E. (1968). *Identity: Youth and crisis.* New York: Norton.

Escobedo, L. G., Remington, P. L., & Anda, R. F. (1989). Long-term secular trends in initiation of cigarette smoking among Hispanics in the United States. *Public Health Reports, 104,* 583–587.

Felix-Ortiz, M., & Newcomb, M. D. (1995). Cultural identity and drug use among Latino and Latina adolescents. In G. J. Botvin, S. Schinke, & M. A. Orlandi (Eds.), *Drug abuse prevention with multiethnic youth* (pp. 147–168). Thousand Oaks, CA: Sage.

Finnegan, L. P. (1979). Women in treatment. In R. I. DuPont, A. Goldstein, & J. O'Donnel (Eds.), *Handbook of drug abuse* (pp. 121–132). Rockville, MD: NIDA.

Fisher, W. R. (1978). Toward a logic of good reasons. *The Quarterly Journal of Speech, 64,* 376–384.

Fitch, F. J., & Papantonio, A. (1983). Men who batter: Some pertinent characteristics. *Journal of Nervous and Mental Disease, 171*(3), 190–192.

Fitzpatrick, M. A., & Badzinski, D. M. (1994). All in the family: Interpersonal communication in kin relationships. In M. L. Knapp & G. R. Miller (Eds.), *Handbook of interpersonal communication* (2nd ed., pp. 726–771). Beverly Hills, CA: Sage.

Flannery, D. J., Vazsonyi, A. T., Torquati, J., & Fridrich, A. (1994). Ethnic and gender differences in risk for early adolescent substance use. *Journal of Youth and Adolescence, 23*, 195–213.

Flay, B. (1985). Psychosocial approaches to smoking. *Health Psychology, 4*, 449–488.

Flay, B. (1986). Mass media linkages with school-based programs for drug abuse prevention. *Journal of School Health, 56*, 402–406.

Forney, M. A., Forney, P. D., & Ripley, W. K. (1989). Predictor variables of adolescent drinking. *Advances in Alcohol Substance Abuse, 8*, 97–117.

Foxcroft, D. R., & Lowe, G. (1995). Adolescent drinking, smoking, and other substance use involvement: Links with perceived family life. *Journal of Adolescence, 18*(2), 159–177.

Freeland, J. B., & Campbell, R. S. (1973). The social context of first marijuana use. *International Journal of Addictions, 8*, 317–324.

Frydenberg, E. L., & Lewis, R. (1993). Boys play sport and girls turn to others: Age, gender and ethnicity as determinants of coping. *Journal of Adolescence, 16*, 253–278.

Furman, W., & Wehner, E. A. (1994). Romantic views: Toward a theory of romantic adolescent relationships. In R. Montemayor, G. R. Adams, & T. P. Gullota (Eds.), *Advances in adolescent development: Relationships in adolescence* (pp. 168–195). Thousand Oaks, CA: Sage.

Gadamer, H. G. (1982). *Truth and method.* New York: Crossroads.

Garfinkel, H. (1967). *Studies in ethnomethodology.* Englewood Cliffs, NJ: Prentice-Hall.

Garton, A., & Pratt, C. (1987). Participation and interest in leisure activities by adolescent school children. *Journal of Adolescence, 10*, 341–351.

Geertz, C. (1973). *The interpretation of cultures.* New York: Basic Books.

Geertz, C. (1976). "From the native's point of view": On the nature of anthropological understanding. In K. H. Basso & H. A. Selby (Eds.), *Meaning in anthropology* (pp. 221–237). Albuquerque: University of New Mexico Press.

Gergen, K. J., & Gergen, M. M. (1986). Narrative form and the construction of psychological science. In T. R. Sarbin (Ed.), *Narrative psychology* (pp. 22–44). New York: Praeger.

Gil, A. G., Vega, W. A., & Biafora, F. (1998). Temporal influences of family structure and family risk factors on drug use initiation in a multiethnic sample of adolescent boys. *Journal of Youth and Adolescence, 27*, 373–393.

Gilchrist, L. D., Snow, W. A., Lodish, D., & Schinke, S. (1985). The relationship of cognitive and behavioral skills to adolescent tobacco smoking. *Journal of School Health, 55*, 132–134.

Gilligan, S. G. (1987). *Therapeutic trances.* New York: Brunner/Mazel.

Gimmestad, B. J., & Dechiara, E. (1982). Dramatic plays: A vehicle for prejudice reduction in the elementary school. *Journal of Education Research, 76*, 45–49.

Glantz, M. D., & Pickens, R. W. (1991). Vulnerability to drug use: Introduction and overview. In M. D. Glantz & R. W. Pickens (Eds.), *Vulnerability to drug abuse* (pp.1–14). Washington, DC: American Psychological Association.

Glaser, B. G. (1992). *Emergence vs. forcing: Basics of grounded theory analysis.* Mill Valley, CA: Sociology Press.

Glaser, B., & Strauss, A. (1967). *The discovery of grounded theory.* Chicago, IL: Aldine.

Glicksman, L., Douglas, R. R., & Smythe, C. (1983). The impact of a high school alcohol education program utilizing a live theatrical performance: A comparative study. *Journal of Drug Education, 13*, 229–248.

Glynn, T. J., & Haenlein, M. (1988). Family theory and research on adolescent drug use: A review. *Journal of Chemical Dependency Treatment, 1*, 39–56.

Goffman, E. (1959). *The presentation of self in everyday life.* New York: Doubleday.

Goffman, E. (1967). *Interaction ritual: Essays on face to face behavior.* Garden City, NY: Doubleday.

Goldstein, A. P., Reagles, K. R., & Amann, L. L. (1990). *Refusal skills: Preventing drug use in adolescents.* Champaign, IL: Research Press.

Goodchilds, J. D., & Zellman, G. L. (1984). Sexual signaling and sexual aggression in adolescent relationships. In N. H. Malamuth & E. Donnerstein (Eds.), *Pornography and sexual aggression* (pp. 233–243). San Diego: Academic Press.

Goodenough, W. H. (1971). *Culture, language, and society.* Reading, MA: Addison-Wesley.

Gordon, D. (1978). *Therapeutic metaphors.* Cupertino, CA: Meta Publications.

Gossett, J. T., Lewis, J. M., & Austin-Phillips, V. (1980). Extent and prevalence of illicit drug use as reported by 56,745 students. In J. E. Mayer & W. J. Filstead (Eds.), *Adolescence and alcohol* (pp. 301–342). Cambridge, MA: Ballinger.

Graber, J. A., Brooks-Gunn, J., & Peterson, A. C. (Eds.). (1996). *Transitions through adolescence: Interpersonal domains and contexts.* Hillsdale, NJ: Lawrence Erlbaum Associates.

Grusec, J. E., & Goodnow, J. J. (1994). Impact of parental discipline methods on the child's internalization of values: A reconceptualization of current points of view. *Developmental Psychology, 30,* 4–19

Gullota, T., Adams, G., & Montemayor, R. (Eds.) (1995). *Substance abuse in adolescence.* Thousand Oaks, CA: Sage.

Guerra, N. G., Huesmann, L. R., & Hanish, L. (1995). The role of normative beliefs in children's social behavior. In N. Eisenberg (Ed.), *Social development. Review of personality and social psychology* (pp. 140–158). Thousand Oaks, CA: Sage.

Haggerty, K. P., Mills, E., & Catalano, R. F. (1991). *Focus on families: Parent training curriculum.* Seattle, WA: Social Development Research Group.

Hale, C. L. (1982). An investigation of the relationship between cognitive complexity and listener-adapted communication. *Central States Speech Journal, 33,* 339–344.

Haley, J. (1976). *Problem-solving therapy.* New York: Harper & Row.

Haley, J. (1986). *Uncommon therapy.* New York: W. W. Norton.

Hansen, W. B. (1991). School-based substance abuse prevention: A review of the state of the art in curriculum, 1980–1990. *Health Education Research, 7(*3), 403–430.

Hansen, W. B., Graham, J. W., Wolkenstein, B. H., Lundy, B. Z., Pearson, J., Flay, B. R., & Johnson, C. A. (1988). Differential impact of three alcohol prevention curricula on hypothesized mediating variables. *Journal of Drug Education, 18*(2), 143–153.

Hansen, W. B., Johnson, C. A., Flay, B. R., Graham, J. W., & Sobel, J. (1988). Affective and social influence approaches to the prevention of multiple substance abuse among seventh grade students: Results from project SMART. *Preventive Medicine, 17,* 135–154.

Hansen, W. B., & Ponton, L. E. (Eds.). (1996). *Handbook of adolescent health risk behavior.* New York: Plenum.

Hanson, D. J. (1982). The effectiveness of alcohol and drug education. *Journal of Alcohol & Drug Education, 27,* 1–13.

Harford, T. C. (1986). Drinking patterns among black and nonblack adolescents: Results of a national survey. *Annals of the New York Academy of Science, 472,* 130–141.

Harrington, N. G. (1995). The effects of college students' alcohol resistance strategies. *Health Communication, 7,* 371–391.

Harrington, N. G. (1996). Strategies used by college students to persuade peers to drink. *The Southern Communication Journal, 61,* 229–242.

Hartup, W. W. (1978) The social worlds of childhood. *American Psychologist, 34,* 944–950.

Hartup, W. W., & van Lieshout, C. (1995). Personality development in social context. *Annual Review of Psychology, 46,* 655–682.

Hawkins, J. D., Arthur, M. W., & Catalano, R. F. (1994). Preventing substance abuse. *Crime Justice, 18,* 197–281.

Hawkins, J. D., Catalano, R. F., Brown, E. O., & Vadasy, P. F. (1991). *Preparing for the drug free years: A program for parents.* Seattle, WA: Developmental Research and Programs.

Hawkins, J. D., Catalano, R. F., & Miller, J. Y. (1992). Risk and protective factors for alcohol and other drug problems in adolescence and early adulthood: Implications for substance abuse prevention. *Psychological Bulletin, 12,* 64–105.

Hays, R. D., & Ellickson, P. L. (1990). Guttman scale analysis of longitudinal data: A methodology and drug use applications. *International Journal of the Addictions, 25,* 1341–1352.

Hays, R. D., & Ellickson, P. L. (1996) Associations between drug use and deviant behavior in teenagers. *Addictive Behaviors, 21,* 291–302.

Hecht, M. L. (1984). Persuasive efficacy: A study of the relationship among type of change and degree of change, message strategies, and satisfying communication. *Western Journal of Speech Communication, 48,* 373–389.

Hecht, M. L. (1993). 2002—A research odyssey: Toward the development of a communication theory of identity. *Communication Monographs, 60,* 76–82.

Hecht, M. L., Alberts, J. K., & Miller-Rassulo, M. (1992). Resistance to drug offers among college students. *The International Journal of the Addictions, 27,* 995–1017.

Hecht, M. L., Andersen, P. A., & Ribeau, S. (1989). The cultural dimensions of nonverbal communication. In M. K. Asanti & W. B. Gudykunst (Eds.), *Handbook of intercultural communication* (pp. 163–185). Beverly Hills, CA: Sage.

Hecht, M. L., Collier, M. J., & Ribeau, S. (1993). *African-American communication: Ethnic identity and cultural interpretations.* Newbury Park, CA: Sage.

Hecht, M. L., Corman, S., & Miller-Rassulo, M. (1993). Evaluation of the drug resistance project: A comparison of film vs. live performance. *Health Communication, 5,* 75–88.

Hecht, M. L., & Driscoll, G. (1994). A comparison of the communication, social, situational, and individual factors associated with alcohol and other drugs. *The International Journal of the Addictions.*

Hecht, M. L., Larkey, L. K., & Johnson, J. N. (1992). African American and European American perceptions of problematic issues in interethnic communication. *Human Communication Research, 19,* 209–236.

Hecht, M., & Ribeau, S. (1991). Socio-cultural roots of ethnic identity: A look at Black America. *Journal of Black Studies, 21,* 501–513.

Hecht, M. L., Ribeau, S., & Alberts, J. K. (1989). An Afro-American perspective on interethnic communication. *Communication Monographs, 56,* 385–410.

Hecht, M. L., Ribeau, S., & Sedano, M. V. (1990). A Mexican-American perspective on interethnic communication. *International Journal of Intercultural Relations, 14,* 31–55.

Hecht, M. L., Trost, M. R., Bator, R. J., & MacKinnon, D. (1997). Ethnicity and sex similarities and differences in drug resistance. *Journal of Applied Communication Research, 25,* 75–97.

Hirschi, R. (1969). *Causes of delinquency.* Berkeley: University of California Press.

Hoffman, M. L. (1980). Moral development in adolescence. In J. Adelson (Ed.), *Handbook of adolescent psychology* (pp. 28–52). New York: Wiley.

Hopper, R., Koch, S., & Mandelbaum, J. (1986). Conversation analysis methods. In G. Ellis & W. A. Donohue (Eds.), *Contemporary issues in language and discourse processes* (pp. 169–186). Hillsdale, NJ: Lawrence Erlbaum Associates.

Houlberg, R., & Bishow, M. L. (1990, April). *Reaching kids who are reaching for drugs: Messages that reduce demand.* Paper presented at the Western States Communication Association Convention, San Diego, CA.

Howard, G. S. (1991). Culture tales: A narrative approach to thinking, cross-cultural psychology, and psychotherapy. *American Psychologist, 46,* 187–197.

Hser, Y., Anglin, M. D., & McGlothlin, W. (1987). Sex differences in addict careers: Initiation of use. *American Journal of Drug and Alcohol Abuse, 13,* 33–57.

Hunter, G. T. (1990). A survey of the social context of drinking among college women. *Journal of Alcohol and Drug Education, 35,* 73–80.

Hymes, D. (Ed.). (1964). *Language in culture and society.* New York: Harper & Row.

Hymes, D. (1972). Models of the interaction of language and the social life. In J. J. Gumperz & D. Hymes (Eds.), *Directions in sociolinguistics: The ethnography of communication* (pp. 35–71). New York: Holt, Rinehart, & Winston.

Irvine, J., & Kirkpatrick, W. (1972). The musical form in rhetorical exchange: Theoretical considerations. *Quarterly Journal of Speech, 58,* 272–284.

Iso-ahola, I., & Weissinger, E. (1987). Leisure and boredom. *Journal of Social and Clinical Psychology, 5,* 356–364.

Jessor, R., Chase, J. A., & Donovan, J. E. (1980). Psychosocial correlates of marijuana use and problem drinking in a national sample of adolescents. *American Journal of Public Health, 70,* 604–613.

Jessor, R., Donovan, J., & Costa, F. (1991). *Beyond adolescence: Problem behavior and young adult development.* New York: Cambridge University Press.

Jessor, R., & Jessor, S. L. (1977). *Problem behavior and psycho-social development.* New York: Academic Press.

Jessor, R., & Jessor, S. L. (1978). Theory testing in longitudinal research on marijuana use (pp. 60–82). In D. B. Kandel (Ed.), *Longitudinal research on drug use.* Washington, DC: Hemisphere-Wiley.

Joanning, H., Quinn, W., Thomas, F., & Mullen, R. (1992). Treating adolescent drug abuse: A comparison of family systems therapy, group therapy, and family drug education. *Journal of Marital and Family Therapy, 18,* 345–370.

Johnson, B. B. (1987). Sexual abuse prevention: A rural interdisciplinary effort. *Child Welfare, 66,* 165–173.

Johnson, C. A., Pentz, M., Weber, M., Dwyer, J., Baer, N., MacKinnon, D., & Hansen, W. (1990). Relative effectiveness of comprehensive community programming for drug abuse prevention with high-risk and low-risk adolescents. *Journal of Consulting and Clinical Psychology, 58*(4), 447–456.

Johnson, J., & Ettema, J. S. (1982). *Positive images: Breaking stereotypes with children's television.* Beverly Hills, CA: Sage.

Johnston, L. D., Bachman, J. G., & O'Malley, P. M. (1993). *Monitoring the future: Questionnaire responses from the nations high school seniors.* Ann Arbor, MI: Institute for Social Research.

Johnston, L. D., O'Malley, P. M., & Bachman, J. G. (1987). *National trends in drug use and related factors among American high school students and young adults, 1975–1986.* Washington, DC: U.S. Government Printing Office.

Johnston, L. D., O'Malley, P. M., & Bachman, J. G. (1989). *Drug use, drinking, and smoking: National survey results from high school, college, and young adult populations, 1975–1988.* Washington, DC: U.S. Government Printing Office.

Johnston, L. D., O'Malley, P. M., & Bachman, J. G. (1996). *National survey results on drug use from the Monitoring the Future study, 1975–1995.* (NIH Pub. No. 97-4139). Rockville, MD: National Institute on Drug Abuse.

Johnston, L. D., O'Malley, P. M., & Bachman, J. G. (1998). *National survey results on drug use from the Monitoring the Future study, 1975–1997. Volume I: Secondary school students.* (NIH Publication No. 98-4345), and *Volume II: College students and young adults.* (NIH Publication No. 98-4346). Rockville, MD: National Institute on Drug Abuse.

Jones, C. L., & Battjes, R. J. (Eds.). (1985). *Etiology of drug abuse: Implications for prevention* (NIDA Research Monograph No. 56, pp. 13–44). Washington, DC: Government Printing Office.

Kaczmarek, M. G., & Backlund, B. A. (1991). Disenfranchised grief: The loss of an adolescent relationship. *Adolescence, 26,* 253–259.

Kafka, R. R., & London, P. (1991). Communication in relationships and adolescence substance use: The influence of parents and friends. *Adolescence, 26*(103), 587–598.

Kalichman, S. C., Tannenbaum, L., & Nachimson, D. (1998). Personality and cognitive factors influencing substance use and sexual risk for HIV infection among gay and bisexual men. *Psychology of Addictive Behaviors, 12,* 262–271.

Kallan, J. E. (1998). Drug abuse-related mortality in the United States: Patterns and correlates. *The American Journal of Drug and Alcohol Abuse, 24,* 103–117.

Kameoka, V. A., & Lecar, S. (1996). *The effects of a family-focused intervention on reducing risk for substance abuse among Asian and Pacific-Island youths and families: Evaluation of the Strengthening Hawaii's Families Project.* Available from the Coalition for a Drug-Free Hawaii, University of Hawaii.

Kandel, D. B. (1983). Commonalities in drug use: A sociological perspective. In P. K. Levison, D. R. Gerstein, & D. R. Maloff (Eds.), *Commonalities in substance abuse and habitual behavior* (pp. 3–28). Lexington, MA: Lexington Books.

Kandel, D. B. (1985). On processes of peer influences in adolescent drug use: A developmental perspective. *Advances in Alcohol and Substance Abuse, 4,* 139–163.

Kandel, D. (1990). Parenting styles, drug use, and children's adjustment in families of young adults. *Journal of Marriage and the Family, 52,* 183–218.

Kandel, D. B. (1995) Ethnic differences in drug use: Patterns and paradoxes. In G. J. Botvin, S. Schinke, & M. A. Orlandi (Eds.), *Drug abuse prevention with multiethnic youth* (pp. 81–104). Thousand Oaks, CA: Sage.

Kandel, D. B. (1996). The parental and peer contexts of adolescent deviance. An algebra of interpersonal influences. *Journal of Drug Issues, 26,* 289–315.

Kaplan, H. B., Martin, S., & Robbins, C. (1982). Application of a general theory of deviant behavior: Self derogation and adolescent drug use. *Journal of Health and Social Behavior, 23,* 274–294.

Kaplan, M. S. (1979). Patterns of alcohol beverage use. *Journal of Alcohol and Drugs, 24,* 26–40.

Katriel, T., & Philipsen, G. (1981). What we need is communication: "Communication" as a cultural category in some American speech. *Communication Monographs, 48,* 301–317.

Kaufmann, E., & Borders, L. (1988). Ethnic family differences in adolescent substance use. Journal of *Chemical Dependency Treatment, 1,* 99–121.

Kellar-Guenther, Y., Moon, D. G., & Trost, M. R. (1998, February). *The role of personal relationships in drug offer situations.* Paper presented at the meeting of the Western States Communication Association, Denver, CO.

Kern, J. M. (1982). Predicting the impact of assertive, empathic-assertive and non-assertive: The assertiveness of the assertee. *Behavior Therapy, 13,* 486–498.

Kleiber, D. A., & Richards, W. H. (1985). Leisure and recreation in adolescence: Limitations and potential. In M. Wade (Ed.), *Constraints on leisure* (pp. 289–317). Evanston, IL: Thomas Publishing.

Kline, S. L., & Floyd, C. H. (1990). On the art of saying no: The influence of social cognitive development on messages of refusal. *Western Journal of Speech Communication, 54*(5), 454–472.

Klingle, R. S., & Miller, M. (1998, April). *Family education efforts and family members' substance use as predictors of adolescent substance abuse.* Paper presented at the Western States Communication Association in Denver, CO.

Knapp, M. (1984). *Interpersonal communication and human relation-ships.* Boston: Allyn &Bacon.

Koch, S., & Deetz, S. (1981). Metaphor analysis of social reality in organizations. *Journal of Applied Communication Research, 9,* 1–15.

Kochman, T. C. (1982). *Black and white: Styles in conflict.* Chicago, IL: University of Chicago Press.

Korzenny, F., McClure, J., & Rzyttki, B. (1990). Ethnicity, communication, and drugs. *Journal of Drug Issues, 20,* 87–98.

Krizek, R. L., Hecht, M. L., & Miller, M. (1993). Language as an indicator of risk in the prevention of drug use. *Journal of Applied Communication Research, 21,* 245–262.

Kumpfer, K. L. (1989). Prevention of alcohol and drug abuse: A critical review of risk factors and prevention strategies. In A. Shaffer, D. Phillips, I. Enzer, & N. Norbert (Eds.), *Prevention of mental disorders due to alcohol and drug use in children and adolescents* (OSAP Monograph #2, DHHS publication # 1646). Washington, DC: Office of Substance Abuse Prevention.

Kumpfer, K. L. (1993). *Resiliency and AOD use prevention in high risk youth.* Unpublished manuscript.

Kumpfer, K. L., & Alvarado, R. (1995). Strengthening families to prevent drug use in multiethnic youth. In G. J. Botvin, S. Schinke, & M. A. Orlandi (Eds.), *Drug abuse prevention with multiethnic youth* (pp. 255–294). Thousand Oaks, CA: Sage.

Kumpfer, K. L., Molgaard, V., & Spoth, R. (1996). Family interventions for the prevention of delinquency and drug use in special populations. In R. Peters & R. McMahon (Eds.), *Preventing childhood disorders, substance abuse, and delinquency.* Thousand Oaks, CA: Sage.

Kumpfer, K. L., & Turner, C. (1990). The social ecology model of adolescent substance abuse: Implications for prevention. *International Journal of Addictions, 25,* 435–463.

Kumpfer, K. L., & Turner, C. W. (1991). The social ecology model of adolescent substance abuse: Implications for prevention. *International Journal of the Addictions, 25,* 435–463.

Kumpfer, K. L., & Turner, C. W. (1993). The social etiology model of adolescents: Implications for prevention. *International Journal of the Addictions,* 610–648.

Kvaraceus, W. (1954). *The community and the delinquent.* New York: World Book.

LaGapia, J. J., & Wood, H. D. (1981). Friendships in disturbed adolescents. In S. W. Duck & R. Gilmour (Eds.), *Personal relationships 3: Personal relationships in disorder.* London: Academic Press.

Lakoff, G., & Johnson, M. (1980). *Metaphors we live by.* Chicago: University of Chicago Press.

Lamb, M. E. (1996). Family, justice, and delinquency. *Family Relations, 45,* 355–380.

Lawrence, P. A. (1998). Psychological risk factors and substance abuse among young adults: A comparison of non-Hispanic Whites and Mexican Americans. In J. G. Power & T. Byrd (Eds.), *United States-Mexico border health: Issues for regional and migrant populations* (pp. 32–51). Thousand Oaks, CA: Sage.

Liddle, H. A. (1996). Family based treatment for adolescent problem behaviors: Overview of contemporary developments and introduction to the special section. *Journal of Family Psychology, 10,* 3–11.

Liddle, H. A., & Dakof, G. A. (1995). Efficacy of family therapy for drug abuse: Promising but not definitive. *Journal of Marital and Family Therapy, 21,* 511–536.

Lloyd, S. A., & Cate, R. M. (1985). Attributions associated with significant turning points in premarital relationship development and dissolution. *Journal of Personal and Social Relationships, 2,* 419–436.

Lollis, S., & Kuczynski, L. (1997). Beyond one hand clapping: Seeing bidirectionality in parent–child relations. *Journal of Social and Personal Relationships, 14* (4), 441–462.

Longshore, D., Grills, C., Anglin, M. D., & Annon, K. (1997). Desire for help among African-American drug users. *Journal of Drug Issues, 27,* 755–770.

MacKinnon, D., Johnson, C. A., Pentz, M. A., Dwyer, J. H., Hansen, W. B., Flay, B. R., & Wang, E. (1991). *Mediating mechanisms in a school-based drug prevention program: First year effects of the Midwestern Prevention Program.* New York: Health Press.

Makepeace, J. M. (1981). Courtship violence among college students. *Family Relations, 30,* 97–102.

Mann, C., Hecht, M. L., & Valentine, K. B. (1988). Performance in a social context: Date rape versus date right. *Central States Speech Journal, 39,* 269–280.

Markus, H., & Nurius, P. (1986). Possible selves. *American Psychologist, 41,* 954–969.

Marsiglia, F. F., Kulis, S., & Hecht, M. L. (1999, May). *Ethnic labels and ethnic identity as predictors of drug use and drug exposure among 7th-grade students.* Report submitted to the National Institute on Drug Abuse, National Institutes of Health, Washington, DC.

Marston, A. R., Jacobs, D. F., Singer, R. D., Widaman, K. F., & Little, T. D. (1988). Adolescents who apparently are invulnerable to drug, alcohol, and nicotine use. *Adolescence, 23,* 593–598.

Masten, A. S., Best, K. M., & Garmezy, N. (1990). Resilience and development: Contributions from the study of children who overcome adversity. *Development and Psychopathology, 2,* 425–444.

Mayer, J. E., & Ligman, J. D. (1989). Personality characteristics of adolescent marijuana users. *Adolescence, 24*, 965–976.

McBride, A. A., Joe, G. W., & Simpson, D. D. (1991). Prediction of long-term alcohol use, drug use, and criminality among inhalant users. *Hispanic Journal of Behavioral Science, 13*, 315–323.

McCurdy, J. (1986). The drug free school: *What school executives can do*. Arlington: National Schools, Public Relations Association.

McGee, L., & Newcomb, M. D. (1992). General deviance syndrome: Expanded hierarchical evaluations at four ages from early adolescence to adulthood. *Journal of Consulting and Clinical Psychology, 60*, 766–776.

McGuire, W. J. (1964). Inducing resistance to persuasion: Some contemporary approaches. In L. Berkowitz (Ed.), *Advances in experimental social psychology* (pp. 191–229). New York: Academic Press.

McLaughlin, M. L., Cody, M. J., & Robey, C. S. (1980). Situational influences on the selection of strategies to resist compliance gaining attempts. *Human Communication Research, 7*, 14–36.

McLaughlin, R. J., Bauer, P. E., Burnside, M. A., & Pokorny, A. D. (1985). Psychosocial correlates of alcohol use at two age levels during adolescence. *Journal of Studies in Alcohol, 46*, 212–218.

McQuillen, J. S. (1986). The development of listener-adapted compliance-gaining attempts. *Human Communication Research, 7*, 14–36.

McQuillen, J. S., Higginbotham, D. C., & Cummings, M. C. (1984). Compliance-resisting behaviors: The effects of age, agent, and types of request. R. N. Bostrom (Ed.), *Communication yearbook 8* (pp. 747–762). Beverly Hills, CA: Sage.

Metcalf, A. (1984). Teaching science through drama: An empirical investigation. *Research in Science and Technological Education, 2*, 77–81.

Meyer, A. L. (1995). Minimization of substance use: What can be said at this point? In T. P. Gullotta, G. R. Adams, & R. Montemayor (Eds.), *Substance misuse in adolescence* (pp. 201–232). Thousand Oaks, CA: Sage.

Mienczakowski, J. (1996). An ethnographic act: The construction of consensual theater. In C. Ellis & A. P. Bochner (Eds.), *Composing ethnography: Alternative forms of qualitative writing* (pp. 244–264). Walnut Creek, CA: AltaMira Press.

Mienczakowski, J., Smith, R., & Sinclair, M. (1996). On the road to Catharsis: A theoretical framework for change, *Qualitative Inquiry, 2*, 439–462.

Miller, M. (1998). The social process of drug resistance in a relational context. *Communication Studies, 49*, 358–375.

Miller, G., Boster, F., Roloff, M., & Seibold, D. (1977). Compliance-gaining message strategies: A typology and some findings concerning effects of situational differences. *Communication Monographs, 44*, 37–51.

Miller, M., Hecht, M. L., & Stiff, J. B. (1998). An exploratory measure of engagement with film and live media. *Journal of Illinois Speech and Theater, 56*, 69–86.

Miller-Rassulo, M. A., & Hecht, M. L. (1988). Performance as persuasion: Trigger scripting as a tool for education and persuasion. *Literature in Performance, VIII(2,)*, 40–55.

Moberg, D. P., & Piper, D. L. (1995, June). *Behavioral outcomes for the Healthy for Life Project*. Paper presented at the Society for Prevention Research, Scottsdale, AZ.

Molgaard, V., Kumpfer, K. L., & Spoth, R. (1994).*The Iowa Strengthening Families Program for pre and early teens*. Ames, IA: Iowa State University.

Moon, D. G., Hecht., M. L., Jackson, K. M., & Spellers, R. (1998). *Ethnic and gender differences and similarities in adolescent drug use and drug resistance process*. Paper presented at the National Communication Association conference in New York.

Moon, D. G., Jackson, K. M., & Hecht, M. L. (in press). Family risk and resiliency factors, substance use, and the drug resistance process in adolescence. *Journal of Drug Education*.

Moore, J. W. (1976). *Mexican Americans*. Englewood Cliffs, NJ: Prentice-Hall.

Morgan, M., & Grube, J. W. (1991). Closeness and peer group influence. *British Journal of Social Psychology, 30*, 159–169.

Mosback, P., & Leventhal, H. (1988). Peer group identification and smoking: Implications for intervention. *Journal of Abnormal Psychology, 97*, 238–245.

Muehlenhard, C. L., & Cook, S. W. (1988). Men's self-reports of unwanted sexual activity. *The Joy of Sex Research, 24*, 58–72.

Muehlenhard, C. L., & Linton, M. A. (1987). Date rape and sexual aggression in dating situations: Incidence and risk factors. *Journal of Counseling Psychology, 34*, 196–199.

National Institute on Alcohol Abuse and Alcoholism. (1986). *Communicating with youth about alcohol: Methods* (DHHS Pub. No. (ADM) 86B1429). Washington, DC: Superintendent of Documents, U.S. Government Printing Office.

National Institute on Drug Abuse. (1989). *Highlights of the 1988 National Household Survey on Drug Abuse* (NIDA capsule 20, #CB86-13.). Washington DC: U.S. Government Printing Office.

National Institute on Drug Abuse. (1992). *National household survey on drug abuse: Population estimates 1991*. Washington, DC: U.S. Government Printing Office..

National Institute on Drug Abuse. (1996). *National household survey on drug abuse: Population estimates 1995*. Washington, DC: U.S. Government Printing Office.

National Institutes on Health. (1997). *Mind over matter*. Publication No. 98-3592.

National School Safety Center. (1986). *Drug traffic and abuse in schools*. NSSC resource paper.

Needle, R., McCuggin, H., Wilson, M., Reineck, R., Lazar, A., & Mederer, H. (1986). Interpersonal influence in adolescent drug use—The role of older siblings, parents, and peers. *The International Journal of the Addictions, 21*(7), 739–766.

Neimeyer, R. A. (1995). Client-generated narratives in psychotherapy. In R. A. Neimeyer, & M. J. Mahmey, (Eds.), *Constructivism in psychotherapy* (pp. 231–246). Washington, DC: American Psychological Association.

Neimeyer, R. A., & Stewart, A. E. (1996). Trauma, healing, and the narrative emplotment of loss. *Families in Society: The Journal of Contemporary Human Services, 45*, 360–375.

Newcomb, M. D. (1992). Understanding the multidimensional nature of drug use and abuse: The role of consumption, risk factors, and protective factors. In M. D. Glantz & R. Pickens (Eds.), *Vulnerability to drug abuse* (pp. 255–297). Washington, DC: American Psychological Association.

Newcomb, M. D. (1995a). Drug use etiology among ethnic minority adolescents: Risk and protective factors. In G. J. Botvin, S. Schinke, & M. A. Orlandi (Eds.), *Drug abuse prevention with multiethnic youth* (pp. 105–129). Thousand Oaks, CA: Sage.

Newcomb, M. D. (1995b). Identifying high-risk youth: Prevalence and patterns of adolescent drug abuse. In E. Rahdert & D. Czechowicz (Eds.), *Adolescent drug abuse: Clinical assessment and therapeutic intervention* (Research Monograph 156). Rockville, MD: National Institute on Drug Abuse.

Newcomb, M. D., & Bentler, P. M. (1986). Substance use and ethnicity: Differential impact of peer and adult models. *Journal of Psychology, 120*, 83–95.

Newcomb, M. D., & Bentler, P. M. (1988). *Consequences of adolescent drug use: Impact on the lives of young adults*. Beverly Hills, CA: Sage.

Newcomb, M. D., Chou, C. P., Bentler, P. M., & Huba, G. J. (1988). Cognitive motivations for drug use among adolescents: Longitudinal tests of gender differences and predictors of change in drug use. *Journal of Counseling Psychology, 35*, 426–438.

Newcomb, M. D., Maddahian, E., & Bentler, P. M. (1986). Risk factors for drug use among adolescents: Concurrent and longitudinal analyses. *American Journal of Public Health, 76*, 525–537.

Newcomer, S. F., & Udry, J. R. (1987). Parental marital status effects on adolescent sexual behavior. *Journal of Marriage and the Family, 49*, 235–240.

Nolan, L. L. (1990, April). *The war on drugs: What we know*. Paper presented at the Western States Communication Association Convention, Sacramento, CA.

Noller, P. (1994). Relationships with parents in adolescence: Process and outcome. In R. Montemayor, G. T. Adams, & T. Gullota (Eds.), *Personal relationships during adolescence* (Vol. 6, pp. 37–77). Thousand Oaks, CA: Sage.

Norman, E. (1995). Personal factors related to substance misuse: Rick abatement and/or resiliency enhancement? In T. P. Gullotta, G. R. Adams, & R. Montemayor (Eds.), *Substance misuse in adolescence* (pp. 15–35). Thousand Oaks, CA: Sage.

Norris, J., & Cubbins, L. (1992). Dating, drinking, and rape: Effects of victim's assailant's alcohol, consumption on judgments of their behavior and traits. *Psychology of Women Quarterly, 16*, 179–191.

Novaceck, J., Raskin, R., & Hogan, R. (1991). Why do adolescents use drugs? Age, sex, and user differences. *Journal of Youth and Adolescence, 20*, 475–492.

Nurco, D. N. (1987). A discussion of validity. In B. E. Rouse, N. J. Kozel, & L. G. Richards (Eds.), *Self-report methods of reporting drug use* (pp. 46–67). Rockville, MD: National Institute on Drug Use.

O'Connor, T. G., Hetherington, E. M., & Clingempeel, W. G. (1997). Systems and bi-directional influences in families. *Journal of Social and Personal Relationships, 14*(4), 491–504.

O'Donnell, J. A., Besteman, K., & Jones, J. (1967). Marital history of narcotics addicts. *International Journal of the Addictions, 2*, 21–38.

Oetting, E. R., & Beauvais, F. (1983). The drug acquisition curve: A method for the analysis and prediction of drug epidemiology. *The International Journal of the Addictions, 18*, 1115–1129.

Oetting, E. R., & Beauvais, F. (1987). Common elements in youth drug abuse: Peer clusters and other psychosocial factors. *Journal of Drug Issues, 2*, 133–151.

O'Keefe, D. J., & Sypher, H. E. (1981). Cognitive complexity measure and the relationship of cognitive complexity to communication. *Human Communication Research, 8*, 72–92.

Olson, C. M., Horan, J. J., & Polansky, J. (1992). Counseling psychology perspectives: The problem of substance abuse (pp. 793–821). In S. D. Brown & R. W. Lent (Eds.), *Handbook of counseling psychology*. New York: Wiley.

Openshaw, D. K., Thomas, D. L., & Rollins, B. C. (1983). Socialization and adolescent self-esteem: Symbolic interactions and social learning explanations. *Adolescence, 18*, 317–329.

Osgood, D. W., Wilson, J. K., Bachman, J. G., O'Malley, P. M., & Johnston, L. D. (1996). Routine activities and individual deviant behaviors. *American Sociological Review, 61*, 635–655.

Padilla, E. R., Padilla, A. M., Morales, A., & Olmedo, E. L. (1979). Inhalant, marijuana and alcohol abuse among barrio children and adolescents. *International Journal of the Addictions, 14*, 943–964.

Page, B. (1990a). Music and lyrics to *"Killing time."* Phoenix, AZ: Wildwest Productions.

Page, B. (1990b). Music and lyrics to *"Don't worry, we're only making a movie."* Phoenix, AZ: Wildwest Productions.

Palermo, J., & Hetherington, C. (1985). Situational drama: A tool for breaking the silence about alcohol use. *Journal of College Student Personnel, 26*, 87–88.

Palmer, R. B., & Liddle, H. A. (1994). Intervention implications of contemporary perspectives about adolescent drug abuse. In T. Gullota, G. Adams, & R. Montemayor (Eds.), *Advances in adolescent development: Problem behaviors of adolescence*. Newbury Park, CA: Sage.

Papp, P. (1982). Staging reciprocal metaphors. *Family Process, 11*, 1453–1467.

Parker, K. (1995a). Predictors of alcohol and drug use: A multi-ethnic comparison. *Journal of Social Psychology, 135*(5), 581–591.

Parker, K. (1995b). Prevalence of cocaine use: A multi-ethnic comparison. *The Western Journal of Black Studies, 19*(1), 30–47.

Patterson, C. J., Vaden, N. A., & Kuperschmidt, J. B. (1991). Family background, recent life events and peer rejection during childhood. *Journal of Social and Personal Relationships, 8*, 347–361.

Patterson, G. R. (1986). Performance models for antisocial boys. *American Psychologist, 41*, 432–444.

Patterson, G. R. (1982). *A social learning approach: Coercive family process*. Eugene, OR: Castalia.

Patterson, G. R., Reid, J. B., & Dishion, T. J. (1992). *A social learning approach for antisocial boys*. Eugene, OR: Castalia.

Patterson, G. R., & Yoerger, K. (1997). A developmental model for late-onset delinquency. In W. D. Osgood (Ed.), *Motivation and delinquency: Vol. 44 of the Nebraska Symposium on motivation* (pp. 119–177). Lincoln: University of Nebraska Press.

Pelias, R. J. (1984). Oral interpretation as a training method for increasing perspective-taking abilities. *Communication Education, 33*, 143–151.

Pentz, M. A., Cormack, C., Flay, B. R., Hansen, W. B., & Johnson, C. A. (1986). Balancing program and research integrity in community drug abuse prevention: Project STAR approach. *Journal of School Health, 56*, 389–393.

Pentz, M. A., Dwyer, J. H., MacKinnon, D. P., Flay, B. R., Hansen, W. B., Wang, E. Y., & Johnson, C. A. (1989). A multicommunity trial for primary prevention of adolescent drug abuse: Effects on drug prevalence. *Journal of the American Medical Association, 261*, 3259–3266.

Pentz, M. A., Trebow, E. A., & Hansen, W. B. (1990). Effects of program implementation on adolescent drug use behavior: The Midwestern Prevention Project. *Evaluation Review, 14*, 264–289.

Perkins, H. W., & Berkowitz, A. D. (1984). Using student alcohol surveys: Notes on clinical and educational program applications. *Journal of Alcohol and Drug Education, 31*(2), 44–51.

Perse, E. M., & Ruben, A. M. (1988). Audience activity and viewing of a dramatic production. *Speech Monographs, 32*, 209–218.

Peterson, A. C. (1988). Adolescent development. *Annual Review of Psychology, 39*, 583–608.

Peterson, G. W., & Leigh, G. K. (1990). The family and social competence in adolescence. In T. P. Gullota, G. R. Adams, & R. Montemayor (Eds.), *Developing social competency in adolescence: Advances in adolescent development* (Vol. 3, pp. 97–138). Newbury Park, CA: Sage.

Peterson, G. W., & Rollins, B.C. (1987). Parent child socialization. In M. B. Sussman & S. K. Steinmetz (Eds.), *Handbook of marriage and the family* (pp. 471–507). New York: Plenum.

Peterson, J. L., & Zill, N. (1986). Marital disruption, parent–child relationships, and behavior problems in children. *Journal of Marriage and the Family, 48*, 295–307.

Petit, G. S., & Lollis, S. (1997). Reciprocity and bi-directionality in parent–child relationships: New approaches to the study of enduring issues. *Journal of Social and Personal Relationships, 14*(4), 435–440.

Philipsen, G. (1975). Speaking "Like a man" in Teamsterville: Culture patterns of role enactment in an urban neighborhood. *Quarterly Journal of Speech, 61*, 13–22.

Philipsen, G. (1976). Places for speaking in Teamsterville. *Quarterly Journal of Speech, 62*, 15–25.

Phillips, G., Hansen, B., & Carlson, D. (1965). A preliminary experiment in measuring attitude shifts as a result of viewing a dramatic production. *Speech Monographs, 32*, 218–232.

Pick, S., & Palos, A. P. (1995). Impact of the family on the sex lives of adolescents. *Adolescence, 30*(119), 667–675.

Pipher, M. (1994). *Reviving Ophelia: Saving the selves of adolescent girls*. New York, NY: Ballantine Books.

Polansky, J. M., Buki, L. P., Horan, J. J., Ceperich, S. D., & Burows, D. D. (1999). The effectiveness of substance abuse prevention videotapes with Mexican-American adolescents. *Hispanic Journal of Behavioral Sciences, 21*, 186–198.

Polich, J. M., Ellickson, P. L., Reuter, P., & Kahan, J. P. (1984). *Strategies for controlling adolescent drug use*. Santa Monica, CA: Rand.

Polkinghorne, D. E. (1988). *Narrative knowing and the human sciences*. Albany, NY: State University of New York Press.

Prus, R. (1996). *Symbolic interaction and ethnographic research : Intersubjectivity and the study of human lived experience.* Albany, NY: State University of New York Press.

Query, J. M. N. (1985). Comparative admission and follow-up study of American Indians and Whites in a youth chemical dependency unit on the north central plains. *International Journal of the Addictions, 20*(3), 489–502.

Rapaport, R., & Rapaport, R. N. (1975). *Leisure and the family life cycle.* Boston: Routledge & Kegan Paul.

Rawlins, W. K. (1992). *Friendship matters.* New York: Aldine De Gruyter.

Rawlins, W. K., & Holl, M. (1987). The communicative achievement of friendship during adolescence: Predicaments of trust and violation. *Western Journal of Speech Communication, 51*, 345–363.

Reardon, K. K., Sussman, S., & Flay, B. R. (1989). Are we marketing the right message: Can kids "just say no" to smoking? *Communication Monographs, 56*(4), 307–324.

Richards, I. A. (1926). *The principles of literary criticism* (2nd ed.). New York: Harcourt, Brace.

Richardson, D. C. (1981). The effect of alcohol on male aggression toward female targets. *Motivation and Emotion, 5*, 333–344.

Riessman, C. K. (1993). *Narrative Analysis* (Vol. 30). Newbury Park: CA.

Ritchie, L. D., & Fitzpatrick, M. A. (1990). Family communication patterns: An epistemic analysis and conceptual reinterpretation. *Communication Research, 18*, 548–565.

Ritter, E. M. (1979). Social perspective-taking ability, cognitive complexity, and listener-adapted communication in early and late adolescence. *Communication Monographs 46*, 40–51.

Roberts, K. (1983). *Youth and leisure.* London: George Allen & Unwin.

Robins, L. N., Helzer, J. E., Croughan, J. L., & Ratcliff, K. S. (1981). National Institute of Mental Health diagnostic interview schedule: Its history, characteristics, and validity. *Archives of General Psychiatry, 4*, 381–389.

Rose, M., Battjes, R., & Leukefeld, C. (1984). *Family life skills training for drug abuse prevention* (DHHS Pub. No. ADM 84-1340). Washington, DC: U.S. Government Printing Office.

Rosenbaum, E., & Kandel, D. B. (1990). Early onset of adolescent sexual behavior and drug involvement. *Journal of Marriage and the Family, 68*, 210–246.

Russell, R. L., & Lucariello, J. (1992). Narrative, yes: Narrative ad infinitum, no! *American Psychologist, 47*, 671–673.

Samet, N., & Kelly, E. (1987). The relationship of steady dating to self-esteem and sex-role identity among adolescents. *Adolescence, 22*, 231–245.

Saville-Troike, M. (1989). *The ethnography of communication.* New York: Basil Blackwell.

Schafran, L. H. (1996). Topics for our times: Rape is a major public health issue. *American Journal of Public Health, 86*, 15–34.

Schinka, J. A., Hughes, P. H., Coletti, S. D., & Hamilton, N. L. (1999). Changes in personality characteristics in women treated in a therapeutic community. *Journal of Substance Abuse Treatment, 16*, 137–142

Schwartz, S. H. (1977). Normative influences on altruism. In L. Berkowitz (Ed.), *Advances in experimental social psychology* (Vol. 10, pp. 221–279). San Diego, CA: Academic Press.

Secretary's Task Force on Black and Minority Health. (1986). *Chemical dependency and diabetes* (Vol. 7). Washington, DC: U.S. Governmental Printing Office.

Simons, R. L., Conger, R. D., & Whitbeck, L. B. (1988). A multistage social learning model of the influences of family and peers on adolescent substance use. *Journal of Drug Issues, 18*, 293–316.

Simons, R. L., Whitbeck, L. B., & Conger, R. D. (1991). The effect of social skills, values, peers, and depression on adolescent substance use. *Journal of Early Adolescence, 11*(4), 466–481.

Skipper, J. K., & Nass, G. (1966). Dating behavior: A framework for analysis and an illustration. *Journal of Marriage and the Family, 28*, 412–420.

Smart, W. E. (1986, October 6). When parting's not such sweet sorrow: Suicide prevention through Romeo and Juliet. *The Washington Post*, pp. 25, 28.

Smeliansky, A. (1995, March). The new narcotic. *American Theatre, 12*, 80.

Smircich, L. (1985). Is the concept of culture a paradigm for understanding organizations and ourselves? In P. J. Frost, L. F. Moore, M. R. Louis, C. C. Lundberg, & J. Martin (Eds.), *Organizational culture* (pp. 55–72). Newbury Park, CA: Sage.

Smith, R. C., & Eisenberg, E. M. (1987). Conflict at Disneyland: A root-metaphor analysis. *Communication Monographs, 54*, 367–380.

Socha, T. J., & Stamp, G. (1995). *Parents, children, & communication: Frontiers of theory and research*. Mahwah, NJ: Lawrence Erlbaum Associates.

Sontag, S. (1989). *Aids and its metaphors*. New York: Farrar, Straus, Giroux.

Spiro, R. (1980). Accommodative reconstruction in prose recall. *Journal of Verbal Learning and Verbal Behavior, 19*, 84–95.

Spitzberg, B. H., & Cupach, W. R. (1984). *Interpersonal communication competence*. Beverly Hills, CA: Sage.

Spitzberg, B. H., & Hecht, M. L. (1984). A component model of relational competence. *Human Communication Research, 10*, 575–599.

Spoth, R., Redmond, C., Haggerty, K., & Ward, T. A. (1995). A controlled parenting skills outcome study examining individual difference and attendance effects. *Journal of Marriage and the Family, 57*, 449–464.

Stearns, D. P. (1990, August 14). Theater troupes enlist for the war on drugs. *USA Today*, p. 17D.

Steinberg, L. (1990). Autonomy, conflict, and harmony in the family relationship. In S. S. Feldman & G. R. Elliott (Eds.), *At the threshold: the developing adolescent* (pp. 255–276). Cambridge, MA: Harvard University Press.

Strauss, A. L., & Corbin, J. (1990). *Basics of qualitative research*. Newbury Park, CA: Sage.

Suit, J. L., & Paradise, L. V. (1985). Effects of metaphors and cognitive complexity on perceived counselor characteristics. *Journal of Counseling Psychology, 32*, 23–28.

Sutker, P. B. (1985). Drug-dependent women. In U.S. Department of Health and Human Services (Ed.), *Treatment services for drug-dependent women* (pp. 25–51). Washington, DC: U.S. Government Printing Office.

Szalay, L., Bovasso, G., Vilov, S., & Williams, R. E. (1992). Assessing treatment effects through changes in perceptions and cognitive organization. *American Journal of Drug and Alcohol Abuse, 18*, 407–428.

Szalay, L., & Deese, J. (1978). *Subjective meaning and culture: An assessment through word associations*. Hillsdale, NJ: Lawrence Erlbaum Associates.

Szalay, L. B., Canino, G., & Vilov, S. K. (1993). Vulnerabilities and cultural change: Drug use among Puerto Rican adolescents in the United States. *The International Journal of the Addictions, 28*, 327–354.

Szalay, L. B., Vilov, S. K., & Strohl, J. B. (1992). Charting the psychological correlates of drug abuse. *Drug and Alcohol Abuse Reviews, 4*, 99–120.

Szapocznik, J., & Kurtines, W. M. (1989). *Breakthroughs in family therapy with drug abusing and problem youth*. New York: Springer.

Teens Kick Off. (1990). *Final report: Fiscal Year 1989*. San Francisco, CA.

Tobler, N. S. (1986). Meta-analysis of 143 adolescent drug prevention programs: Quantitative outcome results of program participants compared to a control or comparison group. *Journal of Drug Issues, 16*, 537–567.

Tobler, N. S. (1989, October). *Drug prevention programs can work: Research findings*. Paper presented at the conference What Works: An international perspective on drug abuse treatment and prevention research, New York.

Tolkien, J. R. R. (1983). *The book of lost tales*. C. Tolkien (Ed.) Boston, MA: Alley & Unwin.

Tobler, N. S. (1995, June). *Interactive programs are successful: A new meta-analysis finding*. Paper presented at the society for prevention research, Scottsdale, AZ.

Toohey, J. V., Dezelsky, T. L., & Baffi, C. R. (1982). The social attitudes of college students toward marijuana: Implications for education. *Journal of Drug Education, 12*, 155–161.

Traupman, J., & Hatfield, E. (1981). Love and its effect on mental and physical health. In R.W. Fogel, E. Harfield, S. B. Kiesler, & E. Shanas (Eds.), *Aging: Stability and change in the family* (pp. 88–107). New York: Academic Press.

Trimble, J. E. (1995). Toward an understanding of ethnicity and ethnic identity, and their relationship with drug use research. In G. J. Botvin, S. Schinke, & M. A. Orlandi (Eds.), *Drug abuse prevention with multiethnic youth* (pp. 3–27). Thousand Oaks, CA: Sage.

Trimble, J. E., & Fleming, C. (1989). Providing counseling services for Native American Indians: Client, counselor, and community characteristics. In P. Pederson, J. Drangus, W. Lonner, & J. Trimble (Eds.), *Counseling across cultures* (3rd ed., pp. 177–204). Honolulu, HI: University Press of Hawaii.

Trost, M. R., Kellar-Guenther, Y., & Bator, R. J. (1997, February). *Relational intimacy and drug use susceptibility in adolescents.* Paper presented at the meeting of the Western States Communication Association, Monterey, CA.

Trost, M. R., Langan, E. J., and Bachman, G. (1998, June). *Addicted to the drug or to the man: Drug resistance in high school dating relationships.* Paper presented at the meeting of the International Society for the Study of Personal Relationships, Saratoga Springs, NY.

Trost, M. R., Langan, E. J., & Kellar-Guenther, Y. (1999). Not everyone listens when you "just say no:" Drug resistance in relational context. *Journal of Applied Communication Research, 27,* 1–19.

Turner, S. (1995). Family variables related to adolescent substance misuse: Risk and resiliency factors. In T. P. Gullotta, G. R. Adams, & R. Montemayor (Eds.), *Substance misuse in adolescence* (pp. 36–55). Thousand Oaks, CA: Sage.

Turner, V. (1980). Social dramas and stories about them. *Critical Inquiry, 7,* 141–168.

U.S. Department of Health and Human Services, National Institute on Drug Abuse. (1988). *National household survey on drug abuse*: Washington, DC: U.S. Government Printing Office.

Valentine, K. B. (1979). Interpretation trigger scripting: An effective communication strategy. *Reader's Theater News, 6,* 7–8, 46–47.

Valentine, K. B., & Valentine, G. E. (1983). Facilitation of intercultural communication through performed literature. *Communication Education, 32,* 303–306.

Vega, W., & Gil, A. G. (1998). *Drug use and ethnicity in early adolescence.* New York: Plenum Press.

Vega, W. A., Zimmerman, R. S., Warheit, G. J., Apospori, E., & Gil, A. G. (1993). Risk factors for early adolescent drug use in four ethnic and racial groups. *American Journal of Public Health, 83,* 185–189.

Wallace, J. M. (1994). Race differences in adolescent drug use: Recent findings from national samples. *African-American Research Perspectives, 1,* 31–35.

Wallace, J. M., & Bachman, J. G. (1993). Validity of self-reports in student based studies on minority populations: Issues and concerns. In M. R. De la Rosa & J. R. Adrados (Eds.), *Drug Abuse among minority youth: Advances in research and methodology* (NIDA Research Monograph 130, pp.167–200). Rockville, MD: National Institute on Drug Abuse.

Wallace, J. M., Jr., Bachman, J. G., O'Malley, P. M., & Johnston, L. D. (1995). Racial ethnic differences in adolescent drug use: Exploring possible explanations. In G. J. Botvin, S. Schinke, & M. A. Orlandi (Eds.), *Drug abuse prevention with multiethnic youth* (pp. 59–80). Thousand Oaks, CA: Sage.

Walls, C. M., & Trost, M. R. (1996, February). *Psychosocial approached to drug prevention: The social norms element.* Paper presented at the meeting of the Western States Communication Association, Pasadena, CA.

Walter, G. A. (1976). Changing behavior in task groups through social learning: Modeling alternatives. *Human Relations, 29,* 167–178.

Warheit, G. J., Vega, W. A., Khoury, E. L., Gil, A. G., & Elfenbein, P. H. (1996). A comparative analysis of cigarette, alcohol, and illicit drug use among an ethnically diverse sample of Hispanic, African American, and Non-Hispanic White adolescents, *Journal of Drug Issues, 26,* 901–922.

Wartella, E., & Middlestadt, S. (1991). Mass communication and persuasion: The evolution of direct effect, limited effects, information processing, and affect and arousal models. In L. Donohew, H. E. Sypher, & W. J. Bukoski (Eds.), *Persuasive communication and drug abuse prevention* (pp. 53–70). Hillsdale, NJ: Lawrence Erlbaum Associates.

Watts, W. D., & Wright, L. L. (1990). The relationship of alcohol, tobacco, marijuana, and other illegal drug use to delinquency among Mexican-American, black, and white adolescent males. *Adolescence, 25,* 171–181.

Werner, E. E. (1990). Protective factors and individual resilience. In S. J. Meisels & J. P. Shonkoff (Eds.), *Handbook of early childhood intervention.* Cambridge, England: Cambridge University Press.

Werner, E. E., & Smith, R. S. (1994). *Overcoming the odds: High risk children from birth to adulthood.* Ithaca, NY: Cornell University Press.

White, G. L., & Mullen, P. E. (1989). *Jealousy: Theory, research, and clinical strategies.* New York: Guilford.

Wildman, B. G. (1986). Perceptions of refusal assertion: The effects of conversational comments and compliments. *Behavior Modification, 10,* 472–486.

Wilhelmsen, L. (1968). One year's experience in an antismoking clinic. *Scandinavian Journal of Respiratory Series, 49,* 251–259.

Wilks, J., Callan, V. J., & Austin, D. A. (1989). Parent, peer and personal determinants of adolescent drinking. *British Journal of Addiction, 84,* 619–630.

William, J., & Smith, J. (1993). Alcohol and other drug use among adolescents: Family and peer influences. *Journal of Substance Abuse, 5,* 289–294.

Willis, T. A., & Vaughn, R. (1989). Social support and substance use in early adolescence. *Journal of Behavioral Medicine, 12*(4), 321–339.

Winner, E. (1988). *The point of words: Children's understandings of metaphor and irony.* Cambridge, MA: Harvard University Press.

Wood, J. (1994). *Gendered lives.* Belmont, CA: Wadsworth.

Wood, J.(1996). *Everyday encounters: An introduction to interpersonal communication.* Belmont, CA: Wadsworth.

Yates, A. (1987). Current status and future directions of research on the American Indian Child. *American Journal of Psychiatry, 144,* 1135–1142.

Youniss, J., & Haynie, D. (1992). Friendship in adolescence. *Developmental and Behavioral Pediatrics, 13,* 59–66.

Zelvin, E. (1999). Applying relational theory to the treatment of women's addictions. *Affilia, 14,* 9–23.

Zuckerman, W., & Link, K. (1968). Construct validity for the sensation-seeking scale. *Journal of Consulting and Clinical Psychology, 32,* 420–426.

Author Index

A

Adams, G., 22, 41, 76, 110
Adelson, J., 31
Agnew, R., 110, 111
Aktan, G., 40
Alberts, J. K., 2, 12, 17, 44, 47, 48, 50, 53, 54, 57, 58, 59, 61, 65, 74, 77, 92, 97, 119, 123, 125, 126, 127, 128, 129, 130, 132, 135, 149, 152, 153
Albrecht, S. L., 19, 40
Allen, O., 71, 118
Alvarado, R., 21, 25, 27
Amann, L. L., 91
Amey, C. H., 19, 40
Anda, R. F., 8
Andersen, P. A., 119
Anderson, L. R., 6, 38
Andrews, J. A., 5, 40
Anglin, M. D., 12, 19, 38, 39
Annon, K., 19
Apospori, E., 119
Apter, T., 26
Aronson, J., 63
Artaud, A., 94, 95
Arthur, M. W., 41
Ary, D., 5, 40, 42
Ashery, R., 40
Austin, D. A., 21, 33, 34, 91
Austin-Phillips, V., 22

B

Bachman, J. G., 1, 3, 7, 18, 19, 36, 40, 67, 118, 119
Backlund, B. A., 37
Badzinski, D. M., 24
Baer, N., 89
Baffi, C. R., 5
Bailey, S. L., 6, 36
Bandura, A., 11, 12, 15, 24, 92
Barber, J. G., 5
Barnett, O. W., 110
Barry, J., 42
Bass, L., 118
Bator, R. J., 8, 17, 19, 47, 50, 52, 53, 54, 55, 57, 63, 64, 66, 68, 119, 136
Battjes, R. J., 18, 27
Bauer, P. E., 21, 22, 77, 89, 128
Baumrind, D., 5, 21, 24, 28, 30, 63, 77, 128
Baxter, L. A., 78, 109, 126
Beauvais, F., 1, 6, 7, 8, 12, 18, 19, 31, 39, 40, 63, 68, 77, 118, 128
Beck, K. H., 25
Bedworth, A. E., 94
Behnke, M., 18
Bell, R. A., 44
Bell, R. M., 12
Benoit, P.J., 110
Benoit, W. L., 110
Bentler, P. M., 1, 7, 8, 30, 36, 38, 39, 63, 68, 76, 118, 119

Subject Index

For Product Safety Concerns and Information please contact our EU
representative GPSR@taylorandfrancis.com
Taylor & Francis Verlag GmbH, Kaufingerstraße 24, 80331 München, Germany

www.ingramcontent.com/pod-product-compliance
Lightning Source LLC
Chambersburg PA
CBHW070401270326
41926CB00014B/2649